Controversies in Second Language Writing:
Dilemmas and Decisions in Research and Instruction

Second Edition

The Michigan Series on Teaching Multilingual Writers

Series Editors
Diane Belcher (Georgia State University) and
Jun Liu (SUNY–Stony Brook)

Controversies in Second Language Writing: Dilemmas and Decisions in Research and Instruction
Second Edition

Christine Pearson Casanave

The Michigan Series on Teaching Multilingual Writers

Series Editors: Diane Belcher and Jun Liu

Ann Arbor
University of Michigan Press

ISBN-13: 978-0-472-03690-5 (paper)
ISBN-13: 978-0-472-12348-3 (ebook)

2020   2019   2018   2017   4   3   2   1

Series Editor Foreword

In the decade or so since the first edition of *Controversies in Second Language Writing* initially appeared in print, not only has there been little to no diminution or clear resolution of the controversies Casanave so accessibly and fair-mindedly laid out for us in that earlier edition, but many of them have become far more complex and intertwined with many other twenty-first century issues that teachers of L2 writing cannot help but be affected by in their real-life and virtual classrooms. The original six chapters of the first edition, as Casanave notes in her new preface, have morphed into eight in the second edition. Topics such as "plagiarism and textual borrowing" and "electronic communication," covered in parts of a chapter in the first edition, now merit, the author has wisely decided, their own chapters, i.e., "Writing from Sources and the Dilemma of Plagiarism" and "Writing in a Digital Era." With these new additions, Casanave helps us more fully appreciate just how rapidly the *how* and *what* of writing are evolving, with the mushrooming of social and multi-media options and of information-technology-enabled content resources, and what the pedagogical implications of these developments may be for those of us who care about L2 writing and writers. The writers themselves, the *who* of L2 writing— formerly known as second language learners but more recently as users of English as a lingua franca and of translingual practices—have also become the subject of increasing debate, which Casanave addresses, again in her thought-provoking and even-handed way, in another new chapter, "What and Whose Standards for Writing?" In other words, far from simply updating with more recent citations, Casanave has, in this new edition, taken a more expansive view, expounding on, with eminently appropriate nuance, topics that were only beginning to be delved into, or even perceived, by the field of L2 writing a decade ago.

Casanave is certainly right to observe, and forewarn, those new to the field (and to remind those familiar with the earlier edition) that they should not expect *Controversies* to serve as a *how-to* manual. It neither tells would-be L2 writing instructors how to teach nor advises them on how to think about issues related to teaching. This is not to say, however, that there are no helpful pedagogical suggestions, as these can indeed be found in the "Classroom Perspectives" section of every chapter. Nor is it the case that guidance through controversies is not offered, for we are engagingly led through multi-perspectival overviews of all the major controversies included in this volume. Casanave's goal, though, in this second edition continues to be, as in the first, to provide a "framework for decision making" (see Chapter 1), to encourage us, whether newcomers or old-timers, to be reflective as writers, teachers of writing, and teachers of teachers of writing, informed by the relevant, often intuition-challenging views and findings of our field and the increasing superdiversity and connectedness of our world.

Diane Belcher
Georgia State University

Jun Liu
State University of New York—Stony Brook

Preface to the Second Edition

This long overdue second edition of *Controversies in Second Language Writing* comes at a time of great change in the fields of first and second language writing, composition, rhetoric, and second language education in general. These changes relate not only to changes in student and teacher populations. They relate as well to pervasive influences of digital technologies developed and expanded since this book was first published (2004) and to issues that cause many of us to wonder what we currently even mean by "writing." To what extent does it still mainly refer to expository prose comprised of words? Does the term "second language writing" still convey what we want it to convey? Has the notion of visual design (e.g., Kress, 2010) finally superseded our understanding of what writing is and does? Other questions, always present in some form or another, puzzle us in different ways than they did in the past. Can L2 writing be assessed electronically both fairly and accurately? Has the dominance of standard "native speaker" English—the Anglo-American English used by educated mother tongue English speakers—finally given way in writing classrooms at all levels to a less prescriptive English, one characterized as more multimodal, diverse, and hybrid? Are the changes so great that it no longer makes sense to use a term like second language writing? Should we consider disposing of the field of second language writing altogether, as suggested by Canagarajah (2013)?

I am not ready to dispose of the term or the field (or the title of this book). However, our notion of writing, whether in a first or second (or other) language, certainly does need to expand to include new forms and functions of print and digital communications. I hope I have addressed some of these expansions in the second edition of *Controversies*. Nevertheless, some practices and attitudes, long entrenched in the L1 and L2 writing fields, have not disappeared, in spite of the apparent glitz and glamour of multimodal-multimedia communication. Although some decades ago we thought the only way to teach L1 and L2 writing was through a process (not single-draft product) approach, that change turned out to be overly simplified because one-shot exam-writing continues to influence students' success or failure in school and work settings. We also thought that the era of the ubiquitous five-paragraph essay in college writing classes was finally over, and that turned out not to be the case. I think it is alive and well in many venues, both in classrooms and on essay tests around the world.

One of the questions underlying this new edition of *Controversies*, then, concerns how much change there has really been in the conceptualizations, teaching, learning, and assessing of second language writing. What issues if any have been resolved? What issues have had lasting power from the past, either because people are resistant to change or because the issues continue to be unresolved ones that writing teachers and scholars need to keep discussing? In all cases, writing teachers benefit from knowing something about the theoretical foundations of second language writing (covered wonderfully in Ferris and Hedgcock (2014), as well as how historical backgrounds have influenced current thinking in the field of second language writing (Matsuda, 2003, 2014; Silva, 1990; You, 2010).

Therefore, in this second edition, readers will find that I continue to use the term "second language (L2) writing," as a convenience, to refer to any writing in any setting that people do in languages that are not their mother tongues, whether or not these "writings" also feature images and sounds. (Most of us do have mother tongues; truly balanced bilinguals are rather rare.) I also continue to believe that writing teachers need some historical perspective on what they do. Moreover, my belief continues from the first edition that most issues in L2 writing are not fully resolved and so are still subject to debate, and that teachers, scholars, and students of L2 writing benefit from debate and discussion within their local contexts more than they do from pat answers to their questions. Without gaps, curiosities, and puzzles, knowledge in a field does not grow. Hence, as was the case for the first edition, readers will not find answers in the book, or guidelines for how and what to teach, or pronouncements about "best methods," or strongly worded opinions about "right" and "wrong" (although I certainly have some strong views that might seep through now and then).

What, then, has changed in this 2nd edition, and what has remained more or less the same? First, all chapters, whether old or new, are updated and refer to works written since the first edition was published. Given the explosion of knowledge production in second language writing in recent years, these updates barely touch the surface of what is available, and by the time this second edition appears, no doubt numerous important pieces will have been published that did not make their way into my reference lists. One of the messages of the book is that readers need to continuously update their own knowledge by locating relevant sources for their own scholarship and teaching, including not only new work, but also significant older work. Don't depend on this (or any other) book as your only source of updates.

Second, a few chapters and sections appear relatively unchanged, if they have some historical or current value. The chapter on Beliefs and Realities (Chapter 1) has not changed much, in that the need to explore what we believe and practice remains the same and deserves ongoing reflection throughout our careers. Likewise, the chapter on contrastive rhetoric (Chapter 2) goes over familiar ground to readers of the first edition, but adds more recent work on intercultural rhetoric. Chapters on Paths to Improvement (Chapter 5) and Assessment (Chapter 7) also cover familiar ground, but I have reorganized these chapters and added new material, including a great deal of newer work that has been done on written corrective feedback and on automated (digital) essay assessment. Finally, I have added a concluding chapter (Chapter 8) that focuses only on the notions of the "Western" notions of critical thinking, individualism, and voice, taken in part from the first edition but expanded to include more recent thinking.

Third, a few chapters are mostly new, such as a chapter devoted to writing in an digital era (Chapter 3), and one on the topic of writing from sources with special attention to updated issues concerning plagiarism (Chapter 6). I have also added a chapter (Chapter 4) that addresses some topics that were touched on in the first edition, the political and ideological topic of whose standards of English (or any other language's) writing we adopt in our teaching and assessing of L2 writing. I devoted a whole chapter to this topic in the second edition, given debates about English as a lingua franca, "translingual literacy practices," and other hybrid uses of English that have been ongoing in the last ten years.

The basic structure of the chapters in this second edition remains similar to that of the first edition. Readers are urged to think about the epigraphs and the leading questions at the beginning of each chapter before they read; to get an overview of issues from an introduction section; to review some of the existing literature on the issues; to see the issues from a classroom perspective; to consider ongoing questions; and to use the chapter-final questions to discuss with others their own beliefs and practices. Also continued from the first edition is my decision to put references at the end of each chapter rather than in a comprehensive bibliography at the end of the book. Changed from the first edition is my decision to include only references that have been cited in these chapter-end lists, rather than other uncited resources. This means that the second edition of *Controversies* is a bit more citation-heavy in places than I would like; I hope it does not affect readability significantly. The chapter-end reference lists are substantial.

Once again, I remind readers that *Controversies in Second Language Writing* is not a book that will teach you how to do things. Rather, it is a book designed to help you think and to wrestle with issues in L2 writing that are not easily resolved by how-to prescriptions. In some ways, it is a book that is designed to make you a bit uncomfortable and to seek out others for ongoing discussion and debate.

References

Canagarajah, A. S. (2013). The end of second language writing? (Disciplinary dialogues). *Journal of Second Language Writing, 22*, 440–441.

Ferris, D., & Hedgcock, J. (2014). *Teaching L2 composition: Purpose, process, and practice (3rd ed.)*. New York: Routledge/Taylor & Francis.

Kress, G. (2010). *Multimodality: A social semiotic approach to contemporary communication*. London: Routledge/Taylor & Francis.

Matsuda, P. K. (2003). Process and post-process: A discursive history. *Journal of Second Language Writing, 12*(1), 65–83.

Matsuda, P. K. (2014). The lure of translingual writing. *PMLA, 129*(3), 478–483.

Silva, T. (1990). Second language composition instruction: Developments, issues, and directions in ESL. In B. Kroll (Ed.), *Second language writing: Research insights for the classroom* (pp. 11–23). Cambridge, U.K.: Cambridge University Press.

You, X. (2010). *Writing in the devil's tongue: A history of English composition in China*. Carbondale: Southern Illinois University Press.

Acknowledgments

As always, people write best when they are supported, encouraged, and critiqued by trusted others. I am fortunate to have such trusted others in my academic life. In preparing this second edition of *Controversies in Second Language Writing*, I have been helped by a number of them, including some who are experts in areas that I have had to learn about and who have generously guided my thinking and writing as I worked on the revisions and on new writing. All have kindly read and commented on one or more chapter drafts, in spite of schedules that are far busier than mine is. I thank you all: Stephanie Vandrick, Deborah Crusan, Lisa Russell-Pinson, Shawna Shapiro, and Sidury Christiansen. John Hedgcock also deserves a special note of thanks for the shared whining and dining at the Crazy Horse Restaurant Salad Bar during our respective struggles with second (and third) editions. The high-quality gossip cheered me up. I also must thank Ann Flower and Kristen Cardoso, main library staff, as well as the student workers, at the Middlebury Institute of International Studies at Monterey, who always had a supportive smile for me during the many months I spent on the second floor of the library revising and writing. I usually entered the library cheerful and energetic, and left haggard and bleary-eyed some hours later. All of you still smiled and welcomed me back next time. And thank you, too, for opening the windows when I needed air!

Finally, this project, both first and second editions, could not have been completed without the support of Diane Belcher, series editor for this book and several other wonderful books on writing, and of Kelly Sippell, Editor Extraordinaire at the University of Michigan Press. I am humbled by your trust in me, and hope I have not let you down.

Contents

Chapter 1

Beliefs and Realities:
A Framework for Decision Making

"...[O]ne of the critical differences between expert and non-expert teachers is their capability to engage in conscious deliberation and reflection. Such engagement involves making explicit the tacit knowledge that is gained from experience." (Tsui, 2009, p. 429)

"[T]eaching experience does not automatically translate into teacher expertise unless teachers consciously and actively reflect on these experiences." (Farrell, 2013, p. 1080)

LEADING QUESTIONS

- What roles do teacher beliefs, assumptions, and philosophies of learning and teaching play in the decision-making process in L2 writing classes?
- To what extent are L2 writing teachers explicitly aware of their own beliefs and practices?
- How can knowledge of relevant issues in L2 writing inform teachers' decisions?
- To what extent do belief systems and practical realities of the classroom support or work against each other?

Introduction to the Issues

The basic issues that teachers confront in face-to-face teaching, and even much online teaching, have not changed much over time. Many parts of Dan Lortie's classic 1975 book, *School-teacher*, seem as fresh and relevant today as they were decades ago (Hargreaves, 2009; Lortie, 1975). Among these unchanging realities is that teachers make hundreds of decisions in their teaching practices every day. Some decisions involve planning. With greater or lesser degrees of control over their decisions, teachers decide what content to teach; what materials to use; what sequences to present content and activities in; what pedagogical activities to set up using different participation structures; what kinds of homework and in-class work to assign; and what kinds of assessments and grading criteria to use. In this digital era, they also need to consider the fundamental question of what they mean by "writing" (see Chapter 3 on writing in a digital era), including the argument that it is no longer just about linguistic matters (Canagarajah, 2013). Other decisions need to be made on the spot: how to respond to students' questions; how to explain an activity if students misunderstand the initial set of instructions; how to handle recalcitrant or overly silent or talkative students on a particular day; how to switch gears mid-class either to take advantage of opportunities that arise unexpectedly or to adjust a lesson plan that cannot be finished in the allotted time; how to respond to a piece of writing that seems plagiarized or that contains disturbing personal information; and generally how to manage and negotiate the countless unforeseen contingencies that arise every teaching day. These decisions are based on teachers' past experiences, their current goals for and beliefs about teaching and learning, their current knowledge of their subject matter and relevant content-based issues, and the constraints of the immediate teaching context.

If asked, teachers can often explain that they are using certain materials in a particular way because they believe, for example, that students will be motivated by this approach and therefore learn more, or that this or that approach has been shown to be effective through research on writing and second language acquisition (SLA), or that the adaptations they make in an approach stem in part from classroom factors such as class size, time constraints, and curricular mandates at the departmental level. Of course, there are unarticulated default beliefs—unexamined assumptions about teaching and learning—that may not seem like beliefs at all, but more like routines and patterns, developed and followed through habit and through teachers' own experiences with learning in their pasts (what Lortie, 1975, referred to as the "apprenticeship of observation") rather than through systematic reflection and conscious choice. Teachers may also choose, or be given, materials, lessons, and assessment tools without reflecting on the assumptions about teaching and learning that underlie those materials and tools. If the materials look good, if they are written by reputable authors and published by good publishers, and if they have been approved by the school or department, they must be good. Many teachers, moreover, pressed for time and short of energy, just hope to get through another day. As important as it is, reflection on beliefs and issues, which requires some intellectual and emotional investment, may not be high on their lists of daily or weekly activities (Farrell, 2007).

Nevertheless, examined or unexamined, within awareness or not, teacher choices and behaviors in the classroom reflect underlying beliefs and assumptions, even when articulated beliefs do not match well with practices (Farrell, 2007; Nishino, 2012). One of my own strong beliefs, and that of many other established scholars in education over the last several decades, is that teachers benefit from bringing underlying beliefs into conscious awareness by articulating those beliefs, reflecting on them, and modifying them as needed (Burns, 1992; Calderhead, 1989; Casanave & Schecter, 1997; Day, Calderhead, & Denicolo, 1993; Farrell, 1999, 2007, 2013; Freeman & Richards, 1996; Gebhard & Oprandy, 1999; Korthagen & Vasalos, 2005; Richards, 1998; Richards & Lockhart, 1994; Ross, 1989; Schön, 1983, 1987; Valli, 1992). Our teaching can thus become more principled, less random, perhaps more experimental and innovative, more connected to the learning of particular students, and more subject to our own critical evaluation of techniques, methods, successes, and failures. With sets of articulated beliefs, we become more able to ask and respond to the important questions such as Why am I choosing to teach in this way? and What effect is my teaching having on my students? and Given the practical constraints in my teaching situation, how can I best implement what I feel to be good decisions?

In this introductory chapter, I lay out several foundational areas for decision-making in the L2 writing class. The areas fall into three broad categories that apply to teaching of any kind: philosophy of teaching and learning; knowledge of relevant issues; and the practical realities of local teaching and learning settings. First, being able to articulate a set of beliefs and assumptions about the teaching and learning of writing will help teachers evolve a consistent philosophy and match their decisions with those beliefs to the extent possible. Second, knowing what the relevant issues are, along with substantive content knowledge, will help teachers make principled decisions that are made in conjunction with what we know to date about the teaching and learning of writing (including decisions that might reject current trends). Finally, recognizing the reality of practical constraints, such as bureaucratic requirements and structural realities, the unique characteristics of particular classes and individual students, and classroom management factors, will help writing teachers make the best decisions possible when perhaps none are optimal.

Building a Philosophy of Teaching and Learning

Getting Started: Literacy Autobiographies

A good place to begin considering beliefs about teaching and learning L2 writing is with a literacy autobiography. A literacy autobiography recounts the history of one's key literacy experiences throughout a lifetime: memories of learning to read and write, influential moments and people that contributed to one's sense of self as a reader-writer, memorable pieces of writing, breakthroughs and blocks, struggles with and joys of writing. For those involved in L2 writing, a literacy autobiography crucially includes one's own experiences learning to read and write in an L2 (Belcher & Connor, 2001; Canagarajah, 2012). It is likely that our own L2 learning experiences influence choices we make today about teaching L2 writing. That L2 may be English, not just the stereotypical "foreign languages" that predominantly monolingual English speakers think of when they hear the term *"second/foreign language."* Some of the most influential published literacy autobiographies in the L2 writing field have been written by scholars for whom English was not a mother tongue (see Belcher & Connor, 2001; Braine, 1999; several of the pieces in Casanave & Vandrick, 2003; Hoffman, 1989; Pavlenko, 1998, 2001). These literacy autobiographies reveal issues and challenges faced by the authors as they developed a professional level of L2 literacy and provide clues about where their beliefs and assumptions about L2 literacy originated. In the broader field of SLA, diary studies that focus on second and foreign language learning achieve a similar purpose (Bailey, 1983, 1990; Carson & Longhini, 2002; Casanave, 2012; Curtis & Bailey, 2009; Hall, 2008; Numrich, 1996). Importantly, literacy practices at the graduate school level also need to learned—they do not come naturally to either L1 or L2 students (Casanave, 2008; Casanave & Li, 2008; Hedgcock, 2008).

The polished form of a published literacy autobiography or of a finished autobiography written as a class assignment in an applied linguistics or composition studies program lends the impression that once written, the literacy autobiography is finished. However, as a piece of writing that can both reveal underlying beliefs and assumptions about writing and contribute to their further development and to the development of a philosophy of teaching and learning, a literacy autobiography can productively be revised many times over a teaching career. In revising and rethinking their own literacy experiences, authors can add new experiences and insights, and reinterpret ones from the past, just as they can from a life story (Bell, 1997; Giddens, 1991; Linde, 1993; Mishler, 2006; Polkinghorne, 1988, 1991). The literacy autobiography is thus a piece of writing in perpetual draft form, ready to be revisited, restoried, and reinterpreted in light of new experiences and of responses of self and others with whom it is shared. It provides the initial airing of beliefs about teaching and learning that can be linked later to decisions in the classroom.

Examining the Sources of Beliefs from the Inside Out

In further articulating a philosophy of L2 teaching and learning, we can also consider sometimes intangible internal factors that may or may not have been addressed in a literacy autobiography. I am thinking here of the rather amorphous factors of personality, cognitive style, emotional proclivities, preferences in learning strategies, and even influences of upbringing as to what behaviors and attitudes are considered efficient, productive, and even moral in leading to future goals for self and students. Whether we realize it or not at the time, these intangible internal factors influence decisions we make in the classroom. Understanding these influences can help us sort the reasoned decisions from knee-jerk responses in the classroom or strongly felt emotional beliefs that appear so normal that they cloud other ways of seeing.

For example, it is possible that a teacher who is fundamentally outgoing, social, and confident will tend to set up class activities that differ from those set up by a teacher who is shy, inward, and solitary by nature. I have sometimes found myself questioning my decisions in the classroom: Should I ask students to do what I could not do at their age, or what I still dislike doing today? For instance, I was, and am, particularly resistant to games and competitions in the classroom, both as a learner and a teacher. A second example, more directly connected to writing, concerns the extent to which a writing teacher is by nature a "radical outliner" or a "radical brainstormer" (Reid, 1984). I have never been able to outline before

I write, at least according to the textbook rules, so for years never asked my students to do outlines either. But by turning my own predisposition into an unreflective belief about how to teach, I was probably limiting students' choices in unfair ways, in that some people benefit greatly from making very detailed outlines. My beliefs about how people plan their writing needed to expand and to become more accessible to self-analysis and critique, and as they did, my messages to students in the writing classroom changed.

The point is that our internal beliefs and predispositions tend to be less clearly visible and articulatable than those we can trace to external influences. They thus merit careful attention through self-observation, interaction with colleagues, reflective journal writing, and open discussion with students. Once articulated, beliefs that develop from the inside-out can be acted upon, or not, as teachers decide how to construct and respond to teaching and learning situations in the L2 writing class.

Examining the Sources of Beliefs from the Outside In

Adding further to the development of an articulated philoso-phy of teaching and learning, we can point to the influence of external factors on our belief systems and concomitant class-room decision-making behaviors (see also the discussion in the next section, "The Reality of Practical Constraints"). For example, teachers may have first learned to teach primarily by using certain textbooks and not others. Textbooks embody (often inconsistent) philosophies of teaching and learning in the kinds of exercises they ask students to do, the sequences of those exercises, and the implicit or suggested roles of teachers. Teachers who are required to use certain textbooks and not others, or who have favorite textbooks, methods, or tasks, or who have free rein to choose and develop materials can profit from examining the assumptions about teaching and learning inherent in those materials and tasks. The assumptions may or may not accord with teachers' own articulated beliefs and may or may not contribute to the development of those beliefs.

Another external influence on teachers' beliefs includes the lessons learned from mentors, master teachers, or colleagues. These influential people may be part of a graduate school program as one's professors and peers, they may be charismatic and inspiring presenters at conferences, or they may be other teachers or even students with whom one is working. As an example, I recall one of my first encounters with second language educator John Fanselow at a conference many years ago, where he was speaking to a hall of enthusiastic admirers. Through his presentation, and later through collegial contact (see Casanave, 2002, Chap. 6, and Fanselow, 1997), I learned to *see* in a different, more open way, even though my teaching style was not modeled on his. Another important influence on me was the persona and work of the late Elliot Eisner, a charismatic teacher and eloquent writer in whom I saw a passion for qualitative inquiry and the arts, and from whom I learned that academic writing can be beautiful and accessible (e.g., Eisner, 1991). An even more profound influence on me was the late Arthur Applebee, whose vast knowledge of writing and composition and gentle persona initially drew me in to the study of writing.

A third external influence on teachers' beliefs comes from books and articles in the field, through self-study or schooling, that express views about approaches to teaching, often regrettably to the exclusion of currently unpopular or "old-fashioned" approaches. For example, strong and persuasive voices in the field can intimidate teachers into believing that attention to grammar is wrong or right, that communicative competence is or is not the central goal of language education, or that students either should or need not learn to express themselves personally in their writing. However, strong and persuasive voices can also advocate openness, flexibility, and change. By attending to and comparing many voices in the field, teachers discover consistencies and conflicts, allies and enemies, inspiration and trivia, and can selectively merge and adapt the views of others as they build their own belief systems.

As an example of some of the early external influences on my beliefs and practices in second language education, when I first began teaching ESL (English as a Second Language) many years ago, my only (lamentable) qualification was that I was a native speaker of English and that I had always liked language and languages. I had not yet studied anything in applied linguistics or education, and relied heavily on the textbook that I was assigned to teach, Robert Lado's now classic audiolingual text series, *English 900*. I "learned" to believe in the primacy of speech, the importance of habit formation and pattern drills, and the need for students to practice, repeat, and practice some more. In the several years that followed I worked as a part-timer with only one other teacher, and she was thoroughly schooled in the same audiolingual behaviorist camp. My teaching and materials development followed in her footsteps. My beliefs in the audiolingual approach began to erode thanks to another external influence, a publisher's review of the draft of a grammar textbook this colleague and I had submitted. Although two of the three reviews had been quite positive, the third claimed in no uncertain terms that our approach was dated, that attention to grammar was passé, and that we needed to go back to the drawing board and familiarize ourselves with the (then) new communicative approach to language teaching. Like many others, I jumped on the communicative language teaching and process-writing bandwagon, read all the right books, didn't talk about grammar for a number of years, and rethought my whole approach to teaching and learning. When I eventually recognized the bandwagon I had jumped on and tried to find more balance in my beliefs and practices, I once mentioned the importance of grammar in communicative approaches to language teaching at a conference talk I was giving, before it became fashionable to do so. I was publicly put down by an assertive-voiced male in the audience who walked out of the room when I countered *his* strongly held belief that grammar did not belong in communicative approaches. Although several members of the audience later expressed support for my then controversial view about the need for grammar study, the experience of not being on the bandwagon was difficult for me as a relatively new scholar in the ESL field.

I am embarrassed today about my earlier bandwagon esca-
pades, but realize that as an inexperienced teacher without a
strong graduate education at the time, I developed my beliefs
and practices in quite normal ways. Now, many years later, I
continue to study and to learn from external sources such as
published literature, colleagues, and even students, but hope
I am not deceiving myself into thinking that I am impervious
to the latest hot topic fads. They lurk around every corner
waiting to capture my attention. Nevertheless, by becoming
close observers of the influences on and characteristics of our
own belief systems, I and other teachers become able to render
these systems into the flexible, dynamic, growing philosophies
of teaching and learning that they deserve to be and that can
contribute to reasoned decision-making in the classroom. The
challenges involve developing a coherent and internally consistent belief system in the first place, then recognizing it not
as dogma, fixed in stone (or print and electronic text, as the
case is more likely to be), but as a dynamic evolving system
that continues to grow over a lifetime.

Knowledge of Relevant Issues

It is not enough to know thyself. Teachers must also know
the content of their fields and which issues are historically
important and currently unresolved. In the field of language
teacher education in general, teachers need to build a knowledge base that includes theories of teaching, knowledge of
teaching and communication skills, subject matter knowledge, pedagogical reasoning and decision-making skills, and
knowledge of the contexts of teaching (Hedgcock, 2002; Mullock, 2006; Richards, 1998). In the broader field of education,
Shulman (1987) added curricular knowledge, knowledge of
educational purposes and philosophies, and (Shulman, 1986)
case knowledge (understanding of specific cases in teaching)
to the knowledge base of effective teachers. In the field of L2
writing, this expertise is based on thorough knowledge about
the target language, including knowledge of the conventions

of writing and rhetoric in the target language and relevant disciplines, and something about the languages, cultures, and writing conventions pertinent to the students they are teaching. It includes as well knowledge about theories of L2 writing, such as they are, about methods and processes of teaching writing, and about key issues in writing research and practice (Ferris & Hedgcock, 2014; Silva, 1990, 1993). Finally, it includes knowledge of the many different kinds of L2 writers from a diversity of contexts we might find in our classrooms, not just the postsecondary students that the L2 writing literature usually focuses on (Belcher, 2012, 2013) and not just ESL, but EFL students as well (Leki, 2001; Reichelt, 2009). In this section, I discuss primarily the need for teachers to build knowledge of relevant content and issues in L2 writing, many of which are taken up in other monographs in this series and which are dealt with in the remaining chapters of this book. With the help of such knowledge teachers are in a position to make principled and informed decisions in the face of sometimes conflicting ideas in the field or dilemmas that arise in the classroom itself. Questions that integrate such information with teaching methods and processes are taken up as well in books on teaching L2 writing (e.g., Ferris & Hedgcock, 2014; Leki, 1992; Reid, 1993; Swales & Feak, 2012).

Where does writing teachers' knowledge come from? One essential source is intuitions about writing processes, products, and problems that teachers develop over a lifetime of their own experiences with writing. Intuitions about writing can be considered a kind of felt knowledge, and may or may not be fully accessible to conscious reflection. (This is one reason why teachers can benefit from writing a literacy autobiography, discussed earlier.) Many of us, for example, can state unequivocally that we find it difficult to write in our first languages, to say nothing of our second (or third) languages. It is not just our students who find writing difficult. However, it is more challenging to try to explain to someone, or to ourselves, just why it is difficult to write. In attempting such an explanation, both teachers and students may identify some of the relevant issues in writing: I worry so much about getting every word and phrase right that I lose the forest for the trees and so become stuck, and can't move on (a problem of fluency and accuracy); I fear being judged (critiqued, assessed, graded) (a problem of assessment); I don't know what is expected of me in terms of content or rhetorical structure in a particular piece of writing (a problem of genre, topic knowledge, and explicitness of instruction); I don't know who I am really writing for or how to incorporate the voices of others in my writing without plagiarizing (problems of audience and writing from sources); I don't know whether I should take a stand or innovate in a piece of writing or just paraphrase the ideas and formal conventions of others (a problem of accommodation, resistance, and standards). The more experience that L2 writing teachers have as writers themselves, the more likely it is they will be able to articulate issues such as these and to help their students identify them as well. But these issues have all been researched in the L2 writing field, so teachers do not need to rely solely on their intuitions and experiences. The books in this series on teaching multilingual writers, and *Controversies* in particular, are designed to help writing teachers and their students identify, bring under conscious control, and put to good use relevant issues in L2 writing.

Perhaps the best way to begin accruing already researched knowledge of the fundamental issues that characterize the field of L2 writing is through a good graduate-level education. Writing teachers and future writing teachers become acquainted with central ideas, issues, and theories through books, journal articles, and lectures and discussions. By learning about relevant content and issues, teachers can then integrate this knowledge with the intuitive and experiential knowledge they have gained throughout their lifetimes. Important conflicts and contradictions will no doubt surface, providing teachers with the opportunity to wrestle with issues at deep levels of analysis and reflection. Reflective journals and learning logs are especially useful for this purpose (Burton, Quirke, Reichmann, & Peyton, 2009; Casanave, 2011; Lee, 2008; Richards & Ho, 1998).

Although a good graduate level education can start novice teachers on the road to a life of study of relevant content and issues, equally important is a commitment to ongoing study after graduate education ends. By continuing to read key books and journals, attending occasional conferences, discussing issues with colleagues, and perhaps writing for publication, teachers build relevant content knowledge over the lifetime of their careers and keep up with current issues and controversies. This knowledge in turn contributes to their evolving intuitions, philosophies, and ability to make reasoned decisions in their classrooms.

Knowledge of relevant issues and content will rarely provide teachers with clear answers, however. As I suggest in this book, there are enough debates and controversies in the L2 writing field to keep L2 writing teachers thinking, studying, learning, and reflecting for many years to come. Building knowledge over our professional lifetimes will complicate, not simplify, our teaching lives. But it will enable us to see, understand, and where practically feasible act on choices that were once invisible.

The Reality of Practical Constraints

Fortunate teachers are able to integrate their beliefs and assumptions about teaching and learning L2 writing, their knowledge of relevant content and issues, and the practical realities of their teaching situations. However, it is often the case that practical realities get in the way of what we believe and know, with the result that teaching materials and practices conflict with deeply held philosophies. Graduate language teacher education programs that have a substantial practicum in actual teaching as part of their requirements can begin to deal with this integration in that novice teachers soon discover that their energies are often taken up more with practical concerns than with content and theory they learned from course work. For instance, teaching journals and follow-up discussions in the practicum class might focus less on the benefits of small group peer reading in a writing class than on how to get students efficiently into groups and interacting productively with each other in the first place. The problem is exacerbated if there are no movable desks in the classroom. Wonderful ideas learned in course work and readings, in other words, may be difficult to implement in specific teaching settings.

Structural and systemic constraints that have plagued my own teaching (some of which took place in Japan) include undergraduate writing classes that met only once a week for 90 minutes, just 13 times a semester, large classes that prevented my being able to work with student writers as closely as I would have liked, and schedules so heavy for students in the Japanese university system that students did not have time or focus to read or write regularly. At the graduate level, where I have felt most strongly the need for students to write regularly, mid-career masters and doctoral students at the American university campus in Japan where I was teaching worked full time and had little time or energy to devote to concentrated writing. These constraints continue to clash with my beliefs that learning to write requires years of practice, not weeks, that writing is a social practice requiring deep engagement with readings and with other writers and mentors, and that focused rather than fragmented time is needed if writers are to move their writing forward. I have myself tried to write a paper along with students within the one-semester time period and found that the "term paper assignment" when applied to myself brings out many of these structural and systemic constraints. Weeks would go by when I did not or could not make time to write; colleagues who were my potential peer readers were busy; other obligations in my life interfered with my ability to concentrate. What got turned in at the end was as much an artificially concluded and incomplete draft as were those drafts that my students turned in, and I had a great advantage over them in that I chose topics about which I already had a great deal of organized knowledge. At the same time, the artificial deadlines imposed by the realities of the classroom situation ensured that we all got something written.

Other institutional realities may require that teachers use materials that have been selected by others, such as administrators or committees of teachers, or that have been selected from a limited pool of choices approved by a government or educational board. Teachers' choices are also severely constrained when there is an institutional mandate to cover a certain amount of material within a semester or a school year, or to work in lockstep with other teachers who are forced to use the same material. A pervasive problem in many settings that further undermines the good ideas and intentions of teachers is institutional (and cultural and parental) concern with students' examination scores rather than with their learning to write (see Chapter 7 on Assessment). In my own experience working with graduate students who are high school teachers in Japan, for example, I find that frustrated teachers may be able to squeeze in just 10 minutes a class session for real writing activities. The rest of the time they follow a mandated, exam-oriented curriculum.

Another practical reality of every classroom concerns classroom management and the ways that interactions with individual students and groups of students influence how teachers' decisions play out and how their beliefs and knowledge are enacted. By listening to teachers talk around the lunch table it is possible to get a sense of how pervasive these concerns are. I seldom hear teachers talking about their beliefs, about current issues in the field, about what it means to learn to write in a second language, about relevant books or articles they are reading, or about ways to enact their beliefs and knowledge in their classes. It is more likely that teachers focus on problem situations that impinge in very real ways on what happens on a day-to-day basis in their classes. How can I get students to stop chatting and to listen to me when I am giving them important information or instructions? What do I do with the disruptive student who refuses to cooperate and who damages the whole atmosphere of the class? How do I get quiet students to participate actively? How do I get students to turn off their mobile phones and devices and make eye contact with me and other students? What if students show no interest in

revising their writing, believing perhaps that what they need is grammar lessons, and so do not turn in required drafts? How do I handle the student who communicates to me or to other students (orally, electronically, or in print) in ways that seem disrespectful? What do I do with the small group of students in the back that insists on chatting or texting rather than on completing in-class writing activities? How do I react to the busy graduate student whose work and personal life get in the way of sustained concentration on reading and writing? These concerns and others can consume the time and energy of well-meaning teachers who really want to be spending every possible precious moment helping their students learn to write in their second language.

In sum, teachers who are forced to follow imposed materials, practices, and deadlines may inevitably find that materials and decisions imposed by others clash in ways that range from frustrating to enraging with their own evolving philosophies about how their students can best learn to write (or speak or read in their second language. Additionally, structural constraints such as large class size, immovable student desks, and minimal time available for writing instruction and practice can easily take precedence over teachers' belief systems and knowledge of their field. And finally, the daily grind of classroom management or the intrusion of students' personal or work lives into their ability to concentrate or develop interest in writing can subvert teachers' enactment of what they believe and know about learning to write in a second language. This picture may sound bleak, but it does not necessarily have to be so. I have found that some teachers working under constraints that make me want to escape the field are able to find clever, inspiring, and forward-looking ways to work with and around the realities of practical constraints. These teachers have developed a strong sense of what they believe about teaching and learning L2 writing, and their beliefs and knowledge help provide them with a vision that gives direction to the daily grind. Their students—in the long run at any rate—benefit.

Ongoing Questions

This chapter has laid out some of the basic factors that influence the decisions that teachers make in their L2 writing classes and in their writing-heavy subject matter classes. It urges that teachers consider not only what they do on a daily basis, but what they believe and know about teaching and learning. Such reflection is part of an ongoing lifetime effort to develop a consistent and coherent belief system that can help guide teachers through the practical realities and constraints they face in each classroom setting and provide a sense of vision when the daily grind seems to want to swallow us up. However, the controversies in L2 writing that I discuss in this book and around which I pose ongoing questions have no easy resolution—hence the word *dilemmas* rather than *problems* appears in my subtitle. Dilemmas, Cuban (1992, p. 6) pointed out long ago, are "often intractable to routine solutions." Dilemmas, therefore, involve decisions and choices that may lead to "good-enough" compromises rather than ideal outcomes (p. 7). Whatever the outcomes, if teachers' decisions are based on thoughtful reflection and a solid knowledge base, L2 writing students stand to benefit.

Many specific questions remain, and I hope readers will approach each chapter in this book, and each book in this series, with questions about their own beliefs and practices. Why am I teaching in the way I do? Why do I believe that this or that kind of exercise will improve my students' writing? Why am I using the particular materials that I have and why in the particular way I am adapting them? Whose voices in the field make most sense to me? Whose agendas am I following, and should I resist or accommodate and encourage my students to resist or accommodate? And perhaps one of the most important questions of all, how do all of my questions pertain to me as a writer, in my first and second languages? What teachers believe about themselves as writers influences their decisions as teachers of writing in ways that can be enlightening and inspiring.

References

Bailey, K. M. (1983). Competitiveness and anxiety in adult second language learning: Looking at and through the diary studies. In H. W. Seliger & M. H. Long (Eds.), *Classroom-oriented research in second language acquisition* (pp. 67–102). Rowley, MA: Newbury House.

Bailey, K. M. (1990). The use of diary studies in teacher education programs. In J. C. Richards & D. Nunan (Eds.), *Second language teacher education* (pp. 46–61). New York: Cambridge University Press.

Belcher, D. (2012). Considering what we know and need to know about second language writing. *Applied Linguistics Review, 3*(1), 131–150.

Belcher, D. (2013). The scope of L2 writing: Why we need a wider lens. *Journal of Second Language Writing, 22*(4), 438–439.

Belcher, D., & Connor, U. (Eds.) (2001). *Reflections on multiliterate lives.* Clevedon, U.K.: Multilingual Matters.

Bell, J. (1997). Shifting frames, shifting stories. In C. P. Casanave & S. R. Schecter (Eds.), *On becoming a language educator: Personal essays on professional development* (pp. 133–143). Mahwah, NJ: Lawrence Erlbaum.

Braine, G. (Ed.), (1999). *Non-native educators in English language teaching.* Mahwah, NJ: Lawrence Erlbaum.

Burns, A. (1992). Teacher beliefs and their influence on classroom practice. *Prospect, 7*(3), 56–66.

Burton, J., Quirke, P., Reichmann, C., & Peyton, J. K. (Eds.). (2009). *Reflective writing: A way to lifelong teacher learning* (e-book). TESL-EJ. http://tesl-ej.org/books/reflective_writing.pdf

Calderhead, J. (1989). Reflective teaching and teacher education. *Teaching & Teacher Education, 5*(1), 43–51.

Canagarajah, A. S. (2012). Autoethnography in the study of multilingual writers. In L. Nickoson & M. P. Sheridan (Eds.), *Writing studies research in practice: Methods and methodologies* (pp. 113–124). Carbondale: Southern Illinois University Press.

Canagarajah, A. S. (2013). The end of second language writing? (Disciplinary dialogues), *Journal of Second Language Writing, 22*, 440–441.

Carson, J. G., & Longhini, A. (2002). Focusing on learning styles and strategies: A diary study in an immersion setting. *Language Learning, 52*(2), 401–438.

Casanave, C. P. (2002). *Writing games: Multicultural case studies of academic literacy practices in higher education.* Mahwah, NJ: Lawrence Erlbaum.

Casanave, C. P. (2008). Learning participatory practices in graduate school: Some perspective-taking by a mainstream educator. In C. P. Casanave & X. Li (Eds.), *Learning the literacy practices of graduate school: Insiders' reflections on academic enculturation* (pp. 14–31). Ann Arbor: University of Michigan Press.

Casanave, C. P. (2011). *Journal writing in second language education.* Ann Arbor: University of Michigan Press.

Casanave, C. P. (2012). Diary of a dabbler: Ecological influences on an EFL teacher's efforts to study Japanese informally. *TESOL Quarterly, 46*(4), 642–670.

Casanave, C. P., & Li, X. (Eds.). (2008). *Learning the literacy practices of graduate school: Insiders' reflections on academic enculturation.* Ann Arbor: University of Michigan Press.

Casanave, C. P., & Schecter, S. R. (Eds.) (1997). *On becoming a language educator: Personal essays on professional development.* Mahwah, NJ: Lawrence Erlbaum.

Casanave, C. P., & Vandrick, S. (Eds.) (2003). *Writing for scholarly publication: Behind the scenes in language education.* Mahwah, NJ: Lawrence Erlbaum.

Cuban, L. (1992). Managing dilemmas while building professional communities. *Educational Researcher, 21*(1), 4–11.

Curtis, A., & Bailey, K. M. (2009). Diary studies. *OnCUE Journal, 3*(1), 67–85.

Day, C., Calderhead, J., & Denicolo, P. (Eds.). (1993). *Research on teacher thinking: Understanding professional development.* London: The Falmer Press.

Eisner, E. W. (1991). *The enlightened eye: Qualitative inquiry and the enhancement of educational practice.* New York: Macmillan Publishing Company.

Fanselow, J. (1997). Postcard realities. In C. P. Casanave & S. R. Schecter (Eds.), *On becoming a language educator: Personal essays on professional development* (pp. 157–172). Mahwah, NJ: Lawrence Erlbaum.

Farrell, T. S. C. (1999). Reflective practice in an EFL teacher development group. *System, 27*, 157–172.

Farrell, T. S. C. (2007). *Reflective language teaching: From research to practice.* Cambridge, U.K.: Cambridge University Press.

Farrell, T. S. C. (2013). Reflecting on ESL teacher expertise: A case study. *System, 41*(4), 1070–1082.

Ferris, D., & Hedgcock, J. (2014). *Teaching L2 composition: Purpose, process, and practice (3rd ed.)*. New York: Routledge/Taylor & Francis.

Freeman, D., & Richards, J. C. (Eds.) (1996). *Teacher learning in language teaching*. Cambridge, U.K.: Cambridge University Press.

Gebhard, J. G., & Oprandy, R. (1999). *Language teaching awareness: A guide to exploring beliefs and practices*. Cambridge, U.K.: Cambridge University Press.

Giddens, A. (1991). *Modernity and self-identity: Self and society in the late modern age*. Palo Alto, CA: Stanford University Press.

Hall, G. (2008). An ethnographic diary study. *ELT Journal 62*(2), 113–122.

Hargreaves, A. (2009). Presentism, individualism, and conservatism: The legacy of Dan Lortie's *Schoolteacher: A sociological study*. *Curriculum Inquiry 40*(1), 143–154.

Hedgcock, J. (2002). Toward a socioliterate approach to second language teacher education. *Modern Language Journal, 86*(3), 299–317.

Hedgcock, J. S. (2008). Lessons I must have missed: Implicit literacy practices in graduate education. In C. P. Casanave & X. Li (Eds.), *Learning the literacy practices of graduate school: Insiders' reflections on academic enculturation* (pp. 32–45). Ann Arbor: University of Michigan Press.

Hoffman, E. (1989). *Lost in translation: A life in a new language*. New York: Penguin Books.

Korthagen, F., & Vasalos, A. (2005). Levels in reflection: Core reflection as a means to enhance professional growth. *Teachers and Teaching, 11*(1), 47–71.

Lee, I. (2008). Fostering preservice reflection through response journals. *Teacher Education Quarterly* (Winter), 117–139.

Leki, I. (1992). *Understanding ESL writers*. Portsmouth, NH: Boynton/Cook.

Leki, I. (2001). Material, educational, and ideological challenges of teaching EFL writing at the turn of the century. *International Journal of English Studies, 1*(2), 197–209.

Linde, C. (1993). *Life stories: The creation of coherence*. New York: Oxford University Press.

Lortie, D. C. (1975). *Schoolteacher: A sociological study*. Chicago: University of Chicago Press.

Mishler, E. G. (2006). Narrative and identity: The double arrow of time. In A. de Fina, D. Schiffrin, & M. Bamberg (Eds.), *Discourse and identity* (pp. 30–47). Cambridge, U.K.: Cambridge University Press.

Mullock, B. (2006). The pedagogical knowledge base of four TESOL teachers. *The Modern Language Journal, 90*(1), 48–66.

Nishino, T. (2012). Modeling teacher beliefs and practices in context: A multimethods approach. *The Modern Language Journal, 96*(3), 380–399.

Numrich, C. (1996). On becoming a language teacher: Insights from diary studies. *TESOL Quarterly, 30*(1), 131–153.

Pavlenko, A. (1998). Second language learning by adults: Testimonies of bilingual writers. *Issues in Applied Linguistics, 9*(1), 3–19.

Pavlenko, A. (2001). "In the world of the tradition, I was unimagined": Negotiation of identities in cross-cultural autobiographies. *International Journal of Bilingualism*, 317–344.

Polkinghorne, D. E. (1988). *Narrative knowing and the human sciences.* Albany: SUNY Press.

Polkinghorne, D. E. (1991). Narrative and self-concept. *Journal of Narrative and Life History, 12* (2 & 3), 135–153.

Reichelt, M. (2009). A critical evaluation of writing teaching programmes in different foreign language settings. In R. Manchón (Ed.), *Writing in foreign language contexts: Learning, teaching, and research* (pp. 183–206). Clevedon, U.K.: Multilingual Matters.

Reid J. (1984). The radical outliner and the radical brainstormer. *TESOL Quarterly, 18*, 529–533.

Reid, J. M. (1993). *Teaching ESL writing.* Englewood Cliffs, NJ: Prentice Hall.

Richards, J. C. (1998). *Beyond training.* Cambridge, U.K.: Cambridge University Press.

Richards, J. C., & Ho, B. (1998). Reflective thinking through journal writing. In J. C. Richards, *Beyond training* (pp. 153–170). Cambridge, U.K.: Cambridge University Press.

Richards, J. C., & Lockhart, C. (1994). *Reflective teaching in second language classrooms.* Cambridge, U.K.: Cambridge University Press.

Ross, D. D. (1989). First steps in developing a reflective approach. *Journal of Teacher Education, 40*(2), 22–30.

Schön, D. (1983). *The reflective practitioner: How professionals think in action.* New York: Basic Books.

Schön, D. (1987). *Educating the reflective practitioner: Toward a new design for teaching and learning in the professions.* San Francisco: Jossey-Bass.

Shulman, L. (1986). Those who understand: Knowledge growth in teaching. *Educational Researcher, 15*(2), 4–14.

Shulman, L. (1987). Knowledge and teaching: Foundations of the new reform. *Harvard Educational Review, 57*(1), 1–22.

Silva, T. (1990). Second language composition instruction: Developments, issues, and directions in ESL. In B. Kroll (Ed.), *Second language writing: Research insights for the classroom* (pp. 11–23). Cambridge, U.K.: Cambridge University Press.

Silva, T. (1993). Toward an understanding of the distinct nature of L2 writing: The ESL research and its implications. *TESOL Quarterly, 27*(4), 657–677.

Swales, J. M., & Feak, C. B. (2012). *Academic writing for graduate students: Essential tasks and skills* (3rd ed.). Ann Arbor: University of Michigan Press.

Tsui, A. B. M. (2009). Distinctive qualities of expert teachers. *Teachers and teaching: Theory and practice, 15*(4), 421–439.

Valli, L. (Ed.). (1992). *Reflective teacher education: Cases and critiques.* Albany: SUNY Press.

Chapter 2

Contrastive and Intercultural Rhetoric

"...[A] group of languages need not in the least
correspond to a racial group or a culture area...." (Sapir,
1921/1949, p. 209)

"The thought patterns which speakers and readers of
English appear to expect as an integral part of their
communication is a sequence that is dominantly linear
in its development." (Kaplan, 1966, p. 4)

"The new term intercultural rhetoric is an umbrella
term that includes cross-cultural studies (comparison of
the same concept in culture one and two) and studies of
interactions in which writers with a variety of linguistic,
cultural, and social backgrounds negotiate through
speaking and writing." (Connor, 2011, p. 2)

"I still don't know what I[intercultural] R[hetoric] really
means..." (Matsuda, in Atkinson & Matsuda, 2013, p. 228)

LEADING QUESTIONS

- What are the main arguments in the historical contrastive rhetoric debate?
- How does the concept of intercultural rhetoric differ from that of contrastive rhetoric? How well has it addressed the critiques of contrastive rhetoric?
- What critiques can be made of the notion of intercultural rhetoric?
- How might aspects of contrastive and intercultural rhetoric continue to inform the researching, teaching, and learning of L2 writing?

Introduction to the Issues

In this introduction, I cover basic ideas of both contrastive rhetoric (CR) and its later incarnation, intercultural rhetoric (IR). Because both of these pedagogical and research projects encompass intuitively compelling ideas that still capture our attention, it pays to know something of the history of their development. These sections are followed by discussions in the literature, including critiques, and then by some classroom perspectives and ongoing questions that have grown out of both projects.

Introduction to Contrastive Rhetoric

Contrastive rhetoric as a field of study began long ago with the publication of Robert Kaplan's 1966 article in *Language Learning*. Kaplan assumed a kind of linguistic relativity, specifically that the rhetorical aspects of each language are unique to each language and culture. In second and foreign language education, this assumption implies that discourse-level features of a learner's first language cause difficulties for learners who are trying to acquire discourse-level patterns in their second languages. In other words, inherent in the CR project is the assumption of negative transfer, particularly of organizational and grammatical structures, from L1 to L2. Understanding such differences, so the claim goes, can help scholars and teachers explain some of the problems that L2 learners have in organizing their writing in ways that will seem acceptable to native speakers.

In the applied linguistics literature, "rhetoric" usually refers to discourse-level organizational patterns rather than to a constellation of techniques for persuasion as Aristotle defined it. Beginning with Kaplan's early article, the five elements of classical rhetoric (invention, memory, arrangement, style, and delivery) were reduced to arrangement—that is, what sentences in speech or writing logically and most effectively come first, second, and so on (Liebman, 1992, p. 142). In Kaplan's work CR is also tied to modes of thinking in the sense that what is considered logical in one culture may not be in another. As Kaplan put it in one of his many statements that generated controversy, "Logic (in the popular, rather than the logician's sense of the word) which is the basis of rhetoric, is evolved out of a culture; it is not universal" (Kaplan, 1966, p. 2).

Kaplan's motivation in looking at rhetorics contrastively was pedagogical, and according to Connor (1998) continued to be so later in his career and in the work of his followers. The work done by Kaplan and his followers, moreover, has been descriptive rather than predictive (Kaplan, 1988, pp. 275–276). As Kaplan pointed out, "the interest was primarily in finding solutions to an immediate pedagogical problem" (Kaplan, 1988, p. 277), one that L2 writing teachers continue to struggle with. He had observed many nonnative–like patterns (e.g., nonlinear organization) in the English language essays of undergraduates at his U.S. university and wished to help teachers design content and instructional materials that would help students write according to expected conventions, especially at the paragraph level. In this sense, his work constituted a pedagogical project. Since that time Kaplan's descriptions of several different culturally based rhetorical patterns, and the accompanying "doodles" of straight lines, circles, and zig zags, have been widely cited for their intuitively compelling "truths" and equally criticized for oversimplifying and overgeneralizing a highly complex idea. Others, and Kaplan himself, later expanded Kaplan's original pedagogical project to one of research in which scholars investigated rhetorical features of writing across many languages (see, for example, the collections in Connor & Kaplan, 1987, and Purves, 1988, and reviews in Connor, 1996, and Grabe & Kaplan, 1996).

Kaplan (1988) noted that the linguistic roots of CR stem from Prague School Linguistics, but he did not discuss the philosophical underpinnings of linguistic relativity in the most widely read of his articles and book chapters. Matsuda (2001, p. 260) commented from his personal communication with Kaplan that Kaplan was "really into Whorf-Sapir at the time." However, Kaplan cited Edward Sapir only twice in the original article, and did not cite Sapir's student Benjamin Whorf at all, either in the original article or in the 1987 "Cultural Thought Patterns Revisited" article (Kaplan, 1987), so these underpinnings are unclear from Kaplan's writings. It may be that Kaplan was more interested in the textual and pedagogical aspects of CR than in the philosophical connections among language, mind, and reality. Matsuda (2001) pointed out that another very strong influence on Kaplan's ideas, including Kaplan's original focus on paragraph structure in ESL students' writing, came from his teacher, Francis Christensen, at the University of Southern California. Christensen (1963, 1965) had authored two influential papers on sentence and paragraph rhetoric, which Kaplan applied to the writing of nonnative English–speaking undergraduate students at USC. According to Matsuda, Kaplan hoped to show that L2 students were not suffering from cognitive deficits, but revealing the influence of different rhetorical traditions in their L1s (Matsuda, personal email communication, Feb. 1, 2002).

Most summaries of CR, however, claim that CR assumes the validity of the so-called "Sapir-Whorf Hypothesis" of linguistic relativity or linguistic determinism (Connor, 1996; Kowal, 1998). As taken up by applied linguistics, the basic idea of this principle is that each language is characterized by a set of rhetorical conventions unique to it, and that these rhetorical conventions influence (control? determine? shape?) how people in those cultures think and write. As reviewed in much literature post-Kaplan 1966, there is a strong version of the Whorfian principle that claims that language determines our perceptions and thoughts. This version, it is generally agreed, is too extreme as well as unprovable. The weaker version, that language influences thought, is more accepted and is considered testable by some (Hunt & Agnoli, 1991). Even though its status as a research program is somewhat uncertain (but see

Connor, 2002), the Whorfian principle remains a comfortable but vague truism. However, it also continues to be debated by more current scholars interested in the still unresolved links among language, culture, and thought (Everett, 2012; McWhorter, 2014).

Regardless of our views on the Sapir-Whorf principle, if we look primarily at structural and organizational features of comparable texts written in different languages, differences have regularly been found (e.g., Bickner & Peyasantiwong, 1988; Clyne, 1987; Connor, 1987, 2000; Connor & Lauer, 1988; Connor, Nagelhout, & Rozycki, 2008; Eggington, 1987; Jenkins & Hinds, 1987; Kachru, 1988, 1995; Kamimura & Oi, 1997; Li, 2008b; Ostler, 1987; Régent, 1985; Söter, 1988; Taylor & Tingguang, 1991). However, the discussions in this work tend to avoid the difficult philosophical and ideological questions. In L2 educational circles, we are perhaps more interested in these structural aspects of our students' writing than in the intractable speculations about the connections among language, culture, mind, and reality. But even at the structural level questions arise as to the sources of differences among languages. The assumption of CR enthusiasts has always been that cultural patterns inherent in the rhetorics of different languages cause L2 students to write in ways that are not "English"-like.

But what is a "cultural" pattern of rhetorical organization in writing? Is this aspect of culture something inside our heads or bodies? Is it something taught in schools? Is it something modeled in certain kinds of literature within cultures? How can we identify a "cultural pattern" when multiple cultures and subcultures, languages, dialects, and text types or genres coexist within most countries of the world? ("Countries" themselves are national and political entities, not necessarily cultural or even linguistic ones.) What, additionally, does it mean to say that there is a "logic" peculiar to English? Does this refer to the language itself or to the users of the language and the text types they create? On the other hand, to what extent are problems that nonnative speakers have in writing the result of cultural influences, low L2 proficiency, schooling, inexperience in writing (a problem that L1 writers also have), or something else? Some of these issues have been addressed in discussions of culture and intercultural rhetoric (e.g., Atkinson, 2004; Atkinson & Matsuda, 2013; Connor, 2004, 2011), and I review them in a subsequent section, but I urge readers to go to some of the original sources, including Whorf (1956), the original Kaplan (1966) article, and some of the subsequent published critiques and research in order to deepen their understanding of how complex the issues are.

Introduction to Intercultural Rhetoric

The shift in labels and in contexts and purposes of inquiry from contrastive to intercultural rhetoric was intended to overcome some of the serious drawbacks of the earlier contrastive rhetoric work (see further discussion of these drawbacks in the next section). Connor (1996, 2002; see also Panetta, 2001) tried to reconstitute CR as a more dynamic contextualized approach to L2 writing, but after continued critiques (e.g., Kubota & Lehner, 2004), decided that shifting the labels and descriptions to "intercultural rhetoric" would deflect the critics and allow the IR reconceptualization of CR to move forward (Connor, Nagelhout, & Rozycki, 2008). "Intercultural rhetoric should not be seen in its 1996, contrastive rhetoric state," Connor (2011, p.23) stated. As she explained (2002, 2004, 2011), even though intercultural rhetoric continues to be primarily a project in which texts of various kinds are analyzed, contrasted, and compared, there is now much greater attention to contexts of production, social, and textual interactions, audience, and comparability of text types, as well as to questions of identity (Li, 2008a). Another change consists of a shift to broader research projects, beyond projects intended just to improve pedagogy in L2 writing.

For example, the influences on IR have expanded to include English for Specific Purposes (ESP) and its textual interest in genres, New Literacy studies and its social and multimodal views of literacy, culture studies including "large" and "small" cultures (Holliday, 1999), and translation studies (Connor, 2011, pp. 14–21). Methods in IR have also expanded. Although IR scholars continue their interest in comparing (comparable) texts using techniques in text linguistics, ways of studying texts and their production have also drawn on both corpus linguistics (quantitative studies of computerized corpora, Belcher & Nelson, 2013; Connor, 2013) and naturalistic (qualitative) studies of texts, writers, and contexts. Concepts such as "cultures" also remain intact in IR, but with greater attention paid by IR scholars to hybrid and dynamic aspects of culture, and to a "blurring of standards and norms in written language" (Connor, 2011, p. 19). Without a concept of culture, intercultural rhetoric as a research and pedagogical project has nothing to study. However, culture is no longer considered only in its "large" incarnation (as nations, languages, and associated language users), but also in its "small" versions (Holliday, 1999), such as the many overlapping discourse communities (personal, work, school) that we all participate in.

To sum up changes that have occurred in the shift from contrastive to intercultural rhetoric:

> The [intercultural rhetoric] field is currently dynamic and exploratory, extending to new genres, widening contextual research through historical and ethnographic inquiry, refining methodology, utilizing electronic corpora of texts, going beyond linguistic patterns to the study of other distinctive differences in writing, and exploring contrasts even beyond writing, such as the differences in Web use between speakers of different languages. (Connor, Nagelhout, & Rozycki, 2008, p. 4)

In the following section, I review some of the literature that has both supported and critiqued the CR and IR projects.

Discussions in the Literature

Kaplan and Early Contrastive Rhetoric

To begin at the beginning of the CR controversy, we need to go back to Robert Kaplan's (1966) original CR article, which these days is still often cited but less often read. I found this article to be a very strange piece of writing. I don't know if I am the only reader who reacted this way, but in spite of the fact that Kaplan discussed the linear nature of English expository prose (or more broadly, "English communication"), I did not find the piece to be particularly linear. Kowal (1998) analyzed the article in some detail, noting that it has three main sections (theoretical position, empirical data, and pedagogical implications) that reveal a "well-orchestrated and engaging argument" (p. 107) and that it is carefully hedged in places, but he did not comment further on its coherence or linearity (or lack of) as an example (or counter-example) of Kaplan's message. True, Kaplan starts and ends with comments about teaching. But what follows is a collection of long quotes from philosophy and rhetoric without his commentary, the promise of research (analysis of 600 student essays) that is not fulfilled, and a conclusion consisting of textbook-like exercises. Even though Kaplan's main evidence rests on the analysis of hundreds of his students' essays, there is no sign of any analysis at all, beyond the statement that these essays were "examined." Moreover, a number of his text samples are not from the student essays, but from the Bible or from published texts.

That being said, Kaplan's point was that nonnative English speakers who write in English violate the norms of English rhetoric, that "each language and each culture has a paragraph order unique to itself, and that part of the learning of a particular language is the mastering of its logical system" (Kaplan, 1966, p. 14). In one of the reprints of this article (Kaplan, 1980) Kaplan included an addendum in which he admitted that some of his claims about the uniqueness of paragraph orders in different cultures were both naive and too strong. He also asserted that "the basic notion remains valid; that is, there is a preferred order in discourse blocs" (p. 416). In a later article still (Kaplan, 1988), he explained and defended the early article, emphasizing that the original goal of CR was pedagogical:

> What was being sought . . . was some clear-cut unambiguous difference between English and any other given language, the notion being that such a clear-cut difference might provide the basis for pedagogical approaches that would solve—within the normative academic space of one or two semesters—the writing problems of speakers of other languages trying to learn to function in written English in the peculiar constraints of tertiary-level education in the United States. (p. 278)

Although the goal of finding such unambiguous differences between English and other languages now seems elusive and misguided, in this article as elsewhere, Kaplan's CR project is mainly focused on form—how paragraphs or longer texts in English and other languages are organized and how textual conventions such as punctuation and indentation make them look. In later work, in response to criticisms, Kaplan was more likely to mention audience, shared knowledge, genre, coherence, function, and so on, in addition to culture, as important factors that influence how people write (Grabe & Kaplan, 1996; Kaplan, 1987, 1988).

In spite of CR's pedagogical goals, Kaplan and his colleagues have been careful to point out that notions of CR cannot be applied directly to instructional decisions, partly because too little research has been done (some of the original CR ideas are not testable) and partly because there is no strong theoretical base for CR, which has always been a *descriptive* pedagogical project, not a research program. Nevertheless, Grabe and Kaplan (1996) defended CR as follows:

> What is clear is that there are rhetorical differences in the written discourses of various languages, and that those differences need to be brought to consciousness before a writer

can begin to understand what he or she must do in order to write in a more native-like manner (or in a manner that is more acceptable to native speakers of the target language). (p. 198)

This view, as "true" and uncontestable as it may seem, avoids some of the difficult issues associated with the CR project, which have been pointed out by various scholars in the debate over many years, some of which I discuss next.

The Critics' Responses to Contrastive Rhetoric

John Hinds (1983) was one of the first to point out some of the flaws in Kaplan's original CR article. In particular, Hinds felt that it was essential to examine the rhetoric of writers' first languages if we wish to make statements about culturally influenced rhetoric. Looking at essays written in English by foreign students simply cannot guarantee that the problems we see result from L1 negative transfer. Audiences may differ and developmental problems may wrongly be assumed to be cultural. Hinds also pointed out that Kaplan (1966) grouped his languages in odd ways (inexplicably excluding Japanese from his "Oriental" category even though they constituted the largest group of students in his study), and mistakenly overgeneralized the term "Oriental" to include four different language families (Hinds, 1983, p. 186). Finally, Hinds (1983) criticized Kaplan for ethnocentrically representing English prose as a straight line. Unlike Kaplan's early article, Hinds' work was restricted to structural features of languages and did not include philosophical or cognitive speculations about writers thinking or logical abilities.

To correct some of these methodological problems, Hinds looked at texts in Japanese, the most well-known studies using a specific popular column from a Japanese newspaper (the *tensei jingo* from the *Asahi Shimbun*). In the Japanese and English translations of those columns, Hinds identified what he saw as a typically Japanese digressive element in the structure of the writing (the "ten" of the *ki-shoo-ten-ketsu* arrangement), in which the writer first begins an argument (*ki*), then develops it (*shoo*), digresses (*ten*), and concludes (*ketsu*). Hinds generalized from this type of newspaper column to "expository prose in Japanese." He further noted that these popular opinion columns demonstrated the reader-responsible nature of Japanese writing (Hinds, 1987), in contrast to English (and modern Chinese), which he described as writer-responsible. In Japanese, he claimed, it is the responsibility of the reader to construct meaning, whereas in English the responsibility lies with the writer to ensure clarity. Japanese writers provide fewer landmarks and transition markers, leaving it to the reader to surmise the connections. Writers of English create unity more overtly, providing "appropriate transition statements so that the reader can piece together the thread of the writer's logic which binds the composition together" (Hinds, 1987, p. 146). In a later article, Hinds (1990) again examined the structure of the tensei jingo newspaper column from Japan's *Asahi Shimbun* (along with several texts written by Chinese, Korean, and Thai writers) and identified in all the texts what he called a "delayed introduction of purpose" or a "quasi-inductive" style. In these texts the conclusions do not seem to follow logically, in the way a reader of English would expect, from the previous statements. He noted that native English–speaking readers expect a deductive style, and not finding this style, will automatically assume the organization is inductive, and thus be baffled at the odd conclusions. Hinds' point in this article was that contrastive rhetoric is in large part about reader expectations.

In short, Hinds followed a CR tradition begun by Kaplan but looked at samples of writing in L1 and translations into L2 in order to generalize about how writers create, and readers understand, coherence and unity in their native languages. ESL writers from a Japanese language background might need to be taught that they should not necessarily assume that there is a "sympathetic reader who believes that a reader's task is to ferret out whatever meaning the author has intended" (Hinds,

1987, p. 152). These kinds of ESL learners, says Hinds, need to learn that "effective written communication in English is the sole provenience of the writer" (p. 152).

Peter McCagg (1996) added to the CR debate by challenging Hinds's (1987) assertion that Japanese is a reader-responsible language and English a writer-responsible one. McCagg used his own translation, as well as that by Hinds, of the same popular newspaper column article used by Hinds (1987), one on the topic of disposable chopsticks. McCagg argued that readers of this text who are deeply familiar with Japanese culture and traditions will not find it necessary to do more work at comprehending than would readers of the English version, as long as both sets of readers share background knowledge. He also argued that the text is not circular and indirect, as CR would predict, but that it quite directly gets to the point and lays out a variety of reasons and explanations. "Writers in every language," noted McCagg, "expect their audiences to contribute to the communicative act according to the conventions of the genre and their shared cultural experiences" (p. 248). This point will hold even if we perceive Japan to be a relatively homogeneous culture (itself a debatable notion) where readers share more background knowledge than they might in a more diverse culture.

Another participant in the debate about CR was Ryuko Kubota, a native-born Japanese who received her PhD in Canada, entered university work in the United States, and later moved again to Canada while retaining strong ties to Japan. As a native speaker of Japanese, she was able to bring in a great many resources in Japanese to add to the literature, such as the advice from Japanese writing experts in published books on how to write in Japanese. In her critique of Hinds, for example, Kubota (1997) revealed that even Japanese scholars do not agree on precisely what the *ki-shoo-ten-ketsu* structure of Japanese prose consists of and that numerous writing books advise students to write clearly and directly. Some years later, Cahill (2003) similarly referred to the "myth of the turn" (the *ten* element) in contrastive rhetoric, further emphasizing disagreements among some scholars. Perhaps more importantly, Kubota asserted that Hinds wrongly implied that the tensei-jingo newspaper column used for much of his research represents Japanese expository prose, which in reality is as diverse as one might expect within any culture and which certainly does not characterize typical academic writing in Japanese schools. (My own MA TESOL students from Japan expressed a wide range of opinions and experiences about the ki-shoo-ten-ketsu structure, some saying that they had never been taught, or used, this structure in school, and others saying they had learned about it only in their early schooling. All recognized it as typical of this particular *Asahi Shimbun* newspaper column, and none found it typical of school writing. See also Matsuda, 2003.)

Kubota (1998) further explored and critiqued the assumptions of CR in her study of the expository and persuasive writing of 46 Japanese students and found no strong evidence that culturally unique patterns either existed or were transferred to students' English writing. Some of the students followed the CR stereotype, but many did not. Some of the students also believed that Japanese essays should be organized inductively, but interestingly her Japanese raters preferred the more deductive (and equally stereotypical?) English organizational style. Kubota speculated that students' poor writing abilities in L1, their low L2 language proficiency, their beliefs about their own writing and about the presumed homogeneity of Japanese culture, and their sparse experience composing in their second language all contributed to the very diverse findings in her study.

These speculations parallel those of other scholars, such as Mohan and Lo (1985), who, in spite of assertions then and later about the influence of culture on L2 writing (Fox, 1994; Matalene, 1985; Mauranen, 1993), attributed some of the rhetorical difficulties that Chinese students in their study had when writing in English to normal developmental problems that inexperienced writers have even in their first language. Mohan and Lo (1985) pointed to other factors as well, such as topic knowledge, language proficiency, and knowledge of writing conventions that are learned in school. They also noted that writing traditions in Chinese are very diverse and that they include both inductive and deductive styles even in classical works such as the *Analects* of Confucius (see also You's, 2010, historical study of Chinese writing and Kirkpatrick and Xu's, 2012, introduction to Chinese rhetoric for language teachers). The famous eight-legged Chinese essay, Mohan and Lo claimed, is no longer an influential genre. Péry-Woodley (1990), too, focused her critiques of Kaplan's (1966) ground-breaking article on its inattention to some important variables other than L1 rhetorical traditions that could influence students' writing problems. Kaplan's early views, stated Péry-Woodley, were done "outside of any question of awareness of projected audience, writer-reader interaction, communication situation, text-type, or ... sociolinguistic factors...." (p. 148). Later work by Kaplan and his followers (e.g., Connor, 1996, 2002; Grabe & Kaplan, 1996; Purves, 1988) attempted to correct some of these deficiencies.

One reason that critiques of Kaplan's early work keep surfacing is that his original, seductively simple ideas and the notion of the "Sapir-Whorf Hypothesis" of linguistic relativity continue to capture people's attention and to help them see their own writing and that of L2 speakers in expanded if simplistic ways. Simple treatments and interpretations of complex issues always invite critique, particularly if they also contain elements of truth. In his book-length treatise, Kowal (1998), presented a critique of Kaplan's position on linguistic relativity and of his simplistic interpretations of the Whorfian principle, in addition to the detailed analysis of the original Kaplan (1966) article, mentioned earlier. (Interestingly, he noted [p. 41] that Whorf did not use the term "hypothesis." It was J. B. Carroll who did so in his introduction to Whorf's [1956] *Language, Thought, and Reality.* The term "Sapir-Whorf Hypothesis" is thus a misnomer, picked up by others and used ever since.)

Kowal reviewed the work of Whorf and several other philosophers, anthropologists, and linguists, and then presented a specific critique of some of Kaplan's underlying assumptions (critiques that can be applied to Hinds as well) such as that of the "native speaker" and of the myth of clearly demarcated linguistic and cultural groups. He argued that these are complex notions, characterized in reality by heteroglossia and great diversity, cross-linguistic and cultural influence, and change. Additionally, for Kaplan's original ideas of "unique paragraph orders" to be plausible, we need to presume that languages must be self-contained systems, "untinctured by influence from other languages" (p. 126) and that the concept of "paragraph" exists across cultures. Kaplan seems to have presumed this, but as Kowal pointed out he also conflated language, nationality, and geography in his odd grouping of languages in his early CR work (p. 131). It is impossible to establish such linguistic purity, of course, given the natural heteroglossia exhibited by every language (see further discussion in Chapter 4 on standards for writing).

Kowal also criticized Kaplan's exclusive focus on written products, and specific grammatical constructions in them, because it led to Kaplan's bypassing the pragmatic intent of writers and the creative ways they can convey meaning. In the main part of his book, he evaluated claims by Kaplan (conference papers cited in Kowal) and Bloom (1981) that Chinese has no overt counterfactual grammatical structure (*If I had...-ed, I would have...-ed*), making it difficult for Chinese speakers to reason counterfactually. To counter this odd assertion, Kowal said that his Taiwanese students, in oral debates and essays in English, rarely used the grammatical counterfactual structure but found many imaginative ways to express counterfactuality (p. 203). (See also an earlier critique by Hunt and Agnoli, 1991, and the debate between Bloom, 1981, 1984, and Au, 1983, 1984.)

In short, Kowal (1998) acknowledged, as do other applied linguists, the contribution of Kaplan in starting the entire field of CR and in pursuing questions related to it for most of his career. He also found, however, that Kaplan reduced complex notions in ways that do not reflect the diversity, change, and heteroglossia that are normal in any group of speakers and writers, and that he overlooked the pragmatic intent of writers if they did not use specific grammatical forms. Kowal claimed as well that most of us vastly oversimplify the complex thinking of Whorf. He urged us to read the original(s).

In two other important critiques of CR from the late 1990s, Leki (1997) and Matsuda (1997) both noted that in spite of the original pedagogical intention of CR, "the insights gained by research have not been effectively translated into the practice of teaching organizational structures" (Matsuda, 1997, p. 45). Matsuda showed that CR has tended to look at L2 writing problems mainly as a problem of negative transfer of L1 rhetorical patterns to L2. The result is a static model of L2 writing, in which the only context for and influence on writing are the writer's and reader's linguistic, educational, and cultural background. The writer's agency is denied, as is the dynamic complexity of decision-making processes that occur in the actual context of writing. In pedagogical applications of CR, the concept of background needs to be expanded, argued Matsuda, to include the writer's and reader's dialect variation, socioeconomic class, knowledge of topic, past writing experiences, and memberships in multiple L1 and L2 discourse communities (p. 53).

For her part, Leki (1997) explained that, at the time she wrote her critique, the contributions of CR to writing instruction had advanced little since 1966, primarily because scholars had paid such scant attention to the ideological implications of their work (p. 244). Rhetorical choices are not linked to thought patterns, she asserted, but "are made in response to social, political, and rhetorical contexts and histories" (p. 236; see also Kubota & Lehner, 2004). What would we be ready to conclude about native English speakers' thinking and reasoning, she asked, from a sample of essays that these students write in a foreign language (p. 236)? She hoped not much. She further noted, as have others, that we need to distinguish between CR problems and problems of low L2 language proficiency, and to determine as well whether L2 students are doing satisfactory work in their subject matter courses. Some evidence shows that students manage fairly well in their subject matter courses and are held back by ESL requirements (see Johns, 1991; Leki & Carson, 1997; Schneider & Fujishima, 1995). She reminded us as well that some elegant academic writing is not necessarily linear (scientist S. J. Gould). Finally, she pointed out that CR's primary focus on differences rather than similarities "has a distancing and exoticizing effect" (p. 242) that contributes little to our understanding of the complexities of writing in L1 and L2.

In more recent discussions, Atkinson (2004) and Matsuda (Atkinson & Matsuda, 2013; Matsuda & Atkinson, 2008) have pointed out that a clear conceptualization of culture is needed if CR is to restore its credibility and if IR is to move ahead. As the basis for CR's claims, a traditional "received" notion of culture links culture seductively to particular nations and languages and presumes homogeneity within territories and groups. Such a received "modernist" view thus misses the complexities, nuances, hybridities, and discontinuities within and across any group (hence the appeal of the "small culture" notion; Holliday, 1999, and more recently, the notion of translanguaging; see Chapter 4, this book).

In short, traditional and even more recent views of CR have continued to be criticized for their seemingly static and essentialized portrayals of cultures, languages, texts, and hence writers, and for insufficient attention to the powerful influences of dominant groups, languages, and text types (Canagarajah, 2013a; Kubota, 2010a, 2010b; Kubota & Lehner, 2004, 2005). Scholars continue to ask whether CR (and now IR) can survive as a purely textual research or pedagogical project, without addressing ideological and social influences and more complex views of how and why people write in L2. That said, the CR project was historically one of the most influential in the development of research and pedagogy in L2 writing (Bloch, 2013) in that it inspired researchers and teachers alike to compare and contrast the organizational aspects of different texts and speculate about reasons for differences.

Ulla Connor, long an ardent CR supporter, has proposed CR's evolution into IR (intercultural rhetoric) (Connor, 2004, 2011; Connor, Nagelhout, & Rozycki, 2008). She has admitted the weaknesses of some early CR work and attempted to correct them (Connor, 1996, 2002), and has helped expand the field of CR to include different languages, comparable text types, genres, and research methods. Bilingual in Finnish and English, Connor and her colleagues first expanded CR by using text analysis, corpus linguistics, and some qualitative techniques to analyze and compare a wide variety of texts in different languages such as grant proposals (Connor, 2000; Connor & Mauranen, 1999), case reports in business management (Connor & Kramer, 1995), and essays by students from different countries (Connor, 1987) (see also the collected essays in Purves, 1988). Then, after shifting terms from CR to IR, she and other IR enthusiasts conducted many other kinds of expanded comparative studies (Connor, 2011, chapter 6; Connor, Nagelhout, & Rozycki, 2008).

In short, one of Connor's most important contributions in response to criticisms of CR has been her ongoing effort to move CR out of the quagmire in which it has been lodged for so long (Connor, 1998, 2002) and to reconstitute it as IR (Connor, 2011, 2013; Connor, Nagelhout, & Rozycki, 2008). No longer using the term CR because its connotations are too narrow, Connor and others now insist that studies under the IR umbrella are context-sensitive, move beyond comparisons of written texts, and include multimodal focuses on how writers and speakers interact. It remains to be seen whether the many new directions in IR can help move it away from accusations that IR continues to reduce languages and cultures to oversimplified portrayals. Continued efforts to move beyond simple comparisons will help teachers of L2 writing understand the many sources of difficulty—not just negative transfer from L1—that students have in learning to write in a second language.

The Intercultural Rhetoric Critics

A number of continuing critiques seem to have prevented a full resolution of the debates surrounding contrastive and intercultural rhetoric. One of these concerns the implication that, by continuing to refer to "languages" and "cultures," overly static entities are presumed, and not sufficiently complexified or situated in a necessarily political context (Canagarajah, 2013a; Kubota, 2010a). Although culture in revised versions of CR and later of IR is no longer treated as a static entity or a product in the way that it was in older CR, some scholars believe it still needs greater development as a fluid and shifting process (Atkinson, 2004) that is simultaneously stable-for-now. Atkinson and Matsuda (2013) are not able to define culture in IR beyond saying that it is a "hodgepodge" (Atkinson, citing anthropologist Lowie, 1920) and that—though we will fail— we must attempt to define this shifting notion for ourselves, situationally, every time we use it. Some critics are not happy with any references to named cultures in IR, finding them still too bounded and essentialized, and now want to get rid of the term "intercultural rhetoric" altogether (e.g., Canagarajah, 2013a). However, boundaries must be drawn somewhere and labels must be applied in order for languages, texts, genres, or contexts to be compared and contrasted. This need for labels makes it difficult to overcome the essentializing and stereo-typing of previous incarnations of contrastive rhetoric and current work in IR. The very term *intercultural* implies two or more identifiable cultures, meaning that we need some kind of understanding of culture in order to pursue the IR project (Atkinson, 2004; Atkinson & Matsuda, 2013).

If the IR label does not satisfy the critics, then the (regret-table?) solution seems to be to create more new labels. Canaga-rajah (2013a) critiqued the term *culture* and the prefix *inter-* as others have, finding that they still connote static bounded groups. He more recently has described culture as a practice or an activity, not a place or set of values or a language and has urged us to adopt terms like *cosmopolitan practice* or *trans-lingual practice* (Cangarajah, 2013a, 2013b, 2013c, 2015) as well as English as a lingua franca (Baker, 2013; Jenkins, 2009, 2014; see further discussion in Chapter 4). Although such terms apply more often to spoken than to written language, they have been suggested by Canagarajah and others (e.g., Gar-cía, & Wei, 2014) as a way to avoid labels that put boundaries around languages and cultures, and to emphasize the active rather than static nature of how negotiation and alignment happens in global contexts when communicators do not share a language or culture. These contexts include ones that may have no geographical or national boundaries at all because they are electronic/internet/Web–based, such that the communicating that happens (written and spoken) is increasingly of a lingua franca variety. In spite of repeated assurances by IR proponents that culture in IR is now treated as dynamic and not necessarily tied to a particular language or geographical location (e.g., Connor, 2011), some other scholars like Baker (2013) still find the field English- and Anglo-dominant and the notion of culture still too constraining (Canagarajah, 2013a). We must remember, however, that written language in school and professional settings always reflects a more stable variety than does informal spoken language (Matsuda, in Atkinson & Matsuda, 2013).

It is likely that the term *intercultural rhetoric* also continues to run into difficulties with the very term *rhetoric* (Canagarajah, 2013a, p. 213). In her update of this term, Connor (2011, p. 5) tried to clarify what she intends, but the comments do more to confuse than clarify. What do proponents of IR in fact mean by *rhetoric*? Text analysis—of organizational structures, words, and phrases—may have little to do with rhetoric, as understood by classical rhetoricians. If it refers to spoken and written language used as a means of speaking and writing persuasively, then far more is involved than structural text analysis.

If intercultural rhetoric continues to pursue a primary goal of descriptive text analysis, then the IR project might survive less scathed by not trying to be all things to all people. Li (2008a) for one noted that a descriptive textual orientation remains viable even without the political and ideological edge that some people have called for (e.g., Kubota, 2010a). (See also work by Hyland, 2000, 2004, 2009, 2015a, 2015b, who has compared texts in academic disciplines written by L1 and L2 authors but who does not use the term IR.) As is clear from the well-articulated overview provided by Belcher (2014), many issues remain to be resolved (see Ongoing Questions).

Classroom Perspectives

Although the principles of CR and IR cannot be applied directly to classroom writing instruction, they can alert teachers to a number of important issues that will help them make decisions in their own classrooms and that will raise students' awareness of discourse patterns (Connor, 1997). I first describe some older suggestions made by others about applications of CR. I then discuss a more recent piece of teacher research by Abasi (2012), who drew on principles of IR in a summary-writing exercise he did with his class of American university students learning Persian.

First, Grabe and Kaplan (1989, 1996) alerted us to some of the kinds of knowledge that CR focused on that will help teachers and students in the L2 writing class. Teachers and students need to be familiar with:

1. Knowledge of rhetorical patterns of arrangement and the relative frequency of various patterns (e.g., exposition/argument, classification, definition, etc.).
2. Knowledge of composing conventions and strategies needed to generate text (e.g., pre-writing, data-collection, revision, etc.).
3. Knowledge of the morphosyntax of the target language, particularly as it applies at the intersentential level.
4. Knowledge of the coherence-creating mechanisms of the target language.
5. Knowledge of the writing conventions of the target language in the sense of both frequency and distribution of types and text appearance (e.g., letter, essay, report).
6. Knowledge of the audience characteristics and expectations in the target culture.
7. Knowledge of the subject to be discussed, including both 'what everyone knows' in the target culture and specialist knowledge. (Grabe & Kaplan, 1996, p. 200)

The authors pointed out that they do not intend to prescribe a method for instruction based on CR, but to suggest the body of knowledge required in the teaching and learning of reading and writing (Grabe & Kaplan, 1989, p. 271) and to suggest as well some pedagogical objectives (Kaplan, 1988). These objectives include making composition teachers aware that different conventions for writing exist in different cultures (note that the "culture" concept is used uncritically here), that discourse-level and coherence features of text production may differ across languages, and that readers and writers may take on different responsibilities in different cultures. They include helping L2 writers learn that it is important to define an audience before writing, that writing types, tasks, and organizational and other conventions may differ in L1 and L2, and that writers need subject matter knowledge and knowledge of the interactive and social nature of writing (Kaplan, 1988, pp. 296–297; Grabe & Kaplan, 1989, pp. 276–277).

Leki (1991) noted, as have others, that CR has a textual orientation, appearing to be concerned primarily with form. However, she clarified that "the true or ultimate focus of a textual orientation, and of contrastive rhetoric studies, and an appropriate pedagogical agenda of a textual orientation in a writing class, is a focus not on form but on audience" (p. 135). Concluding that students must be taught to write in ways that fit audience expectations within the cultures they are learning to write in, she emphasized how important it is for teachers and students to build awareness of the existence, if not the details, of different rhetorics. (An updated argument about teaching students the importance of reader receptivity in genre studies has been made by Tardy, 2016.) Awareness does not necessarily lead to improvement, but it can help students realize that their writing problems do not stem from personal failures (Leki, 1991, p. 138).

When it comes to applying some of these ideas to the L2 writing classroom, however, we lack precise guidelines, mostly because CR descriptive research did not provide us with clear answers to pedagogical questions. There are some well-established techniques in reorganizing scrambled sentences, identifying topic sentences and supports, and other general writing tasks (see Ferris & Hedgcock, 2014; Grabe & Kaplan, 1989, 1996; Reid, 1993). But if we accept the idea that CR and IR deal mainly with questions of what readers expect with regard to organizational and coherence features of different text types in different contexts, genres, and languages, then a sensible place to begin seems to be with carefully planned awareness-building activities of audience expectations of rhetorical features. Teachers using such awareness-building activities would, however, need to resist "constructing and reinforcing the notion of cultural uniqueness" (Kubota, 1998, p. 90). In the L2 writing class when we ask students to consider rhetorical features of different kinds of writing within their own cultures, we risk perpetuating stereotypes if students themselves, as Kubota found, hold overly simple beliefs about their L1 cultures and rhetorics. Teachers, too, may not know enough about rhetorical conventions in students' own languages to counter these stereotypes effectively. I suggest in the next section an "investigative pedagogical approach."

Taking an Investigative Pedagogical Approach in the Classroom

Deciding what to compare and contrast in the L2 writing class depends upon a number of factors. For example, L2 writing teachers should ask early on what students will need to do with their L2 writing. Decisions further depend on whether teachers are themselves bi- or multilingual and can thus participate as insiders on analyses of comparable texts in different languages. Teachers also need to decide if it is easier or more difficult for students to learn write for particular purposes if they have a deep understanding, rather than just a formulaic knowledge, of rhetorical conventions.

Such decisions further depend on practical considerations such as how much time students and teachers have in conjunction with students' needs. For example, students who need to pass a one-time entrance or exit test and who do not need to write in their L2 beyond this, probably do not need to develop a deep understanding of rhetorical differences. On the other hand, students who need to write regularly in settings outside the L2 writing class—in other subject matter classes, in the workplace, or professionally for publication—will probably benefit from an approach that asks them to carefully consider reader expectations and to observe closely how different texts use organizational and linguistic features to fit those expectations—a study of genres in "small cultures" and communities (Connor, 2011; Holliday, 1999; Tardy, 2016). This kind of investigation may involve breaking down students' stereotypes of their L1 and L2 and helping them develop a more complex understanding of how their L1 rhetoric creates meaning. (See, for example, the discussion by Nanri, 2001, on the stereotypical belief held by some Japanese scholars that Japanese texts lack logic, and her analysis of several texts to counter this fallacy.)

If teachers choose not to take the quick route of applying simplistic formulae to students' L2 writing, it makes sense to take an investigative, questioning approach to CR and IR issues in the L2 writing class. Depending on students' L2 proficiency, teachers and students can investigate different kinds of L1-L2 texts, the kinds of writing instruction students received, and the expectations that readers have in L1 and L2. The investigations can be set up as discussions, simple or complex discourse analyses of comparable texts, mini-research projects involving surveys and interviews, and practice writing from models. Existing research on CR and IR can be used as models for class activities.

For example, in a rare example in applied linguistics of students learning a language other than English, one teacher-research study documented how 10 U.S. students whose L1 was English in a class of Persian as an L2 carried out and interpreted a summarizing task (Abasi, 2012). Abasi said he drew on principles of intercultural rhetoric to design and understand this pedagogical activity and students' responses to it. Students first received some basic instruction in the qualities of a good summary (Western, I presume). He then prepared two texts in Persian from current news items on the same topic. One was an original news story in Persian, and the other was the same story from an American newspaper, but translated by Abasi into Persian as closely as he could to the original English. Students had to read both articles as part of two different class activities, and then summarize both articles in Persian. Abasi checked the two summaries for the order in which ideas were presented and for errors, and then interviewed students about which Persian text they found easier or more difficult to understand and summarize, the original or the translated version. Nearly all students commented on the clarity and well-organized presentation of the translated English version and the rambling and vague character of the original Persian text. The translated English version, the students said, was thus easier for them to summarize, leaving them time to check their Persian summaries for errors. Abasi found more errors in the summaries of the original Persian text, and learned that the students took more time to decide how to construct their summaries, leaving them less time to check for errors. Discussions and interviews afterwards in both Persian and English helped students become explicitly aware of differences in the two texts and question why the texts might have been so different. Moreover, a Persian journalist was brought into the discussion to help explain the rambling structure of the original Persian text.

Because Abasi conducted this study as a piece of teacher research, the summarizing tasks done by the students were part of his normal class activities. He was able to learn about his U.S. students' summarizing skills in Persian, and their attitudes about the differences they saw in the two texts. Similar comparative activities could be designed by any bilingual teachers whose students share an L1. Contexts could be outside English-dominant countries in relatively homogeneous classes of L2 English learners, or classes in which L1 English students are learning an L2.

In comparing L1 and L2 texts in class activities like this, it is important for both teachers and students to look at samples in students' L1s alongside L2 samples, or as Abasi did, at samples translated into the L2 that follow the rhetorical conventions of an original L1 sample. Abasi might have drawn on a U.S.

English notion of paragraph (it was not clear in his study), but even the basic concept of paragraph differs across languages (e.g., Clyne, 1987; Régent, 1985). The question to ask students is: Does the concept of "paragraph" exist in their L1s? If it does (as in the case of Abasi's study), does the concept exist in the L2 that is being taught? Discussion and examination of writing samples from students' L1s can help clarify this. The point is that in making comparisons and contrasts, teachers and students should not impose a rhetorical feature from one language directly onto another without investigating whether the feature is comparable.

As another investigative activity, students who need to read and write academic articles within specific fields can conduct their own mini-surveys at the paragraph and the whole text level of published articles in their fields, using corpus analyses (Belcher & Nelson, 2013) or perusing individual published texts. In an EFL setting, students will have access to articles published in their own languages as well as in English, making it relatively easy to secure materials for comparison, but comparisons in English only, across the "small cultures" of disciplines, can be equally revealing (Hyland, 2000, 2015a, 2015b). The work of John Swales (1990a, 1990b; Swales & Feak, 2000, 2012; Swales & Najjar, 1987) as well as Hyland can provide teachers with a great deal of information on structural and linguistic features of academic and research genres, such as the "moves" within research article introductions or other sections of research articles and features of other genres such as grant proposals (see also Connor, 2000; Connor & Mauranen, 1999). In my own writing classes in a Japanese university, some students needed to write theses, conference proposals and presentations, or articles for publication. By comparing readings they did across their various disciplines, primarily in English, according to some of the structural features identified by Swales and others, they developed a text-level sense of what kinds of information typically belong in different sections of academic articles, and a sense as well (important!) that not all academic texts follow the observations made by Swales. At this point the students were able to take control of some of their own decisions, notice similarities and differences within their own disciplines, compare their observations of published English language materials with those in Japanese, and make informed choices in their own writing.

Not all students need to learn to write academic essays or research articles. Students who are interested in journalism (cf. Abasi, 2012, discussed above) could model an investigation of newspaper articles on Ron Scollon's (2000) study of parallel news stories in Chinese and English editions of the same newspaper. Scollon looked at five consecutive days of stories in parallel editions of Chinese and English newspapers and discovered that different genres coexisted within the same papers, and that parallel stories in English and Chinese editions differed in significant ways. Scollon cautioned scholars, and by extension, teachers of L2 writing who look to CR and IR for classroom applications, about making conclusions about genres and about characteristics of writers and of discourse communities (e.g., of journalists) without carefully controlling for genre. But given that many newspapers from different language and culture groups are now available on the internet as well as in libraries, students could use some of Scollon's categories of comparison to do their own investigations of journalistic texts in L1 and L2.

In short, it is important to compare and contrast *comparable* texts, and portions of texts, both across and within languages and across and within disciplines, a commonsense point made by Connor (2004, 2011, 2013) and other followers of IR. In the L2 writing class, such comparisons and contrasts need to be carried out according to what students need and want to learn. Efforts need to be made at every point to capture regularities and differences in texts without succumbing to stereotypes or falsely conveying that English-dominant conventions are superior. This sense of the superiority of English is increasingly difficult to resist in the face of ongoing global trends that are resulting in some merging of Anglophone with non-English rhetorical norms (Kubota, 2010a).

Another investigative activity that can be conducted in L2 writing classes asks what the students' previous instruction in

L1 and L2 reading and writing has been and what their beliefs are about what "good writing" consists of (Li, 1996). Liebman (1988, 1992; Liebman-Kleine, 1987) recommended that L2 writing students become "ethnographers" of their own writing, and that teachers at the very least learn something about their students' previous writing experiences and engage students in discussion about writing in their L1s. For example, Liebman (1992) asked her Japanese and Arabic speaking students about the writing instruction they received in their home countries, using a variety of question types (Likert, open-ended, check list, ranking). She discovered interesting differences in students' previous writing experiences, ones that would be valuable for writing teachers to know as they plan class activities. Although Liebman's questionnaire was used for research purposes, adaptations of it would function wonderfully as the basis for students' mini-research projects and class discussion. It is likely that students will find as much diversity of beliefs and experiences as Liebman found in her research. Students could also analyze the textbooks they used in their home countries in their earlier schooling days for models of reading and writing, following the analyses done on language arts textbooks in Japan, China, the United States, and Canada by Kubota and Shi (Kubota & Shi. 2005; Shi & Kubota, 2007). As did Kubota and Shi, students might find that the models in their textbooks do not display strict stereotypes, but a diversity of organizational features of texts.

A third area of investigation that teachers can pursue in their L2 writing classes, perhaps the most important application of CR and IR to writing classrooms, concerns reader (audience) expectations. Such investigations can involve students in learning how teachers of writing in different cultures respond to writing, or how the students themselves respond. In her ethnographic study, Li (1996) compared the responses of four U.S. and mainland Chinese teachers' to six student essays (personal narratives) written by students in the U.S. and China, a genre she noted is widely used in both countries. The essays themselves were not compared, but the teachers' evaluations of them were. The criteria for "good writing," Li found, were somewhat different for the U.S. and Chinese teachers, the former appreciating logic and a clear opening and the latter appreciating an essay that expressed sentiment, natural scenes, and a moral message. In addition to finding some differences in reader response that could be attributed to culture, she also speculated that responses to writing are deeply personal and individual. Her project involved interviews of teachers in the U.S. and China—an investigative project that could be adapted by students in ESL and EFL settings to be conducted in person, by letter, or by electronic communication.

It is also possible to investigate students' own responses as peer readers to essays by students like themselves. For example, in a revealing study of Japanese undergraduates' perceptions of different features of two compositions written by Japanese students in English, Rinnert and Kobayashi (2001) compared the responses of four groups of readers to different versions of the two compositions, altered to reflect typically American English and Japanese rhetorical patterns (based on some of the literature that I reviewed in this chapter, and similar to the study by Abasi, 2012, of L2 students of Persian). They found that the responses of the four groups (inexperienced L2 writers, experienced L2 writers, Japanese teachers of writing, and native English–speaking teachers of writing in Japan) differed significantly in a number of ways. The inexperienced writers paid more attention to the content of the different versions of the essays than to the organization, logical connections, or language. The more experience the readers had in L2 writing, the more likely they were to respond positively to the typically "American" features of the essays. This study is important for CR and IR because it demonstrates what many scholars have suggested, namely, that reader expectations and audience analysis are needed in L2 writing classes. Whether they are L1 or L2 speakers, if writers misjudge their readers, their writing will not communicate well or will be judged faulty. Teachers can help students design mini-research projects like that of Rinnert and Kobayashi (2001). (See also Kobayashi & Rinnert,

1996, to see how peer readers respond to different kinds of L1 and L2 essays, and Rinnert & Kobayashi, 2009, for a discussion of the role of previous experience and instruction in foreign language writing classes).

Even without doing a mini-research project activity, teachers and students can explore facets of reader expectations across cultures. In discussion, some of my students in Japan echoed what some cross-cultural scholars have observed (Canagarajah, 2002, Ch. 4; Clyne, 1987; Connor, 1999): A writer who is too clear and too redundant risks insulting the intelligence of readers, or as Hinds (1990) implied, does not allow readers to do their own thinking. Alternatively, as Abasi (2012) found, some texts might seem vague or rambling for political reasons, because the writer does not wish to commit strongly to a controversial view. Readers of academic English on the other hand usually do not wish to struggle to understand a writer's message. The subject matter and terminology are often difficult enough. Whether the reader is a teacher-evaluator of an important essay test, a graduate advisor reading a thesis, or a manuscript reviewer reading an article for publication, readers of academic English tend to want to get through the material fast and yet still have their thinking provoked. Friends of mine who used to read TOEFL essays by students from all over the world for the Educational Testing Service sometimes read well more than 200 essays at a sitting (an activity that is disappearing as automated essay scoring systems continue to proliferate; see Chapter 7). If readers have to struggle to find a point, students will surely receive a lower score than if the evaluators can sail through a clearly introduced and structurally coherent essay. On the other hand, the student who gets the structure "right" (following the stereotype of the linear English essay) but fills in formulaic slots with boring content will also probably not receive the maximum possible points. Teachers and students in the L2 writing class can therefore profit greatly by investigating what the expectations of readers are across and within languages and text types, and by bringing those expectations explicitly to the surface. In other words, in addition to comparing texts and portions of texts, teachers and students can compare and contrast the responses of different readers to the same material.

In the L2 writing class, then, it is important to ask students, and ourselves, a great many questions. To start with, teachers need to know something about students' experiences and expectations writing in their L1s. As students learn to write in their L2, they need to know what their readers expect; it is the job of teachers to help make these expectations explicit, and to help students learn to ask appropriate questions of the texts they are reading and modeling their own writing on. If students have stereotypical ideas of what readers expect, it is our job to complicate their understanding and help them recognize that they have choices, and therefore agency. Both within and across cultures, as readers and contexts change, so must our writing. Students who are new to a culture or to a discipline need our help in analyzing the many possible audiences for the many possible types of writing they may need to do. Our goal is to provide students with this help without perpetuating stereotypes.

I have suggested in this section that teachers and students interested in the narrow textual comparisons in CR and the more broadly contextualized IR take an investigative pedagogical approach to differences in L1 and L2 texts, writers' instructional backgrounds, and reader expectations. This approach primarily involves awareness building rather than actual writing, and the need for teachers to consider some very basic questions. Does a one-size-fits all approach make sense even if it does perpetuate stereotypes? It may, if students need only to pass a particular kind of writing test. Does a more complex approach make sense, perhaps involving students in actual analyses of different kinds of texts and readers from their L1 and L2? In such cases, teachers can turn to some of the studies that have been conducted in CR and IR and adopt some of the survey, analysis, and interview methods as techniques in their own classrooms for helping students compare and contrast different kinds of writing.

Ongoing Questions

Teachers of L2 writing, both within English-medium settings and foreign language contexts, may be disappointed that clearer conclusions did not result from the discussions in this chapter. Throughout this book, however, a primary message is that many of the issues are in fact unresolved, and that teachers therefore need to consider them not in isolation as problems to be resolved, but as dilemmas to be dealt with in the context of their own teaching. After all, if everything is clear and resolved, we no longer have anything to think about or to do! In this section of the chapter, I review the key issues and questions, and urge teachers to consider them within the realities of their own classrooms.

First, I think it is important to look closely at the language with which we discuss CR and IR issues. Throughout the older CR literature, from 1966 and occasionally up to the present we see phrases such as "language or culture X prefers such and such rhetorical pattern," or "Japanese is more indirect than English." However, it simply does not make sense to say that "English prefers..." or "Japanese prefers....". Languages and cultures cannot prefer anything, nor is it languages that are inherently direct or indirect. It is people who prefer things, with language, used directly or indirectly, as a vehicle for our preferences. A more accurate and productive question, therefore, is where do our preferences come from, as people, as writers, as readers and importantly as members of not just one homogeneous culture but of multiple and often fuzzily defined subcultures and disciplines, as more recent work in IR has reminded us? Likewise, all of us would benefit from not using terms too loosely, particularly ones that have never been fully defined in an agreed upon way: What does each of us, at a particular moment, mean by *culture* or *rhetoric* or *L1* or *L2*, or *native* or *nonnative speaker*? How can we use such terms without becoming trapped by static views or stereotypes?

Second, with regard to the long-debated issue of possible connections between the rhetorical patterns people use in their writing and the cognitive abilities or patterns in people's thinking, it seems clear that it makes little sense to speculate that our students cannot think "logically" (for example) based on a sample of their L2 writing. It behooves us to ask what we as teachers would want anyone to conclude about our own thinking from a sample of our less-than-proficient second or foreign language writing. What factors do influence the thinking patterns of students and teachers? To what extent might those factors be culturally shared, individual and idiosyncratic, developmentally, or educationally shaped?

Third, much of the literature on CR and IR points to interesting differences in L1 and L2 texts, but questions remain as to the sources of those differences. What are the roles of readers in different cultures, and do these role change according to text type, genre, and purpose for reading? How do multicultural influences, such as international audiences in business, internet communication, and research, affect the rhetorical choices that writers make? Studies have also pointed to important similarities across particular types of L1 and L2 texts. Should we be paying more attention to these similarities in our teaching of L2 writing?

Fourth, what are the educational backgrounds and writing experiences of our students? What have they been taught directly or indirectly about writing in their L1, as well as in their L2? Where do their beliefs about "good writing" come from? To what extent do the problems that L2 students have with writing parallel those that inexperienced L1 writers have, and so cannot be attributed to L1-L2 differences? In other words, do differences indicate linguistic and cultural diversity or do they suggest developmental issues? Whether L1 or L2 users, students who have no experience writing a certain genre or who have little knowledge of a topic will struggle to recognize what the appropriate pieces are and how to fit them together.

Fifth, how are teachers to distinguish among problems of low language proficiency, CR-IR problems, and thinking problems? These problems often mesh in ways that cannot easily be separated for research purposes.

Finally, what role do stereotypical beliefs and formulae for writing play in particular writing classes? How much complexity can a particular group of students deal with, given their particular needs and purposes for learning to write and the time they have to devote to classroom learning? Without undermining our goal of helping students become better writers, how can we help them understand that when someone says "Americans write and think directly" we need to ask: Which Americans? Writing what, and writing for what purposes? If we choose to offer our students rhetorical formulae, how can we help them understand that these formulae may not reflect English in general, or even academic English in general, but are linked to particular types of writing written for particular audiences and purposes?

CR and to some extent IR continue to be primarily textual projects, both assuming differences, but necessarily presuming some uniformity (e.g., "stable for now") within large and small cultures and established varieties of languages. Otherwise, comparisons and contrasts cannot be made. It is up to teachers and students, not just to researchers, to inject diversity and dynamism into their own explorations of rhetorical choices in writing and not fall prey to quick and easy answers.

Beliefs and Practices

Beliefs

1. What are your own beliefs about the connections among language, culture, and thought?
2. What kind of project do you believe CR and IR are: textual analysis or textual analysis augmented by other factors? If the latter, what factors other than L1 factors do you believe cause writing problems in L2?
3. Do you believe that we should stop using the term *contrastive rhetoric* altogether at this point and shift to the term *intercultural rhetoric* or even some other term? Why or why not?

4. To what extent do you believe that current versions of IR are about pedagogy or research? If research, what should the research agenda consist of? Do you believe that the research has direct applications in the L2 writing class? If so, how?

5. After reading some of the CR and IR debates in this chapter, and reading as well some of the original articles, what are your views on the different opinions and evidence that different scholars have presented?

6. What unresolved issues do you see in using the concept of intercultural rhetoric as part of a pedagogy to teach L2 writing? As part of a research project?

Practices

1. In your own experiences writing in L1 and L2 (L3, ...) what CR and/or IR issues have arisen for you? Where do your own problems in writing come from? Have you been consciously aware of the factors that influence your rhetorical decisions? Where does your awareness of these factors come from?

2. In your teaching experiences, have you noticed any features of your students' writing that would lend credence to the claims of CR or IR? If so, describe these, making sure to describe the kinds and purposes of the writing.

3. To what extent do your students have a clear sense of what the audiences for their L1 and L2 writing expect? In a discussion or with a simple questionnaire, try to find out.

4. In your teaching, what kinds of implicit or explicit instruction and explanation do you, or might you, provide students about the features (rhetorical or otherwise) of the kinds of writing you would like students to practice? Share some examples with classmates.

5. Devise a way to learn about your students' writing practices in L1, including any instruction they have received and features of different kinds of L1 writing that they believe are typical. Discuss those L1 writing practices and instruction in class, making comparisons where possible.

References

Abasi, A. (2012). The pedagogical value of intercultural rhetoric: A report from a Persian-as-a-foreign-language classroom. *Journal of Second Language Writing, 21*, 195–220.

Atkinson, D. (2004). Contrasting rhetorics/contrasting cultures: Why contrastive rhetoric needs a better conceptualization of culture. *Journal of English for Academic Purposes, 3*(4), 277–289.

Atkinson, D., & Matsuda, P. K. (2013). Intercultural rhetoric: A conversation—The sequel. In D. Belcher & G. Nelson (Eds.), *Critical and corpus-based approaches to intercultural rhetoric* (pp. 227–242). Ann Arbor: University of Michigan Press.

Au, T. K. F. (1983). Chinese and English counterfactuals: The Sapir-Whorf hypothesis revisited. *Cognition, 15*, 155–187.

Au, T. K. F. (1984). Counterfactuals: In reply to Alfred Bloom. *Cognition, 17*, 289–302.

Baker, W. (2013). Interpreting the culture in intercultural rhetoric: A critical perspective from English as a Lingua Franca studies. In D. Belcher & G. Nelson (Eds.), *Critical and corpus-based approaches to intercultural rhetoric* (pp. 22–45). Ann Arbor: University of Michigan Press.

Belcher, D. (2014). What we need and don't need intercultural rhetoric for: A retrospective and prospective look at an evolving research area. *Journal of Second Language Writing, 25*, 59–67.

Belcher, D., & Nelson, G. (Eds.). (2013). *Critical and corpus-based approaches to intercultural rhetoric.* Ann Arbor: University of Michigan Press.

Bickner, R., & Peyasantiwong, P. (1988). Cultural variation in reflective writing. In A. C. Purves (Ed.), *Writing across language and cultures: Issues in contrastive rhetoric* (pp. 160–174). Newbury Park, CA: Sage.

Bloch, J. (2013). Afterword. In D. Belcher & G. Nelson (Eds.), *Critical and corpus-based approaches to intercultural rhetoric* (pp. 243–252). Ann Arbor: University of Michigan Press.

Bloom, A. H. (1981). *The linguistic shaping of thought: A study of the impact of language on thinking in China and the West*. Hillsdale, NJ: Lawrence Erlbaum.

Bloom, A. H. (1984). Caution—The words you use may affect what you say. A response to Au. *Cognition, 17*, 275–287.

Cahill, D., (2003). The myth of the "turn" in contrastive rhetoric. *Written Communication, 20*(2), 170–194.

Canagarajah, A. S. (2002). *A geopolitics of academic writing*. Pittsburgh, PA: University of Pittsburgh Press.

Canagarajah, A. S. (2013a). From intercultural rhetoric to cosmopolitan practice: Addressing new challenges in lingua franca English. In D. Belcher & G. Nelson (Eds.), *Critical and corpus-based approaches to intercultural rhetoric* (pp. 203–226). Ann Arbor: University of Michigan Press.

Canagarajah, A S. (Ed.). (2013b). *Literacy as translingual practice: Negotiating between communities and classrooms*. New York: Routledge/Taylor & Francis.

Canagarajah, A S. (2013c). *Translingual practice: Global English and cosmopolitan relations*. New York: Routledge/Taylor & Francis.

Canagarajah, S. (2015). Clarifying the relationship between translingual practice and L2 writing: Addressing learner identities. *Applied Linguistics Review, 6*(4), 415–440.

Christensen, F. (1963). A generative rhetoric of the sentence. *College Composition and Communication, 14*, 155–161.

Christensen, F. (1965). A generative rhetoric of the paragraph. *College Composition and Communication, 16*, 144–156.

Clyne, M. G. (1987). Cultural differences in the organization of academic texts: English and German. *Journal of Pragmatics, 11*(2), 211–247.

Connor, U. (1987). Argumentative patterns in student essays: Cross-cultural differences. In U. Connor & R. B. Kaplan (Eds.), *Writing across languages: Analysis of L2 text* (pp. 57–71). Reading, MA: Addison-Wesley.

Connor, U. (1996). *Contrastive rhetoric: Cross-cultural aspects of second-language writing*. Cambridge, U.K.: Cambridge University Press.

Connor, U. (1997). Contrastive rhetoric: Implications for teachers of writing in multicultural classrooms. In C. Severino, J. C. Guerra, & J. E. Butler (Eds.), *Writing in multicultural settings* (pp. 198–208). New York: Modern Language Association.

Connor, U. (1998). Contrastive rhetoric: Developments and challenges. *Studia Anglica Posnaniensia, XXXIII*, 105–116.

Connor, U. (1999). Learning to write academic prose in a second language: A literacy autobiography. In G. Braine (Ed.), *Non-native educators in English language teaching* (pp. 29–42). Mahwah, NJ: Lawrence Erlbaum.

Connor, U. (2000). Variation in rhetorical moves in grant proposals of U.S. humanists and scientists. *Text, 20*(1), 1–28.

Connor, U. (2002). New directions in contrastive rhetoric. *TESOL Quarterly, 36*(4), 493–510.

Connor, U. (2004). Intercultural rhetoric research: Beyond texts. *Journal of English for Academic Purposes, 3*(4), 291–304.

Connor, U. (2011). *Intercultural rhetoric in the writing classroom.* Ann Arbor: University of Michigan Press.

Connor, U. (2013). Corpus linguistics in intercultural rhetoric. In D. Belcher & G. Nelson (Eds.), *Critical and corpus-based approaches to intercultural rhetoric* (pp. 8–21). Ann Arbor: University of Michigan Press.

Connor, U., & Kaplan, R. B. (Eds.). (1987). *Writing across languages: Analysis of L2 text.* Reading, MA: Addison-Wesley.

Connor, U. M., & Kramer, M. G. (1995). Writing from sources: Case studies of graduate students in business management. In D. Belcher & G. Braine (Eds.), *Academic writing in a second language: Essays on research and pedagogy* (pp. 155–182). Norwood, NJ: Ablex.

Connor, U., & Lauer, J. (1988). Cross-cultural variation in persuasive student writing. In A. C. Purves (Ed.), *Writing across language and cultures: Issues in contrastive rhetoric* (pp. 138–159). Newbury Park, CA: Sage.

Connor, U., & Mauranen, A. (1999). Linguistic analysis of grant proposals: European Union research grants. *English for Specific Purposes, 18*(1), 47–62.

Connor, U., Nagelhout, E., & Rozycki, W. (Eds.). (2008). *Contrastive rhetoric: Reaching to intercultural rhetoric.* Amsterdam: John Benjamins.

Eggington, W. G. (1987). Written academic discourse in Korean: Implications for effective communication. In U. Connor & R. B. Kaplan (Eds.), *Writing across languages: Analysis of L2 text* (pp. 153–168). Reading, MA: Addison-Wesley.

Everett, D. L. (2012). *Language: The cultural tool.* New York: Pantheon.

Ferris, D., & Hedgcock, J. (2014). *Teaching L2 composition: Purpose, process, and practice* (3rd ed.). New York: Routledge/Taylor & Francis.

Fox, H. (1994). *Listening to the world: Cultural issues in academic writing.* Urbana, IL: National Council of Teachers of English.

García, O., & Wei, L. (2014). *Translanguaging: Language, bilingualism and education.* New York: Palgrave Macmillan.

Grabe, W., & Kaplan, R. B. (1989). Writing in a second language: Contrastive rhetoric. In D. M. Johnson & D. H. Roen (Eds.), *Richness in writing: Empowering ESL students* (pp. 263–283). New York: Longman.

Grabe, W., & Kaplan, R. B. (1996). *Theory and practice of writing.* New York: Longman.

Hinds, J. (1983). Contrastive rhetoric: Japanese and English. *Text, 3*(2), 183–195.

Hinds, J. (1987). Reader versus writer responsibility: A new typology. In U. Connor & R. B. Kaplan (Eds.), *Writing across languages: Analysis of L2 text* (pp. 141–152). Reading, MA: Addison-Wesley.

Hinds, J. (1990). Inductive, deductive, quasi-inductive: Expository writing in Japanese, Korean, Chinese, and Thai. In U. Connor & A. M. Johns (Eds.), *Coherence in writing: Research and pedagogical perspectives* (pp. 87–110). Alexandria, VA: TESOL.

Holliday. A. (1999). Small cultures. *Applied Linguistics, 20*(2), 237–264.

Hunt, E., & Agnoli, F. (1991). The Whorfian hypothesis: A cognitive psychology perspective. *Psychological Review, 98*(3), 377–389.

Hyland, K. (2000). *Disciplinary discourses: Social interactions in academic writing.* London: Longman.

Hyland, K. (2004). *Genre and second language writing.* Ann Arbor: University of Michigan Press.

Hyland, K. (2009). *Academic discourse.* London: Continuum.

Hyland, K. (2015a). *Academic publishing: Issues and challenges in the construction of knowledge.* Oxford, U.K.: Oxford University Press.

Hyland, K. (2015b). Genre, discipline and identity. *Journal of English for Academic Purposes, 20*, 1–12.

Jenkins, J. (2009). English as a lingua franca: Interpretations and attitudes. *World Englishes, 28*(2), 200–207.

Jenkins, J. (2014). *English as a lingua franca in the international university: The politics of academic English language policy.* New York: Routledge/ Taylor & Francis.

Jenkins, S., & Hinds, J. (1987). Business letter writing: English, French, and Japanese. *TESOL Quarterly, 21*(2), 327–354.

Kachru, Y. (1988). Writers in Hindi and English. In A. C. Purves (Ed.), *Writing across languages and cultures* (pp. 109–137). Newbury Park, CA: Sage.

Kachru, Y. (1995). Contrastive rhetoric in world Englishes. *English Today, 41*(1), 21–31.

Kamimura, T., & Oi, K. (1997). Contrastive rhetoric in letter writing: The interaction of linguistic proficiency and cultural awareness. *JALT Journal, 19*(1), 58–76.

Kaplan, R. B. (1966). Cultural thought patterns in inter-cultural education. *Language Learning, 16*, 1–20.

Kaplan, R. B. (1980). Cultural thought patterns in inter-cultural education. In K. Croft (Ed.), *Readings on English as a second language for teachers and teacher trainees* (2nd ed.) (pp. 399–418). Cambridge, MA: Winthrop Publishers, Inc.

Kaplan, R. B. (1987). Cultural thought patterns revisited. In U. Connor & R. B. Kaplan (Eds.), *Writing across languages: Analysis of L2 text* (pp. 9–21). Reading, MA: Addison-Wesley.

Kaplan, R. B. (1988). Contrastive rhetoric and second language learning: Notes toward a theory of contrastive rhetoric. In A. C. Purves (Ed.), *Writing across language and cultures: Issues in contrastive rhetoric* (pp. 275–304). Newbury Park, CA: Sage.

Kirkpatrick, A., & Xu, Z. (2012). *Chinese rhetoric and writing: An introduction for language teachers*. Anderson, SC: Parlor Press.

Kobayashi, H., & Rinnert, C. (1996). Factors affecting composition evaluation in an EFL context: Cultural rhetorical pattern and readers' background. *Language Learning, 46*, 397–437.

Kowal, K. H. (1998). *Rhetorical implications of linguistic relativity: Theory and application to Chinese and Taiwanese interlanguages*. New York: Peter Lang.

Kubota, R. (1997). A reevaluation of the uniqueness of Japanese written discourse. *Written Communication, 14*(4), 460–480.

Kubota, R. (1998). An investigation of L1-L2 transfer in writing among Japanese university students: Implications for contrastive rhetoric. *Journal of Second Language Writing, 7*(1), 69–100.

Kubota, R. (2010a). Critical approaches to theory in second language writing: A case of critical contrastive rhetoric. In T. Silva & P. Matsuda (Eds.), *Practicing theory in second language writing* (pp. 191–208). West Lafayette, IN: Parlor Press.

Kubota, R. (2010b). Cross-cultural perspectives on writing: Contrastive rhetoric. In N. L. Hornberger & S. L. McKay (Eds.), *Sociolinguistics and language education* (pp. 265–289). Clevedon, U.K.: Multilingual Matters.

Kubota, R., & Lehner, A. (2004). Toward critical contrastive rhetoric. *Journal of Second Language Writing, 13*(1), 7–27.

Kubota, R., & Lehner, A. (2005). Dialogue: Response to Ulla Connor's comments. *Journal of Second Language Writing, 14*, 137–143.

Kubota, R., & Shi, L. (2005). Instruction and reading samples for opinion writing in L1 junior high school textbooks in China and Japan. *Journal of Asian Pacific Communication, 15*(1), 97–127.

Leki, I. (1991). Twenty-five years of contrastive rhetoric: Text analysis and writing pedagogies. *TESOL Quarterly, 25*(1), 123–143.

Leki, I. (1997). Cross-talk: ESL issues and contrastive rhetoric. In C. Severino, J. C. Guerra, & J. E. Butler (Eds.), *Writing in multicultural settings* (pp. 234–244). New York: Modern Language Association.

Leki, I., & Carson, J. G. (1997). "Completely different words": EAP and the writing experiences of ESL students in university courses. *TESOL Quarterly, 31*, 39–69.

Li, X. (1996). *"Good writing" in cross-cultural context.* Albany: SUNY Press.

Li, X. (2008a). From contrastive rhetoric to intercultural rhetoric: A search for a collective identity. In U. Connor, E. Nagelhout, & W. Rozycki (Eds.), *Contrastive rhetoric: Reaching to intercultural rhetoric* (pp. 11–24). Amsterdam: John Benjamins.

Li, X. (2008b). Learning to write a thesis with an argumentative edge. In C. P. Casanave & X. Li (Eds.), *Learning the literacy practices of graduate school: Insiders' reflections on academic enculturation* (pp. 46–57). Ann Arbor: University of Michigan Press.

Liebman, J. D. (1988). Contrastive rhetoric: Students as ethnographers. *Journal of Basic Writing, 7*, 6–27.

Liebman, J. D. (1992). Toward a new contrastive rhetoric: Differences between Arabic and Japanese rhetorical instruction. *Journal of Second Language Writing, 1*(2), 141–166.

Liebman-Kleine, J. (1987). Teaching and researching invention: Using ethnography in ESL writing classes. *ESL Journal, 41*(2), 104–111.

Matalene, C. (1985). Contrastive rhetoric: An American writing teacher in China. *College English, 47*(8), 789–808.

Matsuda, P. K. (1997). Contrastive rhetoric in context: A dynamic model of L2 writing. *Journal of Second Language Writing, 6*, 45–60.

Matsuda, P. K. (2001). On the origin of contrastive rhetoric: A response to "The origin of contrastive rhetoric revisited" by H. G. Ying (2000). *International Journal of Applied Linguistics, 11*(2), 257–260.

Matsuda, P. K. (2003). Coming to voice: Publishing as a graduate student. In C. P. Casanave & S. Vandrick (Eds.), *Writing for scholarly publication: Behind the scenes in language education* (pp. 39–51). Mahwah, NJ: Lawrence Erlbaum.

Matsuda, P. K., & Atkinson, D. (2008). Contrastive rhetoric: A conversation. In U. Connor, E. Nagelhout, & W. Rozycki (Eds.). *Contrastive rhetoric: Reaching to intercultural rhetoric* (pp. 277–298). Amsterdam: John Benjamins.

Mauranen, A. (1993). *Cultural differences in academic rhetoric.* Frankfurt: Peter Lang.

McCagg, P. (1996). If you can lead a horse to water, you don't have to make it drink: Some comments on reader and writer responsibilities. *Multilingua, 15*(3), 239–256.

McWhorter, J. H. (2014). *The language hoax: Why the world looks the same in any language.* Oxford, U.K.: Oxford University Press.

Mohan, B., & Lo, W. A.-Y. (1985). Academic writing and Chinese students: Transfer and developmental factors. *TESOL Quarterly, 19*(3), 515–534.

Nanri, K. (2001). Logical structures of Japanese texts. *Text, 21*(3), 373–409.

Ostler, S. E. (1987). English in parallels: A comparison of English and Arabic prose. In U. Connor & R. B. Kaplan (Eds.), *Writing across languages: Analysis of L2 text* (pp. 169–185). Reading, MA: Addison-Wesley.

Panetta, C. G. (Ed.). (2001). *Contrastive rhetoric revisited and redefined.* Mahwah, NJ: Lawrence Erlbaum.

Péry-Woodley, M. P. (1990). Contrasting discourses: Contrastive analysis and a discourse approach to writing. *Language Teaching, 23*(3), 143–151.

Purves, A. C. (Ed.). (1988). *Writing across languages and cultures: Issues in contrastive rhetoric.* Newbury Park, CA: Sage.

Régent, O. (1985). A comparative approach to the learning of specialized written discourse. In P. Riley (Ed.), *Discourse and learning* (pp. 105–120). London: Longman.

Reid, J. M. (1993). *Teaching ESL writing*. Englewood Cliffs, NJ: Prentice Hall.

Rinnert, C., & Kobayashi, H. (2001). Differing perceptions of EFL writing among readers in Japan. *The Modern Language Journal, 85*(2), 189–209.

Rinnert, C., & Kobayashi, H. (2009). Situated writing practices in foreign language settings: The role of previous experience and instruction. In R. Manchón (Ed.), *Writing in foreign language contexts: Learning, teaching, and research* (pp. 23–48). Clevedon, U.K.: Multilingual Matters.

Sapir, E. (1921/1949). *Language: An introduction to the study of speech.* New York: Harcourt Brace Jovanovich.

Schneider, M., & Fujishima, N. K. (1995). When practice doesn't make perfect: The case of an ESL graduate student. In D. Belcher & G. Braine (Eds.), *Academic writing in a second language: Essays on research and pedagogy* (pp. 3–22). Norwood, NJ: Ablex.

Scollon, R. (2000). Generic variability in news stories in Chinese and English: A contrastive discourse study of five days' newspapers. *Journal of Pragmatics, 32*, 761–791.

Shi, L., & Kubota, R. (2007). Patterns of rhetorical organization in Canadian and American language arts textbooks: An exploratory study. *English for Specific Purposes, 26*, 180–202.

Söter, A. O. (1988). The second language learner and cultural transfer in narration. In A. C. Purves (Ed.), *Writing across languages and cultures: Issues in contrastive rhetoric* (pp. 177–205). Newbury Park, CA: Sage.

Swales, J. M. (1990a). *Genre analysis: English in academic and research settings.* New York: Cambridge University Press.

Swales, J. M. (1990b). Nonnative speaker graduate engineering students and their introductions: Global coherence and local management. In U. Connor & A. M. Johns (Eds.), *Coherence in writing: Research and pedagogical perspectives* (pp. 189–207). Alexandria, VA: TESOL.

Swales, J. M., & Feak, C. B. (2000). *English in today's research world: A guide for writers.* Ann Arbor: University of Michigan Press.

Swales, J. M., & Feak, C. B. (2012). *Academic writing for graduate students: Essential tasks and skills* (3rd ed.). Ann Arbor: University of Michigan Press.

Swales, J. M., & Najjar, H. (1987). The writing of research articles introductions. *Written Communication, 4*, 175–191.

Tardy, C. M. (2016). *Beyond convention: Genre innovation in academic writing*. Ann Arbor: University of Michigan Press.

Taylor, G., & Tingguang, C. (1991). Linguistic, cultural, and subcultural issues in contrastive discourse analysis: Anglo-American and Chinese scientific texts. *Applied Linguistics, 12*(3), 319–336.

Whorf, B. L. (1956). *Language, thought, and reality: Selected writings of Benjamin Lee Whorf* (J. B. Carroll, Ed.). Cambridge: MIT Press.

You, X. (2010). *Writing in the devil's tongue: A history of English composition in China*. Carbondale: Southern Illinois University Press.

Chapter 3

Writing in a Digital Era

"Throughout the developed and in much of the developing world, there is little serious writing that is not done digitally." (Warschauer, Zheng, & Park, 2013, p. 825)

"Despite their widely acknowledged multimodal possibilities such as embedding videos and images, writing is a central element in many Web 2.0 spaces such as the essentially text-based entries in blogs, short status reports on Twitter and Wikipedia entries." (Barton & Lee, 2012, p. 285)

"I keep thinking that what we do now, with this medium of instant delivery, isn't writing, and doesn't even qualify as typing either; it's just sending." (Truss, 2003, pp. 191–192)

LEADING QUESTIONS

- In your current thinking, how do you define or characterize writing?
- Where do you (or do you) draw the line between writing and other forms of representation of meaning?
- What do you think traditional approaches to teaching and learning school-based L1 and L2 writing consist of?
- What traditional aspects of school-based L1 and L2 writing still need to be practiced in the L2 writing class?

- How do digital media resources fit into an L2 writing class given the heavy focus on language learning in many classes?
- Should students' digital literacy practices outside of class be incorporated into L2 writing class activities? If so, how can this be done, and what should the role of teachers be?

Introduction to the Issues

In the first edition of this book, I did not feel the need to include a chapter, even a small one, on how we character-ize writing, particularly in school settings. Conventionally, writing, done with paper and pencil or electronically with keyboard and screen, has generally consisted of constructing essays (argumentative, expository, narrative), reports, exami-nation responses, personal reflections, and perhaps creative writing according to fairly standard genres and formulae. In contrast to his translingual view (see Chapter 4 on standards in writing, this book), Canagarajah (2016) has called this a nor-mative view, which he said is implied by both me in the first edition, and by Ferris and Hedgcock (2014). In this traditional view, students from early years of schooling through graduate school need to have clear beginnings, middles, and ends to their written academic work. They need topic sentences and (in more advanced work) statements of purpose. They need well-formed paragraphs (at least five, in the view of those who teach the infamous five-paragraph essay) that exhibit internal coherence and that connect clearly to paragraphs before and after them. They need to acknowledge where they get their information. They need to follow conventions of grammar in Standard English (an educated variety from the UK or North America), and also need to correct errors in English as they work on multiple drafts of their writing. However, many read-ers of the second edition of this book, as well as their own students, will have grown up with digital technology shaping all aspects of their personal and professional lives, and probably in multicultural environments. Our traditional definitions and activities of writing may no longer be as pertinent as they once were.

Two changes (of many) have occurred in recent years that make a chapter on writing in a digital age seem relevant. One that I will only briefly comment on here is our increasing interest in how L2 writing and L2 language acquisition (SLA) build on each other (Manchón, 2011) in a digital era. This interest obligates us to attend to the ways that language learning, writing, and technology are now inextricably linked (see the journals *Language Learning & Technology* and *Computers and Composition*, among many other resources). In other words, students don't just do L2 grammar exercises until they can pass some kind of proficiency test and only then learn to write. Instead, they learn from early stages how L2 writing and L2 language acquisition build on each other from a vast array of sources, increasingly multimodal and digital, not just written words.

When we consider this change, we can easily get the impression that teaching was much easier when skills for L2 students were neatly separated into grammar study, writing, reading, and so on. In fact, many school programs still function this way—skills are separated and then somehow magically are supposed to come together at some point when "language acquisition" happens. However, a separation-of-skills approach is questioned these days (and has been for some time). Also the intrusion of all kinds of electronic and social media into the lives of students of all ages makes it impossible to justify why we would keep an enormous variety of literacy activities outside the classroom when students could be drawing on them to develop their literacy, language, intellectual, and social skills. In real life, neither L1 nor L2 students separate their learning like this, unless forced to do so in a classroom situation and unless they have no internet or social media resources at all at their disposal.

   The second area of change, which is the focus of this chapter, is the growing prevalence of modes of communication on
digital platforms such as communication on social networks,
and blends of images, sounds, and text. This means that writing—as a kind of symbolic representation of meaning—can
no longer be narrowly defined only as letters, words, and
ideographs on paper and screen; in other words, writing is
no longer solely or even mainly about linguistic dimensions
(Canagarajah, 2013; Kress, 2010; Wolff, 2013). Representation
of meaning has always been multimodal, of course, featur-
ing blends of images and text, but is increasingly so, leading
scholars to refer not to writing, but to multiliteracies (Cope
& Kalantzis, 2000) and design (Kress & van Leeuwen, 1996;
Kress 2003, 2010; Purdy, 2010, 2014). Even more controversial
is the proposal by Kress (2005, 2010) and others that images
are replacing words in multimodal practices. Particularly
outside the traditional school setting, where speech and
writing are conventionally used to "tell the world," depic-
tion in the form of images "shows the world" (Kress, 2005,
p. 16). As Kress (2005, p. 5) noted, the response by critics
has been "anger and nostalgia" at the idea that books and
writing are no longer "the culturally most valued form of
representation."
   How, then, are writing and composition to be viewed in
the school setting and the writing classroom (assuming that
we still have something called "the writing classroom")? If
writing-composition-semiotic representation should no longer
be focused primarily on words, to say nothing of the beloved
(or infamous) five-paragraph essay and on other traditional
school genres, and if images and sound are now an inextricable
part of or even supplanting our written communication and
composition practices (Hafner, 2015), how do we characterize
writing for the purposes of teaching and learning to write in
an L2? In all cases, the common understanding seems to be
that textual production of any kind involves meaning making,
whether meaning is created by words, images, performance, or
sound. Of course semiotic representations of all kinds also con-

struct identities, depict agency, and showcase cultures (Sidury Christiansen, personal communication, August 2016). In both L1 and L2 education, all of us will continue to be interested in meaning making and in effective representation of meaning, but we will need to remember that identities and cultures, not just word-based ideas, inevitably construct meaning as well. We just may not yet agree on what to call an expanded vision of meaning making or how to put digital literacy activities effectively into practice in different kinds of classrooms and for different kinds of students.

Discussions in the Literature

In this section I continue to ask the basic question: Do multimodal digital productions (instructed or uninstructed), communication in social networks, and "products" posted online constitute writing? This basic question involves more than terminological trickery as to what we call the kinds of literacy practices that we engage in these days, although certainly terminology will play a part in how we think about our definitions of these activities. The question is especially important for people like me who are not digital natives, and for anyone (teachers or students) still contending with the demands of institutional expectations and testing corporations. These forces pit traditional print-culture fans (including those of us who love the very smell and feel of books) against so-called digital natives or digital and design enthusiasts, some of whom have lost interest in print culture, in general setting up tensions that some people will not be happy with.

I explore these tensions as I review some of the literature that takes a broader view of writing than traditionalists do, including works that use terms such as *design, multimodality*, and *remix* rather than writing to define some aspects of literacy that fall outside the traditional word-based perspective. I conclude the literature section with a brief look at the concerns voiced by some critics and skeptics. Next, I look at several empirical studies that have investigated ways that digital literacies have been used in classrooms for multimodal projects. The final section poses ongoing questions for readers to consider. More than the other chapters in this book, clear answers will evade us, given the quickly changing evolution of technology. All of us thus need to pay attention to the rapid changes in future developments in first and second language literacy studies regardless of how we characterize writing today.

Writing as Multifunctional Web-Based Literacies

A place to start might be with Wolff (2013), who asked what counts as writing in an age of Web 2.0. Several years ago, Wolff created a huge list of functions of various Web 2.0 applications, 74% of which he and research assistants identified as "writing" (51 of 69 functions; see his Table 2, pp. 215–217). Some of these functions that he claimed fit the category of writing may meet with resistance by some readers. In addition to word-based functions found on blogs, online forums, and sites such as Wikipedia, the list includes all the other categories he identified and the tag names he used for his analysis:

- customizing the layout of personal space in application (tag: *designlayout*)
- controlling who has access to content one creates (tag: *contentsecurity*)
- updating constantly of user activity within application (tag: *newsfeed)*
- subscribing to another's content in order to receive updates (tag: *subscription*)
- adding to one's account games and other apps for entertainment or other purposes (tag: *application*)
- embedding media within a page, post, or other writing space (tag: *embedding*) (Wolff, 2013, p. 214)

It is difficult to conceptualize this list as consisting of writing in ways that we would all agree on, but Wolff argued that "each of the functions identified as a form of writing, or characteristic identified as a writing space, plays a role in the creation of meaning for the writer and/or a specific audience" (p. 217). We can certainly agree that "creation of meaning for self and an audience" lies at the heart of what we would consider writing, but other forms of representation not usually considered writing can also fulfill this function, hence expanding our characterization of writing. Wolff thus wants students (and I trust teachers as well) to "become more digitally sophisticated writers" (p. 222) by recognizing that in this digital era, practices associated with writing are far more complex than they are in print culture. Wolff described the challenges to students (and by extension teachers) as follows:

> Each Web 2.0 application (domain, ecology) challenges users in a similar way by asking them to learn new terms, comprehend new symbols, engage with new writing spaces, recognize relationships among multiple applications, and transfer knowledge from one application to the next—all of which contribute to the interactive complexities of what it means to write in this new environment. (p. 219)

Wolff concluded by asserting that composition today "has more in common with video games, comics, and electronic literature than traditional print-based alphabetic texts and hypertext" (p. 223). Still, as others have pointed out, many forms of online writing are primarily word-based, such as blogs and wikis.

Writing as Blogging and Wiki-Writing

Communicating, constructing, and sharing knowledge through blogs and wikis and other kinds of online writing involve mainly text- and word-based entries (Barton & Lee, 2012). The phrase "online authorship" itself seems to imply that blogs and wikis indeed fall under the umbrella of writing, understood here as word-based meaning making. Jones and Hafner (2012, p. 158) referred to blogs and wikis as "dedicated writing tools" that differ from traditional individualistic notions of print-based writing. For example, unlike traditional writing assignments in schools, which are often done primarily to be evaluated and graded by teachers, online writing activities are much more communicative and collaborative and allow authors access to vast online audiences who will not evaluate or grade what they write. Blogs and wikis should therefore not be used in classrooms in ways that replicate traditional writing activities, cautioned Bloch (2008, pp. 72–73), but should help students explore topics and opinions, write communicatively and collaboratively, and develop an authentic sense of audience and authorship. These purposes differ from the typical evaluative goals of conventional writing assignments that often pay lip-service to the value of communicating with real audiences but that are actually designed for a teacher to read and grade. Students know who their real audience is and with digital writing practices, authentic audiences beyond a single teacher are easily available.

In one example of blogging in an academic writing class, Bloch (2007) found that his generation 1.5 student Abdullah (a Somali immigrant) used blogs to help develop his academic writing and also to provide evidence for his teachers about the strengths and weaknesses of his writing. In the course he described, Bloch aimed to help students use blogs to write in different genres, to discuss plagiarism, to collaborate with and critique each other, and to learn to express their own views to a responsive audience of peers. Learning to write and think critically and to persuade readers of the credibility of one's arguments are fundamental skills in academic writing, so practicing these skills on blogs can feed into more conventional academic writing assignments. However, Bloch is honest in reporting that there was little evidence that Abdullah or other students improved their control of grammar. He concluded nevertheless that "by becoming bloggers, they increased the amount of time they spent writing, reading, and generating ideas as well as demonstrating a variety of complex rhetorical strategies" (p. 137).

In another study that took place in Tokyo with university EFL students, Miyazoe and Anderson (2010) asked students in three classes to participate in three kinds of online writing activities: wikis (collaboratively produced products), blogs (individual posts to a site on a given topic), and forums (collaborative dialogue on a topic) (p. 189). The authors wanted to see how each activity scaffolded students' learning and how students reacted to the different activities in their blended course. Results showed that students found the blended course enjoyable, with wikis as their favorite writing activity. Students also increased the complexity of their sentences over the two semesters of the study. However, results were mixed as to changes in students' vocabulary richness. The authors claimed that the three online activities led to "general success in making qualitative changes in students' writing abilities" (p. 193). Such phrasing indicates that the authors considered all the online writing to fit a view of writing as mainly text- and word-based activities that could scaffold learning and aid language acquisition. However, for reasons the authors could not explain, the students in the different classes had sometimes opposite reactions to the different online activities, as shown in a questionnaire. The authors could not therefore confidently endorse the three online writing activities as clearly beneficial without further research. Similar inconsistent responses were also found in Chen's (2015) study of a blogging project with her Taiwanese EFL students (discussed further below).

In spite of inconclusive research, wikis—as a collaborative form of text-based writing—have been described as beneficial in L2 settings for purposes of collaboratively constructing writing assignments and scaffolding students' writing and learning activities. But should we expect all small wiki-writing groups to be equally successful? Examples with university students in China who composed three writing assignments via wikis (Li, 2013; Li & Zhu, 2013) showed that not all wiki-writing groups worked together successfully. In the three groups studied by Li and Zhu, patterns of interaction differed among the three groups, which influenced the students' perceptions of their learning opportunities. Not surprisingly, the collectively contributing/mutually supportive group perceived the most learning opportunities, and the dominant/withdrawn group the least. Li (2013), in a follow-up study to Li and Zhu (2013) examined the successful group, and reported that in their discussions, these college students pooled their knowledge and resources in genuinely collaborative and scaffolded ways, including making actual changes to writing (adding, deleting, rephrasing, reordering, correcting; see. p. 757). Li referred to this successful writing activity as collective scaffolding. As is the case in any collaborative or interactive activity in the language classroom, teachers thus need to attend carefully to the patterns of interaction among students, whose styles and personalities may or may not mesh in ways that benefit all group members.

Secondary students, too, can use wikis as a collaborative writing activity, as Mak and Coniam (2008) demonstrated with four students in Hong Kong. These students worked together over two months, without much teacher help, and collaboratively produced what eventually became a printed brochure to be distributed to parents that described their school. In the three phases of the project, the students not only added words to their wiki constructions, but amended, reorganized, and corrected what they wrote together. The authors noted that these activities had not previously been common in students' approaches to writing (p. 452). Mak and Coniam described some of the benefits of wiki writing to students' learning as follows:

> One of the great advantages of wikis with regard to language learning, process writing and revision, is that as students work towards the final document, all intermediate copies are retained. This provides an invaluable learning tool for students whereby they can see what errors they initially made – and subsequently corrected. (p. 441)

As is the case with other studies of blogging and wiki writing, these authors did not find convincing evidence that students' grammatical accuracy increased over the phases of the project—accuracy went up in some cases and down in others (p. 452). However, the successful production of a real product (the school brochure) for a real audience boosted students' confidence, allowed them both individual and collective input, and improved students' interest in English. One of the numerous advantages of wiki writing celebrated by its proponents is not just the collaborative and scaffolded nature of learning and meaning making, but also the creation of some kind of genuine product to be shared with a real audience. In addition to blogs and wikis, other kinds of online productions also feature authentic audiences, especially online ones, and continue to expand the view of writing beyond words to include more visual and audio elements, as described in the following sections.

Writing as Multimodal Design

Writing in composition and literacy studies is increasingly being thought of as multimodal and multimedia design (Purdy, 2014). One of the strongest and most contested assertions about the shift from words to multimodal design has been made by Kress, namely that writing is giving way to image. He wrote: "… it seems evident to many commentators that writing is giving way, is being displaced by image in many instances of communication where previously it had held sway" (Kress, 2005, p. 5).As I mentioned in the introduction to this chapter, Kress admitted that such views generate negative responses given the historical domination of print-based writing and powerful book cultures in the West. He noted that these responses range from "outright despair, anger and nostalgia to some still utopian voices on the other end of the spectrum" (p. 5). But multimodality as part of literacy practices is here to stay. Moreover, words have not gone away; we see the explosion of word-based communication across all kinds of digital media, even when images and sound co-occur.

Terms such as *design*, *multimodality*, and *multiliteracies* are not new. As long ago as the late 1990s, such concepts were being espoused by the New London Group (2000) and their followers (Cope & Kalantzis, 2000; Kress 2003, 2005, 2010; Kress & van Leeuwen, 1996) as substitutes for "writing" in the study of literacy. Kress (2010, p. 5) referred to design as "a social-semiotic theory of multimodality" in which individual authorship and ownership disappear; in his view, even the term multimedia no longer suits today's literacy practices because it connotes discrete items rather than mixes and blendings (p. 30). The result is that, in Kress's view, the term plagiarism is anachronistic, "harking back to a different social, semiotic and legal environment" (p. 21) in which individual authors could be seen to own their rhetorical and linguistic creations (see Chapter 6, this book, Writing from Sources).

The connotation of terms like design and multimodality includes not only rhetorical, linguistic, and image-based representations of meaning, but also critical and political aspects, as Janks (2010, Ch. 7) pointed out in her study of children's literacy in South Africa. In her work, students' drawings were the basis of visual and verbal depictions of power and oppression. Janks commented that "...design is the catch-all word that I use for critical text production. It focuses on the production rather than the reception of texts," highlighting the "importance of resisting dominant forms and 'writing back' to power" (Janks, 2010, p. 155). Verbal text accompanied the children's drawings, allowing students to develop these critical multimodal literacy skills. Janks did not discuss how her vision of design might apply to high-stakes writing such as that done by university students, where how a text is received can mean the difference between success and failure.

In another example of word-supported multimodal writing, Barton and Lee (2012) studied the everyday literacies of bilingual Spanish and Chinese users who shared photos supported by words on a Flickr site. The authors noted that "Despite their widely acknowledged multimodal possibilities such as embedding videos and images, writing is a central element in many Web 2.0 spaces such as the essentially text based entries in blogs, short status reports on Twitter and Wikipedia entries" (p. 285). Given this and many other examples of word-supported design (see further examples in the section below on Classroom Perspectives), some of us might take issue with Kress (2005, p. 15) in his assertion that words are "empty of meaning" needing to be filled with meaning by readers, whereas depictions (images, designs) are specific, precise, and full of meaning. As an undergraduate art major and lifelong pen-and-ink artist, I know that images are not always precise and full of meaning. And as a dabbler in Japanese (Casanave, 2012) I know that ideographs can depict meanings quite differently from alphabetic words and sometimes very precisely, but like alphabetic words sometimes ambiguously and polysemously depending on context and purposes of the writer. In the cases of words as well as all but the most mundane and realistic representations of objects, readers and viewers must construct and interpret meanings. The point we cannot argue with is that seeing literacy as multimodal design alters our notions of what it means to learn to communicate via various forms of verbal and visual representation, and so expands our ideas of what it might mean to teach and learn L2 writing and composition (Purdy, 2014).

Writing as Remix

One of the numerous controversies in how we characterize writing in a digital era concerns whether combining objects, sounds, images, and so on from pre-existing sources and adapting the results to fit the composers' needs constitutes writing, composing, or literacy writ large. A remix culture (Manovich, 2007, cited in Jones & Hafner, 2012) has flourished in music for some time (referred to as mashups), and flourishes now on the internet and even in classrooms as students compose projects and presentations from a wide variety of textual, visual, and audio sources (Hafner, 2013, 2015; Jones & Hafner, 2012). Jones and Hafner (2012, p. 45) defined current expanded views of mashups and remixes as "new and original texts or cultural artifacts that have been created out of existing works." (This sounds rather like a description of the compositions of

J. S. Bach.) As did Kress (2010) and Bloch (2008), they have pointed out challenges that confront educators in particular:

> This practice of borrowing and building on existing work has become very common in digital media. Because of the way that mashups and remixes build on the work of others, they pose some interesting questions of both a philosophical and practical nature. They challenge us to rethink beliefs about originality, intellectual property and ethics. (p. 45)

Proponents of remixing in educational settings make the point that traditional text-based writing, as well as speech, have always required writers and speakers to skillfully craft their work from the words and ideas of others (Bakhtin, 1981). The very act of writing from sources (see Chapter 6), and learning how to quote, cite, and paraphrase, involves textual remixing in a sense. The analogy to a multimodal remix culture should not require a major leap of the imagination, they believe. Just as students traditionally have needed to learn to select sources, identify and cite them where appropriate, and weave them together into a coherent whole that tells a story, presents information, or makes an argument, so does digital composing in a remix project. Even traditionalists cannot argue with the fact that writing from sources and assembling a remix project both involve incorporating or adapting existing material for writers' own purposes. As Hafner (2015) explained for the case of English language learners, students need to learn to strategically draw on multimodal resources to construct productions that reach large online audiences (see further description in the Classroom Perspectives section below). It is less clear how, and how extensively, students must evaluate and cite their sources in a remix project. In spite of assertions by Kress (2010) that concepts like plagiarism are anachronistic, legal issues of copyright have not been resolved in a remix culture, particularly in school settings or for commercial purposes, nor have they been resolved for remixes done in the music and film industries for purposes of pleasure and entertainment (Lisa Russell-Pinson, personal communication, August 2016).

I conclude this section on discussions in the literature with a reminder from Bloch (2008, p. 79) that technologies for the L2 composition classroom change so fast and so often that teachers are regularly faced with the same pedagogical questions: "What are the new technologies? What kinds of interaction do they best foster? How can they be best used? What role can they personally, socially, and politically in both the classroom and the society?" And of course, how can any of the non-traditional technologies help students become better writers, presuming we have a broad and flexible definition of writing? These questions extend beyond the dilemma of how we define, learn, and teach writing in a digital era.

Critiques and Fears of Our Growing Love Affair with Digital Literacies

Numerous critiques and worries exist of efforts to bring digital literacies of all kinds into the classroom. One of these is that some teachers and scholars fear that standard practices and instruction in traditional reading and writing (still widely valued) will be replaced by practices that draw primarily on students' informal social networking and entertainment activities from outside the formal school setting. Implicit in this fear is the idea that "the engagement in digital technologies in their personal worlds may impair students' ability to engage in serious academic study, and all that implies in terms of, for example, reading books and writing essays" (Lea & Jones, 2011, p. 378). Deep and engaged reading, which is easier in books when readers are not faced with the millions of distracting temptations online, is thought to be central to a young person's developing intellect (Wolf, 2007), including to a brain that can focus and concentrate (Carr, 2010).

Lea and Jones call this a deficit view, and argue back that "…literacies in higher education, or post-compulsory contexts more broadly, are no longer adequately explained by attention to writing and its significance in terms of both learning and assessment" (p. 381). Moreover, supporters like Lee and Jones argue that without aligning instructional practices with the digital practices that students are steeped in outside of class, teachers will lose their connection to younger generations of students—a powerful incentive for change.

However, many teachers no doubt are still struggling with how they might incorporate digital technologies in their writing classes, as some of the literature reviewed in the previous section demonstrates. Even though many resources address this fear (see the review in Lotherington & Jenson, 2011), resistance to change and anxiety about technological novelty confront teachers who were not schooled in a digital environment, making it difficult for them to shift both attitudes and practices. If, for example, teachers set up some kind of synchronous online interactions among students for purposes of drafting or peer-review, what do teachers do if the students spend most of their interactions in social chat and task management rather than peer review and revision tasks, as happened in Liang's (2010) study of several peer groups in Taiwan? When teachers hope for eye contact and focused in-person discussion but find that students would rather text their friends throughout classtime, what Mueller (2009) calls a "digital underlife," how can writing happen in any meaningful way with such distractions and interruptions? But Mueller claimed that computer technology and the digital underlife can be used to engage students in new and experimental forms of literacy (p. 243), as long as teachers are open to such changes. Another concern is that when students undertake multimodal writing projects, do they become so caught up in the visual and technological aspects of their projects that their attention to actual writing and research suffers, as happened with a class of university students in the United States (Gunsberg, 2015)? In an era when everyone seems to want to promote student autonomy, these questions also lead us to ask how much digital expertise and control writing teachers need when they set up online writing tasks and multimodal projects.

Several studies offer some insights on these questions. Like Liang (2010), Li and Zhu (2013; discussed in the section on blogs and wikis) set up online writing tasks with small groups of Chinese students, but in this case, the students engaged in asynchronous collaborative writing tasks using wikis. As I discussed above, the students' patterns of interaction in the three groups differed greatly, as did the students' perceptions of their learning experiences. Li and Zhu generally reported positive results in the literature they reviewed of collaborative writing using wikis, but their own results were inconsistent, with one of the three small groups exhibiting little scaffolding and revising and reporting little learning. Here, too, we can ask whether teachers need greater control to somehow ensure more consistency in students' experiences and learning, or whether these variable outcomes, based on peer scaffolding in this case, suit all stakeholders unproblematically. Li and Zhu concluded that "not all students are able to take advantage of using computers to engage in collaborative work" and that "the teacher's structuring and evaluation of each member's individual work in the computer-mediated collaborative writing tasks become indispensable to promote positive interactions and support learning" (pp. 77–78). Unfortunately, some teachers do not yet have clear guidelines or training on how to structure and evaluate such tasks.

Similarly, Chen (2015) designed a blogging project for her 33 EFL university students in Taiwan, and also found inconsistent results. Students wrote personal blogs on topics of their choice over a period of 10 weeks, and as part of the assignment, responded to at least two of their classmates' blogs. Topics included "music, arts, travel, sport, health, pop culture and college life" (p. 182). Chen's goals for the activity included motivation and improvement in writing, reading, interacting with others online, self-editing, and building a sense of identity in their writing (p. 183). However, students' responses to a questionnaire and interviews with 10 students indicated that her blogging project did not result in an overall positive response by students. Chen gleaned that her project presumed that students felt confident enough about their topics to participate easily. However, students who did not see themselves as "knowers" of their topics had more negative responses than students who seemed more confident. Also, some of them may not have seen themselves from the perspective of a student-centered learning culture. In other words, learners' predispositions toward the activity and topic influenced how or whether they were able to benefit from the activity. My own dislike of games in language classes, especially the video sort, would make it difficult for me to participate fully and willingly in game activities. Like some of Chen's learners, I would not be engaged. The point is that proponents of digital technologies in writing classrooms need to refrain from any uncritical enthusiasm for the technologies they use and to pay attention to individual students' experiences with them.

None of these studies dealt directly with another possible drawback of online writing activities: that of activity designs that do not consider how to push forward students' knowledge about something they don't already know. In commenting on the articles on multimodality in a special issue of *TESOL Quarterly*, van Leeuwen (2015) asked a very basic question that has not been sufficiently explored by scholars on writing as multimodal design. As I mentioned above, some proponents of writing as multimodal design argue that students' out-of-school literacy practices need to be brought into the classroom, or we risk expanding the divide even further between formal and informal learning. Van Leeuwen agreed with these scholars that "common ground must be established before new territory can be entered" (p. 584). But in re-defining writing as multimodal design (visual literacies, digital literacies), which are practices that young people and adults engage in on their own, we need to recognize that "what children [or adults, I might add] can learn themselves, out of school, informally, need not be taught in school" (pp. 583–584). Van Leeuwen continued with his cautionary statement, noting that "if schools and universities are to contribute something meaningful to the lives of their students, it will have to be something that is not already available elsewhere" (p. 584).

The point then is not just to bring students' informal digital literacy practices into the classroom, but to push students beyond where they would or could have gone without instruction by knowledgeable teachers. We do not need to do the same things in classrooms that we do outside school unless we are adding to and transforming those practices. Making a case for more attention to language in conjunction with multimodal practices, van Leeuwen concluded with the commonsense view that educational institutions need to "both preserve and innovate learning practices and forms of knowledge, and ensure that knowledge is not lost" (p. 587).

At a much more general level, beyond the L1 or L2 writing classroom and even the educational setting, prominent critics are asking even more pointed questions about our addiction to internet technology and social media devices. Language and literacy scholars would be wise to ponder some of the questions asked by these critics. Will we survive the information glut that Shenk (1997) called "data smog," or will we end up spending every waking hour immersed in information, searching, selecting, evaluating, and trying not to be left behind? Is our thinking becoming increasingly shallow as we become lost in tasks that do not engage us in sustained and engaged reading and thinking (Carr, 2010)? Are we losing the ability to be alone, to cherish solitude, to engage in in-person conversations, and to resist interruptions rather than only texting (Turkle, 2011, 2015)? Are we stupifying ourselves, and raising the "dumbest generation" ever (Bauerlein, 2008)? What happens to us and our relationships when we are "always on" (Baron, 2008)? And finally, are we in the midst of a "4th revolution" in which the "infosphere" is profoundly changing how we think of ourselves and our realities, partly by erasing boundaries between our lives online and offline (Floridi, 2014)? These thoughtful critiques deserve to be considered by all educators, including those of us who teach L2 writing.

Classroom Perspectives

In this section, I describe several published examples of projects that conceptualize writing as not just arrangements of words but as arrangements of images and sound supported by or woven through with language. The projects I discuss adopt approaches to learning via sustained engagement with topics, texts, and images, and are most evident in multimodal video projects and digital storytelling. As Hafner (2015, p. 832) pointed out, digital composing practices, with their hypertext, multimedia, collaboration, remixing, and online audiences, "challenge our established notions of what it means to be a writer, and consequently what it means to teach writing in a second or foreign language."

We can ask, for example, how much writing is involved in a digital video project that draws on images, remixing, video production, and oral presentation, such as the project carried out by Hafner and Miller (2011) in a university science class in Hong Kong. First year science students were assigned a simple experiment to conduct in groups. They were then trained in the technological and video production skills they would need to complete a remixed multimodal final project report that would eventually be posted to YouTube. In the planning stage, some students did indeed engage in writing of sorts as they planned out their documentaries on a storyboard, although not all students participated in this activity. They also commented on a course Weblog. The video production and the Weblog established an "authentic audience" for the students, which the authors note was highly motivating (p. 81). However, the focus of this project was not on writing per se, but on how such complex multimodal projects could foster learner autonomy. Moreover, it was not clear how much time students had to spend simply learning the various technological skills they needed to complete this project (a problem if the technical aspects dominate the rhetorical aspects of multimedia production; Sheppard, 2009). For most students, a sense of challenge and enjoyment led to positive results.

Digital storytelling has also been used in L2 writing classes in ways that also lead to a production or product of some kind that is presented in class or posted online. Digital stories can include what we conventionally think of as a story: characters, a setting, a plot, a conflict, a resolution. They can also take the form of other genres, such as persuasive or expository presentations including news broadcasts, ads, cultural investigations, scientific experiments (see Hafner & Miller, 2011, above), and personal journeys, love stories, and fairy tales. In all cases, students use multiple language skills both individually and in groups, prepare scripts and audio narrations, revise in response to peer and teacher feedback, select visual images, and prepare a presentation for a real audience using self-made or downloaded images and sounds.

For example, Christiansen and Koelzer (2016), Christiansen (2017), and Pardo (2014) described multi-step digital storytelling projects they did with their undergraduate students, for the purposes of increasing L2 students' language and literacy skills in English (e.g., grammar, vocabulary, speaking, reading, writing, constructing coherent and persuasive stories) and their ability to communicate with both L1 and L2 users. These authors emphasized that their projects, which were done in the United States with students from Mexico (Christiansen & Koelzer), in the United States with international students from China (Christiansen, in press), and in Spain (Pardo), did not require extensive investment by teachers and schools in software and hardware because the basic technology was widely available and commonly already in the hands of students and teachers. This technology included basic computer facilities, mobile camera phones and smart phones, free editing software that could be downloaded, and commonly used software such as iMovie and Microsoft Power Point.

In the projects described by these authors, traditional writing activities happened as individual students or groups of students prepared storyboards and scripts, which were checked by instructors. In one of their examples that involved quite a bit of writing, Christiansen and Koelzer elaborated the following steps that can be used in a digital storytelling project, following a process-approach to writing. First, small groups of students select a topic based on their interest in a particular culture. Then students individually write a conventional research paper on this culture that receives feedback from the teacher. Students then learn about the technological tools they will need, and work together in groups to construct a script and storyboard with drawings, sketches, or Power Point. From the final drafts of their scripts and storyboards they create a digital story, selecting and arranging videos and images made with their mobile phones. They add audio narrations again using mobile phones or Windows Movie Maker or other easy-to-use websites, and insert their narrations into the visual files. Students finally add music selections (some can be downloaded for free) or record sound effects with their mobile phones. The steps described by Pardo (2014) with his students in Spain were similar: brainstorming ideas; creating a story in the form of a text or script; receiving feedback on the script; selecting visual images; recording a voice narration; and projecting the finished story in class. In Pardo's case, the students also wrote responses to a follow-up questionnaire about procedures and decisions.

Digital storytelling projects are less often described as projects in classes for native English speakers who are learning a foreign language. However, the purposes and process are similar and can be applied to any students who are learning to write in a foreign language. In one case (Castañeda, 2013), 12 fourth-year high school students learning Spanish in the United States worked together with their teacher, with a graduate student, and with a university faculty member over a semester to create and then present digital stories in their L2, Spanish. Like all project-based learning, these digital storytelling projects engaged students in reading, writing, speaking, multimedia technology, and in this case, drama about their experiences at high school. Procedures followed well-known writing process pedagogies such as planning, revising, attending to feedback, and producing a finished product. The students wrote a draft in Spanish of their stories, on which they received grammatical feedback from their teacher. They then formed two story circles and read their stories to each other and discussed them. The following assignment was a second draft, based on teacher and peer feedback. Next, the students spent five days in their computer lab learning how to create a storyboard and a digital draft that incorporated visuals, audio recordings of their reading, music, and titles into their stories with iMovie software. Impressed with students' results, the teacher organized a viewing event for parents and other members of the school community. Students were clearly invested in producing polished productions for their authentic audiences, so attended carefully in their editing not just to the multimedia aspects of the production, but also to the syntactic and lexical aspects of their Spanish.

The students' pride and sense of accomplishment came out in interviews they had with Castañeda, during which she also learned that a few students were not completely happy with the technology part of the project. However, like Sheppard (2009), who argued that time that students spend on learning technical skills is adequately balanced with time spent on rhetorical skills, Castañeda (p. 46) pointed out that in projects like these,

> Digital storytellers spend little time learning and using the software and spend ample time crafting, revising, and narrating the story. Similarly, teachers who infuse these multi-literacy projects spend little time teaching technology because the majority of the time is spent coaching, revising, and providing feedback.

These teachers, and others like them who use digital video projects in their language classes, defined writing for themselves and their students in ways that assume a broader and more multimodal definition of writing than is traditionally used in writing classes and on large-scale essay examinations. The need to expand our conceptualizations of writing seems quite fundamental in this digital era, and should include not only teachers' views, but those of students and possibly parents and administrators as well. In particular, we need to consider how L2 writing is viewed in parts of the world where English instruction in general is still mainly language-based and exam-focused and where views of what writing is are not challenged. Many questions thus remain to be explored.

Ongoing Questions

This review of how we can conceptualize writing in a digital era has raised many questions and provided few answers. I summarize briefly here some of the ongoing questions that instructors, researchers, and students themselves will need to ponder in coming years.

First, as some of the scholarship on digital literacies has asserted, should the boundaries between formal and informal literacy, and between in-class and out-of-class literacy activities no longer be maintained? To what extent do informal digital literacy practices used for social communication and entertainment belong in the L2 writing (or composing, or literacies) class? What do teachers of L2 writing have to offer students who already know more than they do about out-of-school digital practices? These questions make us consider the purposes and practices of education more broadly, because for learning to happen, there needs to be a real gap in what students know and need to know (cf. Vygotsky's Zone of Proximal Development). There needs as well to be a certain amount of challenge and difficulty that engages students in sustained intellectual engagement of some kind, not so difficult as to cause learners to give up, and not so easy and familiar as to bore them (Csikszentmihalyi, 1990). Instructors as more experienced participants in knowledge practices need to scaffold these challenges for students, and provide them with resources and skills they cannot develop on their own (van Leeuwen, 2015). Otherwise educational growth does not happen.

In particular, if teachers allow social media devices and connections in the class that are ordinarily used outside of class, where will they, and students themselves, draw the line between literacy activities that can promote the goals of a lesson (whatever those might be) and those that seem strictly relegated to categories of entertainment or to dabbling, obsessive socializing, and other activities unrelated to lesson goals? More than ever, teachers thus need to clearly conceptualize the goals of their writing-composing classes and lessons, to pay attention to what types of literacy activities are going on in students' lives, and decide what activities belong inside or outside the class. The digital dinosaurs among us, both teachers from older generations and students without experience in digital technologies, are especially challenged by such decisions. I have a strong commitment to literacy activities that involve students in deep and sustained engagement with ideas and language rather than in snippets of informal communication, even if these require symbolic representations in the form of letters, words, images, and emoji. Do long-term digital video and online storytelling projects solve this dilemma of sustained engagement? Will advanced literacy productions required by graduate students and professional academics find ways to routinely incorporate multimodal and multimedia features into their work without compromising depth of engagement? Changes are happening but are not yet resolved.

Second, if classes in writing become classes in digital (video) composing and multimodal design, do teachers of what we once called writing still have ways to address issues of language proficiency in their lessons? The proponents no doubt scoff at the naïveté of such questions, assuming that nothing is quite so beneficial for language instruction as multi-pronged projects that draw on all of students' linguistic and non-linguistic resources. This argument merits attention, in that it is an expanded vision of what we have long called *content-* and *project-based language instruction*: Students practice—often collaboratively—many language and literacy skills at the same time, and expand their content knowledge as well. If we add images and sound, using the latest digital technology, to content- and project-based teaching, will language development, as well as writing improvement, take place as efficiently as it might in a more exclusively language-focused project? Will students' sense of fun and engagement in multimodal projects ensure or at least encourage language acquisition? Will concern for "standards" prevail in this atmosphere, or will lingua franca and "translanguaging practices," with their criteria of negotiability and intelligibility, shift the concerns of writing teachers away from conventional views of accuracy in language acquisition and use (see the discussions in Chapter 4)?

Third, to what extent will students' and teachers' fascination with the technology itself distract our attention and time from helping students learn to engage deeply with content and rhetorical issues? As Lea and Jones (2011, p. 377) expressed it, speaking of undergraduate students, will "web- based technologies in their broader lives" make it difficult for them to engage in "more conventional study practices, such as academic reading and writing essays"? Will students, intrigued by the novelty of a video production (Hafner & Miller, 2011) get lost in efforts to make a beautiful production, and not attend to the challenges of learning to develop, in written language, a coherent and sustained argument, narrative, or exposition? Will they attend more to the visual and technical aspects of a production than to research skills and content (Gunsberg, 2015)? For the purposes of high level reading and writing-composing, language development and intellectual and cognitive development in both L1 and L2 take years of continuous study—a lifetime, in fact. If students of any age need to spend a great deal of time learning the technical skills required to produce a video project, for example, how much time can be devoted to deep thinking, learning in depth about a topic, and critically analyzing, synthesizing, and creating knowledge? Proponents of such projects point to all these skills, and L2 learning as well, as inherent in the projects themselves, with skillful guidance by instructors. Christiansen (2017) is confident that the skills learned in a video project transfer to more traditional academic writing. However, higher order thinking and even language acquisition are not inherent in digital literacy practices, but in how they are designed and used. How, then, do L2 teachers of writing-composing find ways to design engaging and instructive, not just entertaining, projects?

Finally, what are the purposes for which we would design a multimodal digital project in the L2 (writing) class or use digital technology in other less extensive ways? Do our purposes fit with what we believe writing to be and to do, and not just with a goal of amusing students or keeping them awake in class? Mueller (2009, p. 243) wants to "encourage the use of computer technology to foster emerging forms of digital writing and experimentation." This is fine, but do these purposes fit with what our students both need and want? This question inevitably takes us back to demands made on L2 students by examinations and by institutional requirements of disciplinary writing. Where do these demands fit in the digital literacy class, assuming we cannot just dismiss them?

In short, projects that blend language, image, and sound (and performance as well) all potentially involve meaning making, challenge, and intellectual, linguistic, and cognitive growth. Teachers, scholars, and students of L2 writing need to consider these questions in some depth before deciding how they will characterize L2 writing in our current digital era and before planning what to do in their classes. The era of digital literacies is here to stay. How will we define and then use such literacies in pedagogically sensible ways? How will we do this in ways that allow equal access to students and teachers in the developing world so that we avoid widening the digital divide even further?

Beliefs and Practices

Beliefs

1. Having read this chapter and possibly some of the literature that is cited or other literature you have found, what do you believe that a useful definition (or perhaps better—conceptualization) of writing might be? Does your view apply equally to L1 and L2 students?
2. Should we be using different terms for different modes of making meaning? What are some terms that you believe are useful to you in your own experiences and contexts?

3. To what extent do you believe that digital literacies (however you define these) inside school settings and out-of-school digital literacies (however you define these) need, or do not need, to be integrated in school settings? What is your view of van Leeuwen's (2015) statement that we need to challenge students to do things in class that they don't already know how to do outside of class?

4. What do you believe is the place, if any, for extended multimodal video and storytelling projects in an L2 writing class? What do you believe the place is, if any, for brief snippets of writing and communicating via social media?

5. How do you believe teachers should divide class time between teaching students how to use digital and online technology tools for multimodal projects and teaching them content, research skills, and writing and rhetorical principles and processes?

6. What do you believe students in classes you are familiar with want to learn about L2 writing and digital literacies? What do you think they need to learn?

7. What aspects of traditional definitions of writing do you believe need to be preserved?

8. What problems with various forms of digital technologies for writing and project work do you believe have not yet been solved? How serious do you believe these problems are? What solutions can you suggest?

Practices

1. With classmates or students, do a word-association exercise: quickly come up with as many things that come to your mind when you see the word *writing*. Share and discuss these with others.

2. If you have used any digital tools in an L2 writing class, compare with others what those are and what you have done with them. Pay attention to uses that

you are not familiar with or have not tried and that might be valuable in your own teaching.

3. If you believe in the value of multimodal literacy projects such as documentary videos or storytelling, design a semester-long project for a group of L2 students you are familiar with. If possible, consider two versions: In version one, assume you have all the technological resources you could hope for; in version two, assume that technological resources at your institution and among your students are limited.

4. Find out from your students, via questionnaire, discussion, blog, or interview, what their digital literacy practices consist of outside of class. Part of the activity can consist of asking students what they mean by digital literacy practices. Be aware that some students might not consider activities such as texting and Facebook posting to be "literacy practices," so be sure to clarify what you mean before doing this activity or as part of a discussion with them about their own views.

5. Find out from your students what they believe they need and want in an L2 writing class. Try to do this as an in-person discussion so that easy and immediate follow up is possible.

References

Bakhtin, M. M. (1981). *The dialogic imagination: Four essays.* (C. Emerson & M. Holquist, Trans.; M. Holquist, Ed.). Austin: University of Texas Press.

Baron, N. S. (2008). *Always on: Language in an online and mobile world.* New York: Oxford University Press.

Barton, D., & Lee, C. K. M. (2012). Redefining vernacular literacies in the age of Web 2.0. *Applied Linguistics, 33*(3), 282–298.

Bauerlein, M. (2008). *The dumbest generation: How the digital age stupefies young Americans and jeopardizes our future.* New York: Jeremy P. Tarcher/Penguin.

Black, R. W. (2005). Access and affiliation: The literacy and composition practices of English-language learners in an online fanfiction community. *Journal of Adolescent & Adult Literacy, 49*, 118–128.

Bloch, J. (2007). Abdullah's blogging: A generation 1.5 student enters the blogosphere. *Language Learning & Technology, 11*(2), 128–141.

Bloch, J. (2008). *Technologies in the second language composition classroom.* Ann Arbor: University of Michigan Press.

Canagarajah, A. S. (2013). The end of second language writing? (Disciplinary dialogues). *Journal of Second Language Writing, 22*, 440–441.

Canagarajah, S. (2016). Translingual writing and teacher development in composition. *College English, 78*(3), 265–273.

Carr, N. (2010). *The shallows: What the internet is doing to our brains.* New York: W.W. Norton & Company.

Casanave, C. P. (2012). Diary of a dabbler: Ecological influences on an EFL teacher's efforts to study Japanese informally. *TESOL Quarterly, 46*(4), 642–670.

Castañeda, M. E. (2013). "I am proud that I did it and it's a piece of me": Digital storytelling in the foreign language classroom. *CALICO Journal, 30*(1), 44–62.

Chen, R. T.-H. (2015). L2 blogging: Who thrives and who does not? *Language Learning & Technology, 19*(2), 177–196.

Christiansen, M. S. (2017). Multimodal L2 composition: EAP in the digital era. *International Journal of Language Studies, 11*(4), 145–164.

Christiansen, M. S., & Koelzer, M.-L. (2016). Digital storytelling: Using different technologies for EFL. *MEXTESOL Journal, 40*(1), 1–14.

Cope, B., & Kalantzis, M. (Eds.). (2000). *Multiliteracies: Literacy learning and the design of social futures.* London: Routledge/Taylor & Francis.

Csikszentmihalyi, M. (1990). *Flow: The psychology of optimal experience.* New York: HarperPerennial.

Ferris, D., & Hedgcock, J. (2014). *Teaching L2 composition: Purpose, process, and practice* (3rd ed.). New York: Routledge/Taylor & Francis.

Floridi, L. (2014). *The 4th revolution: How the infosphere is reshaping human reality.* Oxford, U.K.: Oxford University Press.

Gunsberg, B. (2015). The evaluative dynamics of multimodal composing. *Computers and Composition, 38*, 1–15.

Hafner, C. A. (2013). Digital composition in a second or foreign language. *TESOL Quarterly, 47*(4), 830–834.

Hafner, C. A. (2015). Remix culture and English language teaching: The expression of learner voice in digital multimodal compositions. *TESOL Quarterly, 49*(3), 486–509.

Hafner, C. A., & Miller, L. (2011). Fostering learner autonomy in English for science: A collaborative digital video project in a technological learning environment. *Language Learning & Technology, 15*(3), 68–86.

Janks, H. (2010). *Literacy and power.* New York: Routledge/Taylor & Francis.

Jones, R. H., & Hafner, C. A. (2012). *Understanding digital literacies: A practical introduction.* London: Routledge/Taylor & Francis.

Kress, G. (2003). *Literacy in the new media age.* London: Routledge/Taylor & Francis.

Kress, G. (2005). Gains and losses: New forms of texts, knowledge and learning. *Computers and Composition, 22*, 5–22.

Kress, G. (2010). *Multimodality: A social semiotic approach to contemporary communication.* London: Routledge/Taylor & Francis.

Kress, G., & van Leeuwen, T. (1996). *Reading images: The grammar of visual design.* New York: Routledge/Taylor & Francis.

Lea, M. R., & Jones, S. (2011). Digital literacies in higher education: Exploring textual and technological practice. *Studies in Higher Education, 36*(4), 377–393.

Liang, M.-Y. (2010). Using synchronous online peer response groups in EFL writing: Revision-related discourse. *Language Learning & Technology, 14*(1), 45–64.

Li, M. (2013). Individual novices and collective experts: Collective scaffolding in wiki-based small group writing. *System, 41*(3), 752–769.

Li, M., & Zhu, W. (2013). Patterns of computer-mediated interaction in small writing groups using wikis. *Computer Assisted Language Learning, 26*(1), 62–81.

Lotherington, H., & Jenson, J. (2011). Teaching multimodal and digital literacy in L2 settings: New literacies, new basics, new pedagogies. *Annual Review of Applied Linguistics, 31*, 226–246.

Mak, B., & Coniam, D. (2008). Using wikis to enhance and develop writing skills among secondary school students in Hong Kong. *System 36*(3), 437–455.

Manchón, R. M. (Ed.). (2011). *Learning-to-write and writing-to-learn in an additional language.* Amsterdam: John Benjamins.

Miyazoe, T., & Anderson, T. (2010). Learning outcomes and students' perceptions of online writing: Simultaneous implementation of a forum, blog, and wiki in an EFL blended learning setting. *System, 38*(2), 185–199.

Mueller, D. N. (2009). Digital underlife in the networked writing classroom. *Computers and Composition, 26*(4), 240–250.

The New London Group (2000). A pedagogy of multiliteracies: Designing social futures. In B. Cope & M. Kalantzis (Eds.), *Multiliteracies: Literacy learning and the design of social futures* (pp. 9–37). London: Routledge/ Taylor & Francis.

Pardo, B. S. (2014). Digital Storytelling: A case study of the creation, and narration of a story by EFL Learners. *Digital Education Review*, (26), 74–84. Accessed July 20, 2016, http://greav.ub.edu/der/

Purdy, J. P. (2010). Changing space of research: Web 2.0 and the integration of research and writing environments. *Computers and Composition, 27*, 48–58.

Purdy, J. P. (2014). What can design thinking offer writing studies? *College Composition and Communication, 65*(4), 612–641.

Shenk, D. (1997). *Data smog: Surviving the information glut.* New York: HarperCollins.

Sheppard, J. (2009). The rhetorical work of multimedia production practices: It's more than just technical skills. *Computers and Composition, 26*(2), 122–131.

Truss, L. (2003). *Eats, shoots & leaves: The zero tolerance approach to punctuation.* New York: Gotham Books.

Turkle, S. (2011). *Alone together: Why we expect more from technology and less from each other.* New York: Basic Books.

Turkle, S. (2015). *Reclaiming conversation: The power of talk in a digital age.* New York: Penguin Press.

van Leeuwen, T. (2015). Multimodality in education: Some directions and some questions. *TESOL Quarterly, 49*(3), 582–589.

Warschauer, M., Zheng, B., & Park, Y. (2013). New ways of connecting reading and writing. *TESOL Quarterly, 47*(4), 825–830.

Wolf, M. (2007). *Proust and the squid: The story and science of the reading brain.* New York: HarperCollins.

Wolff, W. I. (2013). Interactivity and the invisible: What counts as writing in the age of Web 2.0. *Computers and Composition, 3*, 211–225.

Chapter 4

What and Whose Standards for L2 Writing?

> "The assumption is that S[tandard]W[ritten]E[nglish] doesn't belong to any one community. This orientation to the neutrality of writing is bolstered by the notion that written language is not native to anybody. [...] However, multilinguals are increasingly questioning the attitude to written language as being standardized or neutral." (Canagarajah, 2013b, p. 108)

> "I feel that it is unfortunate that 'standard English' has so often been equated with 'native speaker English'. [...] Native speakers are frequently among the most non-standard of users, and a large number of non-native speakers use standard English with far greater skill and accuracy." (Maley, 2009, p. 198)

> "While it is clearly inappropriate to foist native-speaker norms on students who neither want nor need them, it is scarcely more appropriate to offer students a target which manifestly does not meet their aspirations." (Timmis, 2002, p. 249)

LEADING QUESTIONS

- To what extent does L2 writing reflect political and ideological concerns about standards for writing? Where do these standards come from?
- To what extent are (written) English grammar and lexis stable or dynamic and changing?

- What standards, if any, are appropriate for L2 writing in an era when the overwhelming majority of users of English worldwide are so-called nonnative speakers?
- How do the different anti-monolingualist or linguistically more inclusive views (e.g., World Englishes, English as an international language, English as a lingua franca, English as translingual practice) apply to L2 writing and not just to oral communication?
- To what extent do scholars and teachers of L2 writing need to attend to the desires of students to learn a particular variety of written English?
- Should scholars and teachers of L2 writing model nontraditional standards in their own writing and publishing?

Introduction to the Issues

As I wrote in the first edition of *Controversies*, discussions have gone on for some time about the extent to which English language education is a political and ideological enterprise, one that encompasses both idealistic visions of diversity and resistance to native speaker standards on the one hand, and, on the other, pragmatic orientations designed to help students acquire, not resist, the standards that will help them succeed in the school and workplace. This question persists and in fact has intensified in current debates about who is and who is not a native speaker of a language, what standards should be adopted for oral and written communication by institutions, teachers and students, testers, and textbook writers, whether new concepts and terms are needed to explore such questions, and what students themselves might want and expect to learn.

Whether or not we agree that English language education is always political and ideological (Benesch, 1993, 2001a, Morgan, 2009, Motha, 2014, and Pennycook, 1994/2013, among others believe it is), discussions about so-called native- and nonnative speakers of English as teachers of English, in particular as teachers of L2 writing, have been going on for many years. Stereotypes and prejudices abounded in the past about the privileged status of the native speaker from the West and the desire of students, parents, institutions, and commercial language schools for white instructors whose mother tongue is English (Appleby, 2013; Bailey, 2006; Kubota, 1998, 2011; Motha & Lin, 2014; Ruecker & Ives, 2015). Many of these discussions continue to lump native speakers into one group and nonnatives into another, an unfortunate dichotomy because it does not distinguish among many dialects of native English according to users' levels of education, regional accents, grammar, and lexis, some of which would be considered nonstandard by traditional purist criteria (Maley, 2009), or among indigenized varieties of English such as those in India (Pandey, 2013). When we see calls for "native English speakers" in job ads, then, we have to presume that educated British and North American dialect speakers of white or Anglo ethnicity are what is being sought. The prejudices and preferences in favor of these dialects and of certain races over others continue worldwide, although recent discussions acknowledge more than in the past how oversimplified previous discussions were and how complex, contested, and racially based the issues really are (Motha, 2014).

Moreover, discussions since the early 2000s have tried to introduce new terms and concepts as a way to highlight some of the political and social realities and complexities of what it means to be a multilingual teacher or learner of English. Such discussions have also tried to move beyond the monolingual bias that has existed for so long. (Note that the term *monolingual bias* could refer to native English speakers who don't know any other languages or to institutional and societal pressures that favor only an educated Anglo-American standard.) At the center of this debate about what kind(s) of English and whose standards should be taught, learned, and used in L2 education—particularly in L2 writing—are concepts and terms from past and present that more often than not have added to the confusion. Similar arguments from the past seem to have been forgotten (see, for example, the extensive work by Cummins on bilingualism; Cummins, 1981, 1996, 2000; Cummins & Swain, 1986). *Multicompetence-multilingualism-plurilingualism, World Englishes, English as an international language, English as a lingua franca, metrolingualism, code-meshing, translingualism* and *translanguaging*, and *cosmopolitan practices* are just some of the terms in current use. It is not clear whether we need so many new terms and concepts. For example, Matsuda (2014) and I say there is no need for new terms like *translingualism*; Creese and Blackledge (2010), García and Wei (2014), and Canagarajah (2013a, 2013c) say there is. Regardless of terms, what they share is an embracing of the hybrid, variable, and dynamic nature of language (documented phenomena in sociolinguistics for 50 years or more), and a disdain for monolingual standards that promote and permit only a narrow range of educated native-speaker English of the U.S. or U.K. varieties, particularly on standardized (international) tests and in academic writing.

Much of the discussion from a lingua franca perspective and some of the translingualism work, however, pertain most directly to oral communication in English and to U.S.-based bilingual education, and less specifically to finished products of writing. I have had trouble finding my way into and through some of the arguments to see how they might apply to academic writing (see the discussion in the next section). This gap is beginning to change as scholars and educators wrestle with the question of whether written English in school settings needs, or does not need, to follow formal conventional standards (Canagarajah, 2011, 2013a, 2015; Velasco & García, 2014). One problem is that the published literature arguing for relaxing the standards for L2 students is itself written in traditional standard English, and so is not a model for what authors are proposing, nor do these authors, with only a few exceptions, provide models from the writing of others that might be appropriate in academic settings. Additionally, profit-driven textbook and testing industries as well as universities that are competing for lucrative international student tuition are not likely to loosen the standards of formal English that for so long have dominated these enterprises. Many teachers themselves as well are likely to accommodate rather than resist conventional standards, either by choice or because they are not fully aware of the issues. Finally, those who promote English as a lingua franca or translanguaging practices do not seem to be talking much about what students and their (often nonnative) teachers want, expect, and need during their short time in language or writing classes (Timmis, 2002). It is unclear, therefore, where changes in standards will come from. We cannot ask students to flout existing standards (a bottom-up approach) when scholars, testers, publishing conglomerates, and teachers are not themselves changing standards of evaluation or providing models for how English can be used flexibly and multilingually and still be accepted in schools and workplaces without risk to users. Moreover, even if writing scholars and teachers relax standards, there is no guarantee that faculty in the disciplines will go along.

In the sections that follow, I first review some of the literature that has discussed the political and ideological nature of English language education, as a way to provide a foundation for the controversies that follow. I next review some specific discussions about different views of standards in English, particularly as they pertain to L2 writing. These views feature discussions about the global diversity of English and its use primarily by nonnative speakers worldwide, including English as a lingua franca, English as an international language, and translingual literacy practices. Subsequent sections address classroom perspectives and ongoing questions.

Discussions in the Literature

Politics and Ideology: Idealism or Pragmatism?

It is clear that at some level questions of power and influence affect the L2 writing class, as scholars of Critical EAP (English for Academic Purposes) have described for some time: Who determines students' purposes for writing and the kinds and standards of writing they will do? How is students' writing evaluated? What are students' and teachers' relationships with the dominant discoursal and cultural practices of literacy in the context in which teaching and learning takes places? Are they, or should they be, agents for change or followers of long-standing traditions (e.g., Benesch, 2001a, 2001b; Morgan, 2009; Shapiro, Cox, Shuck, & Simnett, 2016)?

In discussions about the politics and ideology of L2 writing, and of English language education more generally, one side of the argument holds that all education and language use is political and ideological, whether or not we realize it in the day-to-day practices of our teaching (Benesch, 1993, 2001a; Jenkins, 2014; Kubota & Lin, 2009; Pennycook, 1989, 1994/2013; Shor, 1992). English language education in particular is fraught with political minefields, given that English is a dominant international language associated with economic and political power, subjugation of minorities, injustice, and globalization (Blommaert, 2010; Canagarajah, 1999, 2002; Kubota, 2014; Motha, 2006, 2014; Phillipson, 1992). Some critical EAP educators believe it is the responsibility of L2 educators to help pre-service EAP and ESL teachers become aware of such issues and to become "transformative practitioners" (Morgan, 2009), and for all L2 educators to consider who "owns" the English language if so-called native speakers no longer do (Seidlhofer, 2003, 2011). Still, the reality is that English increasingly dominates worldwide enterprises of science, business, and much international education.

The language of research publications in print and on the internet is also predominantly English, thus potentially limiting the participation of non-English users in international research communication (Flowerdew, 2008; Gibbs, 1995; Hyland, 2015a; Lillis & Curry, 2010; Swales, 1997; Warschauer, 1999). But evidence of real discrimination is sparse (Casanave, 2008; Hyland, 2015a), causing Hyland (2016) to refer to the "myth of linguistic injustice." Nevertheless, teachers who hold strong beliefs about the inseparability of language and politics claim that L2 writing students and novice scholars need to be aware of the ways that the English language is implicated in issues of power. They also need to recognize that they have the right, or perhaps the obligation, to question, resist, and challenge the status quo (Benesch, 2001a, 2001b; Jenkins, 2014). They believe as well that our teaching can be neither neutral nor objective. All choices we make in the classroom are therefore laden with political and ideological implications.

Another view claims that writing teachers are entrusted with a very pragmatic goal—that of assisting students to develop the language and writing proficiency they need to survive in the environments in which they will be using their second language, such as an English-medium academic institution or an international company. In this view, students need to learn prevailing discourse conventions as efficiently as possible, including lexical, syntactic, and rhetorical norms of the discourse communities they will participate in (Horowitz, 1986; Maley, 2009; Ruecker, 2014; Santos, 1992, 2001). Teachers who ascribe to this accommodationist view, as it is sometimes called, do not necessarily deny that political and ideological issues lurk behind every educational corner. Rather, they believe that teachers must concern themselves with the kinds of language, writing, and thinking that students need to succeed, avoid imposing particular political agendas in classrooms, and work to maintain neutrality and objectivity to the extent possible in how and what they teach. Teachers also need to consider time factors as well as what students need and want in deciding whether to teach standard or diverse norms in the writing class (Ruecker, 2014, p. 116). In the case of L2 students, teachers also need to distinguish between language learning and language use (MacKenzie, 2014), remembering that L2 writers are continuing to learn the language as they learn to write (Manchón, 2011). It may not be feasible to address everything in the short time that students are in classes.

Writing teachers need to be fully aware of these issues, reflect regularly on their own stances, and remain open to discussion and opposing views. Where possible, acquainting students with political and ideological aspects of English as well as with choices open to them—a kind of critical pragmatism (Benesch, 2001b)—does not seem controversial, assuming we have time and opportunity for such meta-instruction. Awareness and choice always seem beneficial, as long as we listen to what students and their sponsors need and expect. We cannot totally reject pragmatic choices. As is the case with most of the other issues in this book, there are no right and wrong solutions on which teachers can base decisions about what to teach in L2 writing classes or how to design and carry out lessons. However, the stances that different educators take involve moral and ethical issues about what we believe is right, fair, just, and culturally appropriate (Hafernik, Messerschmitt, & Vandrick, 2002). Educators also need to reflect on the "invisible" privilege enjoyed by racially and ethnically mainstream educators and students and taken for granted by them, but denied to ESL students (Vandrick, 2009, 2015). Passions can therefore run high as we struggle to understand the links among politics, ideology, culture, technology, and language and as we inquire into our own standards for language use in speech and writing. Whatever stances we take, they influence greatly what we do in the classroom.

Native Speaker Debates, Englishes, and Standards in L2 Writing

Debates about who is and is not a "native speaker of English" and what the roles of native and nonnative teachers of English are in the worldwide enterprise of English language teaching flourished in the 1990s and early 2000s (Braine, 1999; Cook, 1999; Davies, 2003; Leung, Harris, & Rampton, 1997; Liu, 1999; Rampton, 1990). It has become clear since then that, with the burgeoning of English language education worldwide, the majority of English language teachers and users are not mother-tongue users of English. In spite of this reality, the model English language instructor continues to be the white native speaker (Appleby, 2013; Houghton & Rivers, 2013; Kubota & Fujimoto, 2013; Kubota & Lin, 2009; Kusaka, 2014; Llurda, 2009; Motha, 2006; Ruecker & Ives, 2015). These discussions about "native speakerism" have influenced what we consider to be appropriate standards for L2 students to use in their spoken and written English.

For some years now, compelling arguments have been made by a number of scholars against what they call the monolingual bias in English language education throughout the world and against the Anglo-American norms of standard spoken and written English that textbooks and teachers have adopted. Such norms, they argue, are part of a colonial legacy that no longer suits the diverse world we live in, where people speak Englishes, not a single variety of English, where most of the world's English users are now nonnative speakers, and where communicative function and ability to negotiate are often more important than formal accuracy. Discussions began and have continued about what scholars call World Englishes or nonnative varieties of English (Bolton & Kachru, 2006; Hamp-Lyons & Zhang, 2001; Jenkins, 2006; Matsuda, 2003, 2012; Seidlhofer, 2009) and English as an International Language (Alsagoff, McKay, Hu, & Renandya, 2012; Llurda, 2009; Matsuda, 2012; Matsuda & Friedrich, 2011; Sharifian, 2009). Other anti-monolingualist voices promote English as lingua franca, using the unfortunate acronym ELF (Baker, 2009, 2011; Jenkins, 2007, 2014; Jenkins, Cogo, & Dewey, 2011; Mauranen, 2012; Seidlhofer, 2011) and what some people in composition studies refer to as translingual practices (Canagarajah, 2013a, 2013b, 2013c; García & Wei, 2014; Horner, Lu, Royster, & Trimbur, 2010; Lu & Horner, 2013). The proliferation of terminology, initials, and acronyms alone can puzzle even the sincerest of second language educators.

Points of agreement among such scholars include the indisputable fact that many varieties of English are indeed used worldwide, that these varieties are used primarily by nonnative speakers of English outside what Kachru called the "Inner Circle" of users in the developed Anglo-American world (Kachru, 1985/2006), and that the varieties are as rich and diverse as its users are. Also uncontroversial is the fact that most studies of English as a lingua franca concern the Englishes that are spoken and written for functional and communicative purposes during interactions among nonnative speakers, not those between a nonnative and native user, and not for purposes of instructing L2 learners (Shapiro et al., 2016). As Mauranen (2012, p. 4) put it, "Using a lingua franca means being a user of an L2 but not a learner." Native speaker standards are not relevant in this functional view, nor is the concept of an L2 as a separate identifiable entity. We need to look carefully, then, at how these arguments apply to L2 writing instruction.

Other questions are more controversial. For instance, we know that language change is normal, but to what extent do languages change in significant ways or are instead basically stable over our lifetimes? What are the attitudes of teachers and students toward different varieties of English (including grammar, lexis, and accent)? And what is the role of Anglo-American and other elite standards for written English versus diversity and variety in second language writing instruction for L2 users who are still learning the spoken and written L2? Even the literature on English as a lingua franca, with its primary focus on oral uses of English for functional rather than instructional purposes, has underlying arguments that apply to standards in the L2 writing class.

Arguments about the Instability or Stability of English

We know that all languages, English in particular, have evolved historically from many different linguistic roots. English has never been pure or uncontaminated in any sense of the word. We also know from decades of work in sociolinguistics that languages are not static; they change over time in both spoken and written forms. However, documents and literature written in English from 200 or more years ago are generally accessible to modern readers today. If English has been relatively stable over 200 or more years, does an argument for its current instability make sense (Canagarajah, 2013c)? Do recent lexical innovations or the abbreviated styles of text messaging in the digital era constitute evidence of fundamental change in English? To what extent do arguments against the stability of English or against its existence as a "thing" that can be learned and taught (Pennycook, 2007) find their way into the L2 writing field?

Pro-Instability Positions/Anti-Standards Positions

Written language is often viewed as more stable than oral language. Once written, language seems, at least for a time, quite fixed and stable, especially in educational settings. (Note that I am not talking here about the rapid changes in communication via social media.) The fact that most L1 and L2 users learn to write as part of their formal education (i.e., written language is a second language to everyone) gives written English—any written language learned in school for that matter—an aura of stability and neutrality. However, this is a view that some scholars strongly disagree with. They base their disagreement on at least three arguments. One is that written language, like all language, does indeed change over time and across genres. Another is that there is no such thing as separate languages because all languages are blends of many elements (Canagarajah, 2013a, p. 1), and so the very notion of "English as an international language" is a myth (Pennycook, 2007). A third is that the norms of standard written English seem more stable than they actually are or should be, because they follow those of Inner Circle communities, which have a vested interest in maintaining stability and ownership. In multilingual communities, however, change and diversity are increasingly evident in the current era of "superdiversity" (Blommaert, 2013), "cosmopolitan relations" (Canagarajah, 2013c), and "metrolingualism" (Otsuji & Pennycook, 2010). It makes little sense, from this perspective, to follow narrow and elite standards of English that do not reflect current global diversity.

Ownership

If most communication in English throughout the world no longer includes native speakers (Seidlhofer, 2011), it can be argued that it makes no sense to teach native speaker norms (whatever these are) for purposes of international oral or written communication. This fact, and the fact that languages are endlessly creative, dynamic, and performative, means that English above all, given its global reach and multiple varieties and functions, can no longer be owned by elite inner circle native speakers. As Ammon (2009, p. 116) phrased it:

> I would like to challenge the inner-circle countries' exclusive control of the standards of International English. It seems to me that there is no real justification for this kind of control in a world with a growing majority of speakers of the language outside the inner-circle countries.

In this view, it is not possible for native speakers of English to simultaneously promote their own native speaker standards while acknowledging the many varieties of English in the world and still maintain ownership over English (Seidlhofer, 2011, p. 65). If we adopt a diverse and functional use of English, as Jenkins, Seidlhofer, Canagarajah, Pennycook, and others advocate, our writing classes along with the institutions housing them and the textbook publishers supporting them, will have to change in radical ways. We will need to accept, teach, and learn multiple practices in addition to standard forms. We will also need to view the concepts of diversity and hybridity themselves in critical ways. Kubota (2014) for one believes that these concepts have already taken on a privileged and elite status that their supporters had hoped to avoid.

Change

The lingua franca and translingual practices scholars have emphasized the view that, particularly for oral language, English as a lingua franca or English as an international language is so changeable and dynamic that it no longer makes sense to treat English as a singular stable entity. For instance, as a communicative vehicle among nonnative users of English, English as a lingua franca is negotiated among users as needed in particular settings and for specific oral (and less often, written) purposes (Baker, 2009; Jenkins, 2009; Seidlhofer, 2011). As described by Cogo and Dewey (2012, pp. 11–12), English as a lingua franca has been defined "in terms of its settings, which we see as contexts in which English is used as the principal contact language; second, in terms of its function, which we see as a means of communication among different first language speakers in such settings." It is easy to see how this functional and communicative use of English as a lingua franca could be used in business and workplace written exchanges and on social media among people from different language backgrounds.

Studies of English as a lingua franca have drawn on large corpora of oral data from workplace and education settings (see Jenkins, 2014, Seidlhofer, 2011, and some of the studies in Mauranen & Ranta, 2009). Some scholars have tried to codify features of lingua franca varieties (e.g., Cogo & Dewey, 2012; Mauranen, 2012; Prodromou, 2008; Seidlhofer, 2011), but given the functional nature of lingua franca English, such codification does not make much sense: We would expect great diversity in how nonnative English users communicate with each other such that lingua franca features could not sensibly be codified or taught. For this reason, scholars study practices, not just forms of language. As Cogo and Dewey (2012, p. 169) explained, "Any consideration of the pedagogic implications of ELF research must therefore take as its starting point the premise that effective communication is not contingent on the application of fixed language forms and conventionalized pragmatic norms." Users of lingua franca varieties of English should therefore not be considered deficient users of a standard variety, but effective communicators in their own right. From an English as a lingua franca perspective, there is no standard or even newly codified variety that could be taught in an L2 writing class.

Supporters of translingual literacy practices go further by applying notions of change, diversity, and hybridity in language to ways they believe written language should be treated in educational settings (Canagarajah, 2013a, 2013c; García, & Wei, 2014). They insist we need to depart from native speaker standards in written English, honor the diversity of cultures and languages of students, and grant these students agency in their literacy practices because of the increasing multilingual diversity, particularly in U.S. composition classrooms (Lu & Horner, 2013; Shapiro, et al., 2016). They emphasize that language is not stable, but continuously changing, rhetorical, and negotiated (Canagarajah, 2015, p. 427). In this view, both oral and written English need to be understood as practices, not as forms or varieties that can be codified (Park & Lee, 2011). Moreover, proponents of this view believe that multilingual nonnative users have special abilities to negotiate meanings in the presence of other multilingual interlocutors (Canagarajah, 2007).

Mixing, meshing, and blending of ever-changing language resources should therefore, in this view, be considered normal and somehow worked into the pedagogies of L1 and L2 writing classrooms (García & Wei, 2014; Lee, 2014). Some scholars have concluded that the notions of a "standard English speaker" and "Standard Written English" must be termed "bankrupt concepts" (Horner, Lu, Royster, &Trimbur, 2010, p. 305). Horner et al. continued, stating that "all speakers of English speak many variations of English, every one of them accented, and all of them subject to change as they intermingle with other varieties of English and other languages. Likewise, standards of written English are neither uniform nor fixed. What constitutes expected norms—for example, Edited American English— varies over time and from genre to genre" (p. 305). Even critics will not deny such diversity in language; their disagreements arise over how fast and how extensively language actually changes and what kinds of changes should be accepted for different purposes in educational and professional settings.

Separateness and Blendings

In addition to discussing the extent to which languages are stable or changing, some scholars ask whether languages can even be considered to be separate entities. Pennycook (2007) argued against the thingness of English, calling English as an international language a "myth." He similarly called monolingualism a myth (Pennycook, 2010), given what the field of sociolinguistics has taught us about dialects, registers, styles, and genres. In his view, we perform English in a variety of creative ways according to local and contextual needs, rather than by following a monolithic stable system called English. Canagarajah, too, wants us to give up the myth that languages are separate systems, in spite of the pull of labels that name languages and grammar books that describe them. A more accurate characterization of spoken and written English as a lingua franca and as translingual practice is that it is blended, functional, and practice-oriented (versus form-oriented) (Canagarajah, 2013a; García & Wei, 2014; Horner et al., 2010; Lu & Horner, 2013). Translingual practices thus mix, mesh, and blend languages and dialects, including in classroom pedagogy through techniques like code-meshing (Canagarajah, 2011; Lee, 2014; Young, 2004, 2013), unlike in conventional bilingual instruction, which uses separate languages alongside each other (Creese & Blackledge, 2010, 2015; García & Wei, 2014). Grammars are thus not predefined or static, claimed Canagarajah, but "negotiated, rhetorical, and changing ...." (Canagarajah, 2015, p. 427). The more common term *multilingual* is therefore misleading in his view for an orientation that features meshing of various language resources, because the term *multilingual* "has been traditionally conceived as multiple languages enjoying their separate identity and structure even in contact" (Canagarajah, 2015, p. 419). But languages, in the translingual view, are not separate, nor does communication rely only on language, given the many semiotic systems and modes we use (Canagarajah, 2015, p. 419; Fraiberg, 2010; Kress, 2010). In all of this work, scholars have argued that standard (educated native speaker) English is not the only acceptable model for students.

The Intelligibility Criterion

Traditional L2 writing teachers may be wondering at this point what they are supposed to be doing in their classes. In the writing class, said Canagarajah (2015, p. 425), "What translingual pedagogies favor is deconstructing Standard English to make students aware that it is a social construct." He fears that "students may feel intimidated" if standard English is presented as a stable norm and that "they may adopt it mechanically, feeling that they don't have spaces for creativity." He has advocated what he calls shuttling "between different dialects or language repertoires" at the same time that standard English is taught (p. 425).

In another view, Jenkins (2014, p. 202), like Ammon (2009), argued strongly that the "only criterion [for international students in an Anglophone institution of higher education] should be mutual intelligibility among the relevant international academic community members inside and outside the institution instead of blanket conformity to a particular version of native English." She would have the criterion of mutual intelligibility rather than a formal standard apply to English language entry and exit examinations and theses as well, asking that institutions allow international students more time and provide more academic support. Of her own approach to PhD theses that she supervises, she said that she follows a practice of "ignoring grammar deviations from native English and only indicating intelligibility problems" (p. 193). I wondered when I read this if her students sail through their thesis defenses when others on their committees evaluate the work. Do all faculty agree with this criterion of intelligibility or do students have to seek proofreading help elsewhere, possibly at great cost? I turn now to some pro-standards arguments.

The Skeptics and Pragmatists Speak: A Friendlier View of Standards

Skeptics and pragmatists who critique the strong anti-monolingualist positions taken by the lingua franca–translingual practices advocates do not deny, to my knowledge, the inherent diversity of languages. That users of English, even within a single English-dominant context (e.g., Canada, the United States, Great Britain, Australia, New Zealand), speak many varieties of English, with many different native-speaker accents is undeniable (see an example from the United States in Lippi-Green, 1997). They also do not deny that a privileged native speaker variety continues to exert a powerful influence worldwide. This is a reality we all must face.

However, the term *native English speaker* to mean one privileged variety is a misnomer because without further qualifications it would have to include speakers of different dialects from all social classes, educational groups, and regional contexts if they were born into families where some variety of English was used as the mother tongue. But, of course, this is not what educators mean by the term *native speaker*, implying instead an educated variety associated with so called inner circle elites, and standardized in formal education, the corporate news media, in some workplaces, and in tests and examinations of language. This is the uncomfortable reality that lingua franca and translingual scholars resist and wish to change. But for better or worse, such conservatism and privilege not only characterize how English is used in many venues throughout the world, but other languages as well. In some countries, the privileged variety of language is protected from excessive change and "corruption" from foreign words by "royal academies" and other institutions that regulate language (e.g., Spain, France; see the impressive worldwide list on https://en.wikipedia.org/wiki/List_of_language_regulators).

It is also undeniable that we can find differences in the English used across genres and disciplines (Hyland, 2009, 2015b), and that we can indeed observe changes over time in how written language is used in the worlds of academia. But here too, changes are slow, and the academic world in reality is not so flexible, and regulates itself in ways that sometimes feel oppressive including to novice scholars trying to learn to write for publication (Canagarajah & Lee, 2014; Hyland, 2015a). Moreover, genre conventions in academic institutions resist innovation and change more than outside academia, making it tempting for L2 writing instructors to teach formulaic and template-like varieties (Tardy, 2009, 2016). Gatekeepers in the book and journal publishing worlds also make it difficult for writers to employ the kinds of innovative or blended practices that some scholars promote (see, for example, some attempts in Canagarajah, 2013c, and some chapters in Canagarajah, 2013a). We can also look to the stranglehold that textbook publishers and the testing industry have on what kinds of English will be taught. It is no wonder that political and ideological controversies have arisen about who is a real native speaker and about what varieties and standards should be taught in schools. We can understand the unfairness of such prescribed standards, particularly strict for written English, but are faced with some challenges if we are writing instructors who wish to make ethical and pragmatic choices that will fit our students' needs and expectations. Let us look at some of these challenges.

First, as to the changeability of English versus its basic stability, we can see concrete evidence of change by trying to read Chaucer, or even Shakespeare, or just by taking a course in the history of English. However, it is difficult to find examples of rapid major changes in the English grammatical system even over several hundred years: The Declaration of Independence (1776) is written in clear and lucid English, comprehensible today in both its grammar and lexis, where Chaucer (who died in 1400) is not. But it is also clear that in order to teach and learn a second language in an instructional setting, particularly its written forms, we need to presume that a language is relatively stable at least for the moment. That moment might be 200 or more years. Although the lexicon clearly changes more quickly as terminology is introduced in the media, the digital world, and the professional and disciplinary worlds, grammar and syntax are more stable. How pervasive are the "new grammars and new meanings" that Canagarajah (2015) refers to in his translingual perspective? How profound is their influence on how English is used in education and workplaces? Even when we consider how images have become infused into our textual practices, basic (dare I say standard) grammar remains fairly stable.

Likewise, in his critique of English as a lingua franca from a teacher's perspective, Maley (2009), a lifelong world-wide English language educator, asserted that some of the claims made by Jenkins and Seidlhofer are both statistically and theoretically flawed. Among other critiques, Maley noted from his review of attempts to codify features of English as a lingua franca that there really are only a "handful of new features" in an otherwise rather standard looking list (Maley, 2009, p. 192). Like MacKenzie (2014), he pointed out that many varieties of English share a standard native speaker core. In MacKenzie's (2014) critique of assertions of newness, change, and innovation in global Englishes as portrayed in the lingua franca literature, he commented that fluent users of English as a lingua franca and users of standard English share most features (95-96 percent) of English (p. 6). Maley (2009, p. 193) continued: "These findings are hardly supportive of Jenkins' claim that 'ELF . . . is self-determining and independent of Anglo-American English' (Jenkins, 2007, p. 35)." Pragmatists in the L2 writing class, then, hope to help both learners and users of English develop a variety of English that seems fundamentally stable and based on an Anglo-American standard if this is what they need and expect.

Another important critique that has been made by Maley (2009), MacKenzie (2014), and others is that the distinction between "errors" and "new grammars-lexicons" (Maley, 2009, p. 193) has not been sufficiently explored. What Canagarajah calls creativity and innovation in written and spoken language may in fact be cases of errors or incomplete proficiency—we would not know without knowing our students' L2 proficiency levels well and without checking with each of our students about their so called hybrid creativity in their writing (Shapiro et al., 2016). Canagarajah (2013c) did this with one of his multilingual students, Buthainah, reported in numerous publications, who apparently used some Arabic phrases intentionally in her peer-reviewed essay (an example critiqued as linguistic tourism by Matsuda, 2014), but few other examples of intentional innovation by L2 writers exist. MacKenzie (2014, p. 143) asserted that:

> It is all too rarely acknowledged in ELF research that what can be described, when seen from one angle, as the active, skillful, innovative, creative and resourceful adapting, blending, manipulating, reshaping and co-constructing of lexicogrammatical and pragmatic forms and speakers' linguistic resources to produce localized repertoires can also be reasonably analysed in terms of a lack of proficiency, incomplete learning, fossilization or learner language.

MacKenzie's points are worth remembering in the L2 writing class, namely, that an enormous amount of native English and standard English forms are "shared by indiginized varieties…" (p. 169), and that from the perspective of language learners, creativity that results in nonstandard English may or may not reflect intentional innovation rather than incomplete proficiency that students would prefer correcting. We need to ask students and to observe them closely over time, and help them develop the agency to make informed choices (Shapiro et al., 2016). It is not enough to have the testimony of just one student. When Jenkins (2014) stated that she worried only about the intelligibility of her PhD students' theses, not their formal accuracy, she did not tell us how her students felt about this, or whether they felt compelled to get someone else to proofread and edit their work. Connor, in a case study of four Chinese professionals studying English, presented at the end of her 2011 book, learned directly from these mature scholars what they wanted: They demanded to be taught standard English, a wish she was obligated to accede to. The point is that we need to ask L2 students and their teachers as well about their choices and their preferences in their writing and speaking.

Several attitude surveys did query students and teachers about their preferences for standard (native-like Anglo-American) features of their English. The opinions of learners, from the few studies that have commented on these, "tend to show that learners prefer to be taught what they perceive as a standard variety" (Maley, 2009, p. 194). Timmis (2002), for example, administered a questionnaire to 400 students from 14 countries and found that two-thirds of the students wished to acquire a native-like pronunciation in their English and to aim for fully native control of English grammar, with the exception of students from India, Pakistan, and South Africa, of whom one-third aimed for native speaker standards.

The opinions of teachers follow the same pattern, assuming teachers are aware of these issues. Maley (2009, p. 195) commented that "most teachers worldwide are, I suspect, far more concerned with improving their level of communicative effectiveness in English and of finding more effective ways of teaching it than with issues like ELF." Some existing studies confirm these predictable attitudes and beliefs. For instance, in his 2002 study, in addition to surveying students worldwide, Timmis also surveyed teachers (180 responses from 45 countries) as to their wishes for their students' accents and control of grammar. In this case, teachers' preferences for pronunciation balanced more evenly among native standards, intelligibility standards, and no preference, reflecting perhaps the teachers' understanding of realistic versus idealistic goals. However, more than half of the teacher respondents expressed the desire that their students acquire full control of the standard grammar of native speakers.

Even Jenkins, who has focused mainly on accent and pronunciation in her work, found in both surveys and interviews that respondent teachers had ambivalent attitudes about which accents they preferred. For example, she interviewed eight teachers (2005) and found that the teachers supported English as a lingua franca in theory, but still considered nonnative pronunciation to be "incorrect" (p. 540). She also interviewed 17 teachers as part of a larger questionnaire study and found similar ambivalent attitudes and beliefs about accent and pronunciation. In the questionnaire study, she surveyed more than 300 teachers' preferences from 12 countries for their own accents in English and found that the great majority of them preferred to aim for native-like U.S. or U.K. accents (Jenkins, 2007, 2009; see also Llurda, 2009). She commented on her results from the questionnaire study that

> Many of the respondents thus reveal strongly held positions about the correctness, pleasantness, and international acceptability of English accents (sometimes on the basis of limited familiarity), and firm linguistic beliefs about the locus of the 'best' English accents (i.e. the US and UK). (Jenkins, 2007, p. 186)

Another survey and focus group study was done in Hong Kong of 107 students and teachers (Li, 2009), with findings that mirrored those of Jenkins: Respondents overwhelmingly favored a native speaker accent (78–84 percent; p. 109). Li made the important point that nonnative speakers are perfectly capable of making their own choices about accent, and that we need to learn more about their choices and attitudes rather than imposing on them the views of scholars.

Although these studies were done on pronunciation, we can easily extrapolate to conventional writing studies. In this work, educated native speaker standards of correctness pervade the L2 writing field as can be seen in the hundreds of studies and presentations on written corrective feedback and error treatment. All of these studies presume an accepted standard of some sort (e.g., Bitchener, 2012; Bitchener & Ferris, 2012; Bitchener & Storch, 2016; Ferris, 2011; see also Chapter 7 on Assessment in this book, and some work in the journal edited by Ferris, *Journal of Response to Writing* (http://journalrw. org/index.php/jrw). In other words, second language development along with writing development, not just functional and communicative intelligibility, is the goal of most L2 writing students. If such development is not targeted at some kind of educated native speaker standard, the error treatment enthusiasts are left without a purpose or point of reference for their corrections. There is nothing to correct without an agreed-upon standard.

Taken together these studies indicate that most L2 students, including professionals who study English in the United States or United Kingdom, want efficient and direct instruction in speaking and writing in Standard English (now a pejorative term in some circles) and development of their linguistic proficiency, particularly if there is little time to offer them options (Ruecker, 2014, fn 12, p. 116).The same apparently holds for L2 teachers worldwide, whose own standards favor those of U.S.- or U.K.- educated native speakers. Outside conventional school settings and on social media, however, and in creative writing and journal writing tasks in schools, it is possible to find numerous examples of hybrid, code-meshed writing that are used to support a lingua-franca/translingual approach to literacy practices.

The point is that from the pragmatists' perspective, the interests and pronouncements of researchers and philosophizing scholars seem to have predominated over students' and teachers' wishes, needs, and expectations. My own reading of much of the lingua franca and translanguage literature is that researchers have been trying to tell us what L2 students and nonnative teachers of English want without asking them about their wishes and expectations and without investigating the beliefs that teachers bring with them into the diverse classroom. When teachers do ask, students often prefer an educated Anglo-American speaker standard, just as many teachers themselves do. Are scholars who have adopted a more critical, diverse view supposed to tell students and their teachers that their wishes are wrong? We can opt for awareness-building with L2 students and with teachers in teacher education programs, of course (Canagarajah, 2016), and let students and teachers choose their own target standards, assuming that there is interest and time, and assuming that there are no penalties for creative mixing and meshing of languages on written assignments and exams. No one is arguing against the benefits of greater awareness and choice in how all of us use language.

Classroom Perspectives

What are L2 writing instructors to do? Reflecting on their own beliefs is clearly a place to start. However, beyond this, they may or may not have choices. As often happens in L2 writing instruction, teachers may not be free to decide on their own about curricula such as what standards will be followed in teaching materials, tests, and graded written work. Even if standards are not overtly prescribed by an institution or department, they will be obvious from the kind(s) of English presented in textbooks assigned by the institution and expected on written work and examinations. Standards might also be prescribed by states, provinces, or national governments, as has happened in the United States with the Common Core standards. These are likely to follow the educated British or American native speaker standards that some of the scholars previously discussed have been dismissing as bankrupt concepts. Ethically, then, L2 writing teachers need to find out if there are required standards that they and their students must (or want to) follow, and then teach accordingly or find ways to resist that do not harm students.

One of the first steps classroom L2 writing instructors can do, therefore, is to learn whether their schools or departments adhere to any standards, what those standards are, and whether decisions to adhere to certain standards were made with full understanding of the issues I have described in this chapter. In general, we need to learn what the ideological stance of a school or department is toward English-only monolingualism, separate bilingualism, or blended multi-plurilingualism for both its L1 and L2 students. In other words, does a school or department honor and strive for diversity in more than name only, or instead pragmatically insist on students' need and right to acquire a standard educated variety as efficiently as possible?

A second step in the classroom is to find out what students themselves believe, need, and expect in their L2 writing. Such questions are rarely asked of students, although expectations can be assumed in some cases. For example if international students are studying English in order to achieve certain scores on tests or to read and write about particular subject matter in ways that schools or workplaces expect, or if they are being sponsored by governments or by companies, or if tuition-paying parents believe that there is one "correct" English that their children should learn, then educated native speaker standards will be expected, not questioned. L2 students and other stakeholders may have little doubt as to what kind(s) of English they want to learn, and what "correct" grammar and pronunciation mean. They are likely as well to hold strong beliefs about what "correct" language means in their own native languages and what variety they would use if they were teaching their L1s to foreigners in their cultural and national contexts. L2 writing teachers, therefore, need to learn enough about their students to be able to understand what they know about the many varieties of English, indeed of all languages including theirs, and to know what their needs, wishes, and expectations are in their L2 writing classes and other situations and contexts where English is used. If teachers believe that students who adhere to native speaker standards are "misinformed" (Jenkins, 2007) and need instruction in ways to move beyond or outside those standards, they will need to provide class time for such instruction in awareness of multiple varieties of English and code-meshing techniques, and in some views, actually teach code-meshing, as Lee (2014) did in her U.S. university classroom. Here are some questions, followed by a few specific examples.

English Only, Separation of Languages, or Blends

Will the L2 writing classroom as a whole be an English-only (educated native speaker standard) environment, including group discussion and collaboration on writing tasks, or will students' home languages and dialects be brought in to be drawn on separately for particular tasks? If home languages and dialects are not separated, how can they be blended into some or all of the writing activities? English-only classes continue to be preferred in some educational and political circles, in spite of being strongly condemned by the lingua franca/world Englishes/translanguage practice scholars.

In other cases, a blend of languages, styles, and stances can easily happen without affecting students' overall acquisition of (for example) standard conventions in academic writing. Journal writing (Casanave, 2011) is the best example, in which ungraded writing can be done freely in any way students wish, for the purposes of exploring and reflecting on ideas and topics. Blends can be accomplished in academic writing too, in which both lexical and rhetorical features flout the native English-only standard. Young (2004, 2013) named this strategy *code-meshing*, a concept picked up by Canagarajah (2006). Unlike code-mixing, which Canagarajah (2006, p. 614) described as including nonstandard lexical items in a piece of writing, code-meshing "can include mixtures of larger structural and rhetorical units and may still symbolize something 'marked' in the dominant language of the text." (Note that Matsuda, 2014, has commented that code-mixing and code-meshing are nearly synonymous.) Teachers and students in linguistically and culturally diverse writing classes would need to decide whether glosses or translations should be included in code-meshed writing, or whether peer readers and teachers should be left to admire or puzzle at the mixes and meshes.

In her university class, for example, Lee (2014) had students that included users of African-American Language (her term) first build awareness of many varieties of English in the world. She then asked them to record, transcribe, and analyze the language of someone they knew, study existing models of code-meshed writing, and then write their own narratives in any variety they wished, providing readers with a "translation table" of non-standard usages as needed. Although we don't know what her students needed or wanted from their composition classes, she reported that they felt legitimated in being able to use their home varieties. She referred to her instructional writing strategy of code-meshing as a "temporary pedagogical remedy for the harm that traditional monolingualist composition curricula have inflicted on students whose home languages and language varieties" differ from the standard privileged varieties (p. 318). This view and these arguments are especially prevalent in the United States.

Errors or Innovation?

As I discuss in more detail in Chapter 7 on Assessment, students' and teachers' attitudes toward error will be salient in decisions that we make about standards in L2 writing in actual classroom practice. Without some fairly sophisticated study of sociolinguistics, most people believe there are correct and incorrect ways to speak and write a language. It is difficult to change such a belief—I tried it once with an educated friend of mine. She would have none of it—nonstandard varieties and dialects of English are simply incorrect, she insisted. This is a view that many writing teachers still hold. If scholars of the lingua-franca/translanguage practices ilk want teachers and students to view deviations from standard norms as creative use of multiple language resources rather than errors, we will need to commit time and effort to first distinguishing in our own minds what is an error and what is a creative innovation. Second we will need to convince students that at least in certain kinds of writing what they thought were errors may not be errors, but creative blendings and meshings from their non-English language resources. Third, we will need to ask students, in discussions of their own writing, what they intended with any deviations from Standard Written English: Were the deviations intentional (and hence creative and innovative), or unintentional errors in their minds that they hope to correct? Once we understand our own views of errors versus innovations and the views of our students about their own writing, what kinds of writing tasks will we assign, and for what purposes? How will a blended writing assignment be assessed?

Models of Standard Written English, Code-Mixing, and Code-Meshing

One way to encourage students to blend their many linguistic resources in their writing would be to provide models of different kinds. For instance, teachers could provide models for students to analyze of the same basic paragraph written in three ways: Standard Written English, code-mixed (with non-native lexical items included), and code-meshed (a blend of nonstandard lexical and rhetorical features). They could also model different practices in their own writing and share this with students, if this is something they themselves practice. Likewise, teachers could share some of the scholarly literature with advanced students on the debates about standards in English writing. However, the vast majority of scholarly literature on code-meshing, lingua franca, and translanguage practices is itself written in fully standard English. Models are hard to come by. The example of Young (2013) is rare. Insertion of a few lexical items from other languages or adopting a personal rather than academic tone does not come close to modeling hybrid and creative practices as discussed in the literature, including the literature on genre innovation (Tardy, 2016). In particular, if, as L2 writing instructors and scholars, we ourselves do not model creative meshing and blending of multiple language resources, why are we pushing our students to write like this? For whom are they writing?

Still, as Lee (2014) did, Canagarajah has made a strong argument that code-meshing can be used in the L2 writing class without sacrificing students' need to acquire the dominant code:

> The power of codemeshing is that it enables us to acknowledge the reality of established codes in formal literate institutionalized contexts, while also making spaces within the text for alternative discourses. [...] Seeing the inclusion of their own language norms in elite and formal institutionalized texts, minority students and scholars will gain more ownership and voice in academic writing. (Canagarajah, 2013c, p. 113)

He then admitted that bits of oppositional code need to be introduced gradually into minority students' and scholars' texts, so as not to exclude such writers from the mainstream: "To be really effective, I need to work from within the existing rules to transform the game. [...] The qualified use of alternate codes into the dominant discourse will serve to both play the game and also to change its rules" (Canagarajah, 2013c, p. 114). It sounds like students first need to learn the rules to be able to then transform them.

In other words, even in Canagarajah's view, it is likely that students will need to express their ideas in primarily standard written English—to work within the existing rules. I might add here that I am not sure it is the students' responsibility to "change the rules." In short, L2 writing instruction needs to proceed with full awareness on the part of teachers and students as to what standards are possible, needed, expected, and desired, and only then to decide, with full awareness, which standards are practiced or resisted.

Ongoing Questions

Ongoing questions arising from the discussions in the chapter are numerous. Should or should not students and teachers worldwide be encouraged to pursue the standards of their choice, particularly if their choices involve the very real blendings of languages and styles used in Englishes worldwide? Do L2 writing instructors and their students comply with or resist the pull of powerful standards of English that are still dominated by the myths of the (monolingual) native speaker (Pennycook, 2010) and of the homogeneous native English speaker (Matsuda, 2006)? If we believe that L2 students and teachers need fast and efficient access to the powerful discourses of traditional standard varieties, how do we manage to pursue the kinds of translingual practices supported by Canagarajah, Jenkins, and others, given the limited time and energy of both students and teachers? Jenkins (2007) has commented on a fact that we are all familiar with: Beliefs about proper language use are deeply engrained in all of us. How much effort and time do we expend in the L2 writing class to try to convince students that their beliefs are wrong or at the very least narrow, especially if teachers themselves need to be convinced? Once liberated from narrow beliefs, will they feel free to experiment and innovate in positive and creative ways?

Is helping students and teachers increase their awareness of the normality of hybrid and code-meshing practices enough to instigate changes in their beliefs? With time, with sensitive instruction, and with models, learners can certainly be exposed to options they might not have been aware of. The idealists hold to such a goal, and to instruction that at the very least includes scaffolding and blending in students' own languages and dialects, even if the ultimate target is acquisition of standard written English (see Canagarajah's, 2015, discussion of how multilingual adolescents are instructed in New York Common Core standards and Velasco & García's, 2014, study of young bilingual learners). But pragmatic constraints weigh heavily on students who need to efficiently write papers and take tests in conservative educational institutions and on professionals who need to write and publish in academic and workplace genres. If learners are aware of their choices (and depending on how they are instructed, they may not be), the pragmatists believe they need to be allowed to choose what they feel is best for them and that instructors need to acknowledge students' wishes. We must ask, therefore, whether L2 students should be agents of their choices to the extent possible (Morgan, 2009; Shapiro et al., 2016). Whether they opt for conventional native speaker standards or creative code-meshed blends of languages, don't L2 writing instructors need to honor their choices?

Ultimately we can probably all agree that teachers and learners need to be aware of these deeply political, ideological, and emotional debates about standards, to the extent that time permits. Discussions in L2 writing classes about how everyone feels about standard and nonstandard features of spoken and written English for the purposes they are pursuing merit attention. But both L1 and L2 educators and scholars themselves can also ask what standards of L2 they would demand for themselves and their children if they were learning to speak and write an(other) L2. As a language learner in Japan, would I want to learn varieties of Japanese that would identify me as uneducated or as a speaker-writer of a regional dialect that is not favored by educated users? Probably not, but if I am aware of differences, I can choose. We really don't do enough perspective-taking in the field of second language education (Casanave, 2010) and would benefit from putting ourselves in the shoes of L2 learners to see what our own standards might be for the speaking and writing we learn and practice.

Beliefs and Practices

Beliefs

1. After reading some of the arguments in this chapter, and I hope some of the cited readings, do you believe there is something called a native English standard that should be practiced in the L2 writing class? Where do you now think this standard comes from? Should this standard be applied to all the writing that students do, or to certain tasks and genres?

2. What do you believe the phrase *monolingual bias* refers to?

3. If you believe the educated native speaker standard should be changed (made more diverse, flexible, hybrid), how do you think those more flexible standards can be explained to skeptical students and colleagues? How do you believe these more flexible standards might be applied to L2 writing tasks?

4. If English is not your mother tongue, do you believe there are standards in your native language(s) that need to be followed in school writing tasks? (i.e., is there a "correct" way to speak and write your language?) If so, where do you think these standards came from? Should they be changed to account for diversity of dialects, registers, and influences from other languages in your home country or culture?

5. If you have strong beliefs about the need for error treatment in L2 writing, according to what standards do you make corrections?

6. Do you believe that scholars who write about English as a lingua franca, English as an international language, and translingual literacy practices should publish their work in standard English or in the more flexible hybrid styles they espouse for their multilingual students? Why or why not?

7. What practices do you believe a student who is a monolingual L1 user of English should follow in a class that teaches hybrid and blended language standards?

Practices

1. Consult with teachers and colleagues at your own institution to ask their views of standards in written English. This can be done through informal or formal interviews or a short questionnaire (try to include open ended questions).

2. Try to find some published or unpublished examples of academic writing that do not follow standard written English. Analyze the features of this writing to identify the deviations from the standard and to assess how well the writing works (as a message about a topic to a particular audience and as a model for student writers).

3. Draft a short piece of academic writing (even just a few paragraphs) on a topic that interests you, blending styles and languages that you are familiar with so as to exemplify and model code meshing. Consider lexicon, grammar, organization, and style (e.g., formal or personal). Share these examples with classmates or colleagues and discuss their effectiveness as pieces of writing.

4. Design two writing activities for L2 students, one that would encourage creative code meshing and one that follows a formal standard for written English. Make sure you consider who the audience for this writing would be. If you are currently teaching, try these activities out with students and discuss their reactions to each kind of writing. Do they (and you) have strong views about them?

References

Alsagoff, L., McKay, S. L., Hu, G., & Renandya, W. (Eds.). (2012). *Principles and practices for teaching English as an international language*. London: Routledge/Taylor & Francis.

Ammon, U. (2009). Towards more fairness in international English: Linguistic rights of non-native speakers? In R. Phillipson (Ed.), *Rights to language: Equity, power, and education* (pp. 111–116) Mahwah, NJ: Lawrence Erlbaum.

Appleby, R. (2013). Desire in translation: White masculinity and TESOL. *TESOL Quarterly, 47*(1), 122–147.

Bailey, K. (2006). Marketing the eikawa wonderland: Ideology, akogare, and gender alterity in English conversation school advertising in Japan. *Environment and Planning D: Society and Space, 24*(1), 105–130.

Baker, W. (2009). The cultures of English as a lingua franca. *TESOL Quarterly, 43*(4), 567–592.

Baker, W. (2011). Intercultural awareness: Modelling an understanding of cultures in intercultural communication through English as a lingua franca. *Language and Intercultural Communication, 11*(3), 197–214.

Benesch, S. (1993), ESL, ideology, and the politics of pragmatism, *TESOL Quarterly, 27*, 705–717.

Benesch, S. (2001a). *Critical English for academic purposes: Theory, politics, and practice*, Mahwah, NJ: Lawrence Erlbaum.

Benesch, S. (2001b). Critical pragmatism: A politics of L2 composition. In T. Silva & P. K. Matsuda (Eds.), *On second language writing* (pp. 161–172). Mahwah, NJ: Lawrence Erlbaum.

Bitchener, J. (2012). Written corrective feedback for L2 development: Current knowledge and future research. *TESOL Quarterly, 46*(4), 855–860.

Bitchener, J., & Ferris, D. R. (2012). *Written corrective feedback in second language acquisition and writing*. New York: Routledge/Taylor & Francis.

Bitchener, J., & Storch, N. (2016). *Written corrective feedback for L2 development*. Bristol, U.K.: Multilingual Matters.

Blommaert, J. (2010). *The sociolinguistics of globalization*. Cambridge. U.K.: Cambridge University Press.

Blommaert, J (2013). *Ethnography, superdiversity and linguistic landscapes: Chronicles of complexity*. Bristol, U.K.: Multilingual Matters.

Bolton, K., & Kachru, B. J. (Eds.). (2006). *World Englishes: Critical concepts in linguistics.* London: Routledge/Taylor & Francis.

Braine, G. (Ed.), (1999), *Non-native educators in English language teaching,* Mahwah, NJ: Lawrence Erlbaum.

Canagarajah, A. S. (1999), *Resisting linguistic imperialism in English teaching,* Oxford, U.K.: Oxford University Press.

Canagarajah, A. S. (2002), *A geopolitics of academic writing,* Pittsburgh, PA: University of Pittsburgh Press.

Canagarajah, A. S. (2006). The place of World Englishes in composition: Pluralization continued. *College Composition and Communication, 57*(4), 586–619.

Canagarajah, A. S. (2007). Lingua franca English, multilingual communities, and language acquisition. *The Modern Language Journal, 91*(5), 923–939.

Canagarajah, A. S. (2011). Codemeshing in academic writing: Identifying teachable strategies of translanguaging. *The Modern Language Journal, 95*(3), 401–417.

Canagarajah, A. S. (Ed.). (2013a). *Literacy as translingual practice: Between communities and classrooms.* New York: Routledge/Taylor & Francis.

Canagarajah, A. S. (2013b). Negotiating translingual literacy: An enactment. *Research in the Teaching of English, 48*(1), 40–67.

Canagarajah, A. S. (2013c). *Translingual practice: Global English and cosmopolitan relations.* New York: Routledge/Taylor & Francis.

Canagarajah, A. S. (2015). Clarifying the relationship between translingual practice and L2 writing: Addressing learner identities. *Applied Linguistics Review, 6*(4), 415–440.

Canagarajah, A. S. (2016). Translingual writing and teacher development in composition. *College English, 78*(3), 265–273.

Canagarajah, A. S., & Lee, E. (2014). Negotiating alternative discourses in academic writing and publishing: Risks with hybridity. In L. Thesen & L. Cooper (Eds.), *Risk in academic writing: Postgraduate students, their teachers and the making of knowledge* (pp. 59–99). Bristol, U.K.: Multilingual Matters.

Casanave, C. P. (2008). The stigmatizing effect of Goffman's stigma label: A response to John Flowerdew. *Journal of English for Academic Purposes, 7*(4), 264–267.

Casanave, C. P. (2010). Perspective taking. In A. Stoke (Ed.), *JALT 2009 Conference Proceedings* (pp. 1–11). Tokyo: Japan Association for Language Teaching.

Casanave, C. P. (2011). *Journal writing in second language education.* Ann Arbor: University of Michigan Press.

Cogo, A., & Dewey, M. (2012). *Analysing English as a lingua franca: A corpus-driven investigation.* New York: Continuum.

Connor, U. (2011). *Intercultural rhetoric in the writing classroom.* Ann Arbor: University of Michigan Press.

Cook, V. (1999). Going beyond the native speaker in language teaching, *TESOL Quarterly, 33*(2), 185–209.

Creese, A., & Blackledge, A. (2010). Translanguaging in the bilingual classroom: A pedagogy for learning and teaching? *The Modern Language Journal, 94*(1), 103–115.

Creese, A., & Blackledge, A. (2015). Translanguaging and identity in educational settings. *Annual Review of Applied Linguistics, 35,* 20–35.

Cummins, J. (1981). The role of primary language development in promoting educational success for language minority students, In California State Department of Education (Ed.), *Schooling and language minority students: A theoretical framework* (pp. 3–49). Los Angeles: Evaluation, Dissemination and Assessment Center, California State University.

Cummins, J. (1996). *Negotiating identities: Education for empowerment in a diverse society.* Ontario: California Association for Bilingual Education.

Cummins, J. (2000). *Language, power and pedagogy: Bilingual children in the crossfire.* Clevedon, U.K.: Multilingual Matters.

Cummins, J., & Swain, M. (1986). *Bilingualism in education.* New York: Longman.

Davies, A. (2003). *The native speaker: Myth and reality.* Clevedon, U.K.: Multilingual Matters.

Ferris, D. R. (2011). *Treatment of error in second language student writing* (2nd ed.). Ann Arbor: University of Michigan Press.

Flowerdew, J. (2008). Scholarly writers who use English as an additional language: What can Goffman's "stigma" tell us? *Journal of English for Academic Purposes, 7*(2), 77–86.

Fraiberg, S. (2010). Composition 2.0: Toward a multilingual and multimodal framework. *College Composition and Communication, 62*(1), 100–126.

García, O., & Wei, L. (2014). *Translanguaging: Language, bilingualism and education.* New York: Palgrave Macmillan.

Gibbs, W. W. (1995, August). Lost science in the Third World. *Scientific American,* 92–99.

Hafernik, J. J., Messerschmitt, D. S., & Vandrick, S, (2002). *Ethical issues for ESL faculty: Social justice in practice*, Mahwah, NJ: Lawrence Erlbaum.

Hamp-Lyons, L., & Zhang, B. W. (2001). World Englishes: Issues in and from academic writing assessment. In J. Flowerdew & M. Peacock (Eds.), *Research perspectives on English for academic purposes* (pp. 101–116). Cambridge, U.K.: Cambridge University Press.

Horner, B., Lu, M.-Z., Royster, J. J., & Trimbur, J. (2010). Opinion: Language difference in writing: Toward a translingual approach. *College English, 73*(3), 303–321.

Horowitz, D, (1986). What professors actually require: Academic tasks for the ESL classroom. *TESOL Quarterly, 20*, 445–482.

Houghton, S. A., & Rivers, D. J. (Eds.). (2013). *Native speakerism in Japan: Intergroup dynamics in foreign language education*. Bristol, U.K.: Multilingual Matters.

Hyland, K. (2009). *Academic discourse*. London: Continuum.

Hyland, K. (2015a). *Academic publishing: Issues and challenges in the construction of knowledge*. Oxford, U.K.: Oxford University Press.

Hyland, K. (2015b). Genre, discipline and identity. *Journal of English for Academic Purposes, 20*, 1–12.

Hyland, K. (2016). Academic publishing and the myth of linguistic injustice. *Journal of Second Language Writing, 31*, 58–69.

Jenkins, J. (2005). Implementing an international approach to English pronunciation: The role of teacher attitudes and identity. *TESOL Quarterly, 39*(3), 535–543.

Jenkins, J. (2006). Current perspectives on teaching World Englishes and English as a lingua franca. *TESOL Quarterly, 40*(1), 157–181.

Jenkins, J. (2007). *English as a lingua franca: Attitude and identity*. Oxford, U.K.: Oxford University Press.

Jenkins, J. (2009). English as a lingua franca: Interpretations and attitudes. *World Englishes, 28*(2), 200–207.

Jenkins, J. (2014). *English as a lingua franca in the international university: The politics of academic English language policy*. Abingdon, U.K.: Routledge.

Jenkins, J., Cogo, A., & Dewey, M. (2011). Review of developments in research into English as a lingua franca. *Language Teaching, 44*(3), 281–315.

Journal of Response to Writing (http://journalrw.org/index.php/jrw).

Kachru, B. (1985/2006). Standards, codification and sociolinguistic realism. In K. Bolton & B. J. Kachru (Eds.), *World Englishes: Critical concepts in linguistics* (pp. 241–269). London: Routledge/Taylor & Francis.

Kress, G. (2010), *Multimodality: A social semiotic approach to contemporary communication*. London: Routledge/Taylor & Francis.

Kubota, R. (1998). Ideologies of English in Japan, *World Englishes, 17*(3), 295–306.

Kubota, R. (2011). Learning a foreign language as leisure and consumption: Enjoyment, desire, and the business of eikaiwa, *International Journal of Bilingual Education and Bilingualism, 14*(4), 473–488.

Kubota, R. (2014). The multi/plural turn, postcolonial theory, and neoliberal multiculturalism. *Applied Linguistics, 35*(3), 1–22.

Kubota, R., & Fujimoto, D. (2013). Racialized native speakers: Voices of Japanese American English language professionals. In S. A. Houghton & D. Rivers (Eds.), *Native speakerism in Japan: Intergroup dynamics in foreign language education* (pp. 196–206). Bristol, U.K.: Multilingual Matters.

Kubota, R., & Lin, A. (Eds.). (2009). *Race, culture, and identities in second language education: Exploring critically engaged practice.* New York: Routledge/Taylor & Francis.

Kusaka, L. L. (2014). *Negotiating identities: An interview study and auto-ethnography of six Japanese American TESOL professionals in Japan.* Unpublished doctoral dissertation, Temple University, Philadelphia, Pennsylvania.

Lee, M. (2014). Shifting to the World Englishes paradigm by way of the translingual approach: Code-meshing as a necessary means of transforming composition pedagogy. *TESOL Journal, 5*(2), 312–329.

Leung, C., Harris, R., & Rampton, B. (1997). The idealized native speaker, reified ethnicities, and classroom realities. *TESOL Quarterly, 31*(3), 543–560.

Li, D. C. S. (2009). Researching non-native speakers' views toward intelligibility and identity: Bridging the gap between moral high grounds and down-to-earth concerns. In F. Sharifian (Ed.), *English as an international language: Perspectives and pedagogical issues* (pp. 81–118). Bristol, U.K.: Multilingual Matters.

Lillis, T., & Curry, M. J. (2010). *Academic writing in a global context: The politics and practices of publishing in English.* London: Routledge/Taylor & Francis.

Lippi-Green, R. (1997). *English with an accent: Language, ideology, and discrimination in the United States.* New York: Routledge.

Liu, J. (1999). Nonnative-English-speaking professionals in TESOL. *TESOL Quarterly, 33*(1), 85–102.

Llurda, E. (2009). Attitudes towards English as an international language: The pervasiveness of native models among L2 users and teachers. In F. Sharifian (Ed.), *English as an international language: Perspectives and pedagogical issues* (pp. 119–134). Bristol, U.K.: Multilingual Matters.

Lu, M.-Z., & Horner, B. (2013). Translingual literacy, language difference, and matters of agency. *College English, 75*(6), 281–315.

MacKenzie, I. (2014). *English as a lingua franca: Theorizing and teaching English.* New York: Routledge/Taylor & Francis.

Maley, A. (2009). ELF: A teacher's perspective. *Language and Intercultural Communication, 9*(3), 187–200.

Manchón, R. M. (Ed.). (2011). *Learning-to-write and writing-to-learn in an additional language.* Amsterdam: John Benjamins.

Matsuda, A. (2003). World Englishes in teaching English as an international language. *TESOL Quarterly, 37*(4), 719–729.

Matsuda, A. (Ed.). (2012). *Principles and practices of teaching English as an international language.* Bristol, U.K.: Multilingual Matters.

Matsuda, A., & Friedrich, P. (2011). English as an international language: A curriculum blueprint. *World Englishes, 30*(3), 332–344.

Matsuda, P. K. (2006). The myth of linguistic homogeneity in U.S. college composition. *College English, 68*(6), 637–651.

Matsuda, P. K. (2014). The lure of translingual writing. *PMLA, 129*(3), 478–483.

Mauranen, A. (2012). *Exploring ELF: Academic English shaped by non-native speakers.* Cambridge, U.K.: Cambridge University Press.

Mauranen A., & Ranta, E. (Eds.). (2009). *English as a lingua franca: Studies and findings.* Newcastle upon Tyne, U.K.: Cambridge Scholars Publishing.

Morgan, B. (2009). Fostering transformative practitioners for critical EAP: Possibilities and challenges. *Journal of English for Academic Purposes, 8,* 86–99.

Motha, S. (2006). Decolonizing ESOL: Negotiating linguistic power in U.S. public school classrooms. *Critical Inquiry in Language Studies, 3*(2 & 3), 75–100.

Motha, S. (2014). *Race, empire, and English language teaching: Creating responsible and ethical anti-racist practice*. New York: Teachers College Press.

Motha, S., & Lin, A. (2014). "Non-coercive rearrangements": Theorizing desire in TESOL. *TESOL Quarterly 48*(2), 331–359.

Otsuji, E., & Pennycook, A. (2010). Metrolingualism: Fixity, fluidity, and language in flux. *International Journal of Multilingualism, 7*, 240–254.

Pandey, A. (2013). When "second" comes first—[Hindi word] to the eye? Sociolinguistic hybridity in professional writing. In A. S. Canagarajah (Ed.), *Literacy as translingual practice: Between communities and class-rooms* (pp. 215–227). New York: Routledge/Taylor & Francis.

Park, J., & Lee, L. (2011). A practice-based critique of English as a lingua franca. *World Englishes, 30*(3), 360–374.

Pennycook, A, (1989). The concept of method, interested knowledge, and the politics of language teaching, *TESOL Quarterly, 23*(4), 589–618.

Pennycook, A. (1994/2013). *The cultural politics of English as an international language*, New York: Routledge/Taylor & Francis.

Pennycook, A. (2007). The myth of English as an international language. In S. Makoni & A. Pennycook (Eds.), *Disinventing and reconstituting languages* (pp. 90–115). Clevedon, U.K.: Multilingual Matters.

Pennycook, A. (2010, August 10). The monolingual myth. Posted on Language on the Move website. http://www.languageonthemove.com/recent-posts/the-monolingual-myth

Phillipson, R. (1992), *Linguistic imperialism*, Oxford, U.K.: Oxford University Press.

Prodromou, L. (2008). *English as a lingua franca: A corpus based analysis*. New York: Continuum.

Rampton, M. B. H. (1990). Displacing the 'native speaker': Expertise, affiliation, and inheritance. *ELT Journal, 44*(2), 97–101.

Ruecker, T. (2014). "Here they do this, there they do that." *College Composition and Communication, 66*(1), 91–119.

Ruecker, T., & Ives, L. (2015). White native English speakers needed: The rhetorical construction of privilege in online teacher recruitment spaces. *TESOL Quarterly, 49*(4), 733–756.

Santos, T. (1992). Ideology in composition: L1 and ESL. *Journal of Second Language Writing, 1*, 1–15.

Santos, T. (2001). The place of politics in second language writing. In T. Silva & P. K. Matsuda (Eds.), *On second language writing* (pp. 173–190). Mahwah, NJ: Lawrence Erlbaum.

Seidlhofer, B. (Ed.). (2003). *Controversies in applied linguistics*. New York: Oxford University Press.

Seidlhofer, B. (2009). Common ground and different realities: World Englishes and English as a lingua franca. *World Englishes, 28*(2), 236–245.

Seidlhofer, B. (2011). *Understanding English as a lingua franca*. New York: Oxford University Press.

Sharifian, F. (Ed.). (2009). *English as an international language: Perspectives and pedagogical issues*. Bristol, U.K.: Multilingual Matters.

Shapiro, S., Cox, M., Shuck, G., & Simnitt, E. (2016). Teaching for agency: From appreciating linguistic diversity to empowering student writers. *Composition Studies, 44*(1), 31–52.

Shor, I. (1992). *Empowering education: Critical teaching for social change*. Chicago: University of Chicago Press.

Swales, J. M. (1997). English as *Tyrannosaurus rex*. *World Englishes, 16*(3), 383–382.

Tardy, C. (2009). *Building genre knowledge*. West Lafayette, IN: Parlor Press.

Tardy, C. (2016). *Beyond convention: Genre innovation in academic writing*. Ann Arbor: University of Michigan Press.

Timmis, I. (2002). Native-speaker norms and international English: A classroom view. *ELT Journal, 56*(3), 240–249.

Vandrick, S. (2009). *Interrogating privilege: Reflections of a second language educator*. Ann Arbor: University of Michigan Press.

Vandrick, S. (2015). No "knapsack of invisible privilege" for ESL university students. *Journal of Language, Identity, and Education, 14*(1), 54–59.

Velasco, P., & García, O. (2014). Translanguaging and the writing of bilingual learners. *Bilingual Research Journal, 37*(1), 6–23.

Warschauer, M. (1999). *Electronic literacies: Language, culture, and power in online education*. Mahwah, NJ: Lawrence Erlbaum.

Young, V. (2004). Your average nigga. *College Composition and Communication, 55*, 693–715.

Young, V. (2013). Keep code-meshing. In A. S. Canagarajah (Ed.), *Literacy as translingual practice: Between communities and classrooms* (pp. 139–145). New York: Routledge/Taylor & Francis.

Chapter 5

Paths to Improvement

"... [W]riters' ability to produce their texts fluently seems to be different from their ability to produce texts of high quality. That is, some students who write high-quality texts may not be able to produce these texts fluently." (Abdel Latif, 2009, p. 550)

"[W]e find it difficult if not impossible to identify anything that is learned without feedback." (Evans, Hartshorn, McCollum, & Wolfersberger, 2010, p. 447)

"[A]ffective factors play an important role in uptake and retention of feedback." (Storch & Wigglesworth, 2010, p. 304)

"[A]s yet there is little evidence that the effects of AWE [automated writing evaluation] transfer to more general improvements in writing proficiency." (Stevenson & Phakiti, 2014, p. 51)

"[S]tudents cannot possibly perfect their writing in a classroom that over-emphasizes written accuracy." (Lee, 2013, p. 116)

LEADING QUESTIONS

- In L2 writing classes, what do we mean by "improvement"? How can teachers best help students improve?
- To what extent do we need to distinguish between improvement in language and improvement in writing?
- In what ways are fluency, accuracy, and complexity linked to improvement in writing?

- How do the central arguments in the process-product debate relate to aspects of improvement in writing?
- Of the many kinds of responses to student writing, what evidence is there that error correction leads to improvement, either in research you have read or in your own experiences?
- What kinds of practices and responses to writing might help students improve writing beyond the level of linguistic accuracy?

Introduction to the Issues

Perhaps the most consuming of all dilemmas for L2 writing teachers is how to best help their students improve their writing. The dilemma involves not only the need for teachers to have a sense of what they mean by improvement but also an idea of what the diverse and sometimes competing and controversial opinions are in different disciplines and contexts about the meaning of improvement and the approaches and practices that best lead to improvement. For example, some work has concerned how students can increase their fluency and syntactic complexity, both thought to signal improvement in spoken and written language. The field of L2 writing has been consumed for many years by the process-product debate, the history of which is beneficial for writing teachers to know about, given that proponents of both views wish to find ways to help students improve their writing. Fans of genre approaches, and post-process theorists, too, are ultimately concerned about helping writers develop contextualized awareness and strategies for improving their writing.

But the view of improvement in the L2 writing field that has dominated in recent years concerns the role of feedback, in particular how teachers can help students improve the linguistic accuracy of their writing, i.e., decrease their grammatical and lexical errors. These concerns fall under the purview of SLA, with less attention to larger rhetorical issues in writing. Research abounds on feedback, response, and error correction in L2 writing, reflecting the deeply held beliefs of many writing teachers, researchers, and students that students' writing will not improve without feedback (in spite of earlier debates about the questionable efficacy of grammar correction, an area I cover in this chapter). I cover these issues in this chapter, but regrettably do a less thorough job of addressing other kinds of improvements, such as the development of content knowledge needed for particular subject matter areas, rhetorical and genre sophistication, knowledge of argument and persuasion, and creativity. Where possible, I will remind readers to continue thinking about these important areas in which all writers, including the most experienced, hope to improve, and that go well beyond the conventional emphases on processes and products, and on fluency, complexity, and accuracy. Some of these larger concerns are captured in the analytical criteria we find on rating scales and rubrics (see Chapter 7 on Assessment), but we seem to have trouble figuring out how to do research on or respond effectively to the less concrete and visible elements of writing such as "development of an argument" or "sophistication." It is much easier to count errors.

This is not to diminish the importance of error-free writing, particularly in high-stakes writing such as dissertations (Rogers, Zawacki, & Baker, 2016), but to point out that the L2 writing field's obsession with language-level errors as a primary path to improvement obscures other more challenging areas in which writers need to improve. As a field historically made up of many people in applied linguistics who have a long-term interest in SLA (as opposed to composition, rhetoric, and the disciplines), and as one driven in many parts of the world by an exam/test culture, L2 writing does what it knows best— research and instruction on *language* development, not just writing and knowledge development. Much of this work also presumes that a primary goal of L2 written language development is native or near-native linguistic competence (Bitchener & Storch, 2016). This is so in spite of arguments against such standards (see Chapter 4) and in spite of arguments by scholars of disciplinary writing that form and content knowledge develop in tandem (Hyland, 2013; Hyland & Hyland, 2006, p. 4). We thus have much to share with people in composition, rhetoric, and discipline-based writing about the importance of language-level improvements in students' writing. But they also have much to share with us about larger issues, as numerous scholars have pointed out and as L2 writing researchers interested in students' overall writing development are coming to understand (Ferris, 2010). I urge readers, therefore, to read widely not only in the SLA and L2 writing fields, but beyond, and to develop a perspective on improvement in writing that can apply beyond concerns about processes, products, and linguistic accuracy, including perspectives that can apply to our own writing.

I thus present in this chapter only some of the issues related to improvement that have been debated in the L1 and L2 writing literature. As part of this introduction, I include a section that tries to define what we mean by improvement in writing. Without some sense of what we mean by this, we have no way to instruct writing students or to help them improve what they write. The section on Discussions in the Literature begins with the tensions among the goals of fluency, accuracy, and complexity in writing. This section is followed by a historical look at the process-product debate, which explores in part how much attention writers pay to the processes by which they achieve fluency, accuracy, and complexity, among other things, versus how focused they are mainly on the products of their writing, as is the case for one-shot exam writing. Subsequent discussions of genre continue the social turn that began during the era of the process-product debates. The next issue encompasses a more volatile debate on the role of response—written corrective feedback in particular—in helping students improve the linguistic aspects of their writing. Many L2 writing teachers cannot imagine *not* correcting at least some of their students' errors, and many L2 students apparently feel the same way. Although I discuss the correction debate at some length, at the expense of broader discussions of response, I remind readers that corrective feedback is only one kind of response to writing.

Underlying these debates are several less controversial assumptions concerning how students' (and our own) writing improves. I won't discuss them much in this chapter, but these assumptions merit attention by writing instructors and students. I will assume in this chapter that writing of all kinds, by all kinds of writers, improves with practice. Thus, regardless of what beliefs writing teachers hold about the controversial paths to improvement in their students' writing, practice, and more practice, is considered essential. I will further assume that all writers have trouble improving their writing if they do not know their topics well or if they have little interest in their topics or their writing tasks. Topic knowledge and interest underlie improvements in all kinds of writing (Langer, 1984; Newell & MacAdam, 1987; Yang, Lu, & Weigle, 2015). I will also assume that reading and writing are linked (Belcher & Hirvela, 2001; Carson & Leki, 1993; Hirvela, 2016), and that people who read and reflect on examples of good writing can improve their own writing. Finally, I will assume that some writers, both L1 and L2, can improve their writing by studying some of the classic and more recent books about how to write well (e.g., Strunk & White, 1959; Sword, 2012; Williams, 1997; Williams & Colomb, 2012; Zinsser, 2005) and how to write badly (Billig, 2013; Frankfurt, 2005; Pinker, 2014). My own writing has benefited greatly from the insights provided in these sources.

Trying to Define Improvement

Before delving into the more controversial issues in detail, I discuss the difficulties we face in trying to figure out what we mean by improvement. In order to do this, we need to have a sense of what "good writing" is and a way to capture changes in the assessments we make of students' writing (see Chapter 7, Assessment). Broadly, improvement can be defined as positive change over time, or as Pennington (2014, p. 175) expressed it, change, development, and progress. However, a fundamental dilemma, one that influences how writing teachers approach specific paths to improvement, concerns how researchers and teachers identify specific characteristics of improvement in writing (Currie, 1994), including what we mean by change, development, and progress. To do this, we need to have some idea of what we consider good writing to be. It turns out to be quite difficult to characterize good writing in a clear and unambiguous way that would allow teachers to apply the characterizations to writing pedagogy, other than saying that good writing is "error free" (not always true). And some characterizations seem opposite. One view: Good writing is simple, clear, and jargon-free and full of strong verbs and clear agents for actions. An opposite view: Good writing is complex and lexically and syntactically sophisticated, and full of nominalizations and the grammatical metaphor that nominalizations provide.

As Leki (1995) and others have noted, instructors in universities often hold tacit views of what constitutes good writing in their fields. In other words, they can recognize it when they see it but have trouble explaining their criteria. Li (1996) is one of the few writing scholars to conduct an in-depth cross cultural study to try to get at the heart of what "good writing" consists of in the perceptions of teachers from two cultures, China and the United States (see details in Chapter 2). Li's own experience as a writer in two cultures, however, convinced her that even if readers believe that objective standards exist, deciding what good writing consists of "is a messy and complex issue, anything but pure and simple" (Li, 1996, p. xiii). One thing that I can say about my own criteria for good writing is that it keeps me awake and makes me want to turn to the next page. Figuring out how to improve my own writing so that it keeps readers awake and interested is the challenge.

In addition to asking readers to give reasons why they judge some writing as good and other writing as less successful, we can turn to assessment rubrics to see the criteria by which student writing is actually judged (see Ch. 7; see also Crusan, 2010, 2015; Chapter 6 in Ferris & Hedgcock, 2014, on assessment; and Weigle, 2002). By setting up criteria for assessment, writing teachers and evaluators necessarily characterize what they believe good writing to consist of. Criteria may be described in analytic schemes that focus on how effectively writers address a topic, provide a coherent and well-organized discussion, and use vocabulary and grammar to achieve their purposes. Holistic rubrics describe similar criteria but generally without breaking the features into discrete categories. Other criteria include maturity and flair (Casanave, 1994), style and grace (Williams, 1997), and "wit, humor, surprise, originality, [and] logical reasoning" (Haswell, 2006, p. 70), all of which are criteria that are themselves difficult to define. It soon becomes obvious that criteria for good writing, particularly those that relate to thinking skills and topic knowledge, such as coherence, flow, logic, clarity, depth of treatment, and maturity, cannot themselves be easily characterized in ways that would satisfy the assessor or researcher or computer essay evaluator who wishes to count and quantify unambiguously what good writing is. It is perhaps for this reason, particularly in L2 writing, that teachers seem to focus so persistently on features of writing that can be seen and counted by teachers or by automated essay evaluation software and easily corrected: grammar, vocabulary, and mechanics.

Finally, teachers and researchers of L2 writing need to try to distinguish between two very different conceptions of improvement in writing. One has to do with the quality of writing and its overall effectiveness, including its reception by readers (Tardy, 2016), however that effectiveness is measured or characterized. This challenge faces both L1 and L2 writing teachers and researchers (Ferris, 2010). The second has to do with the development of students' second language proficiency, an issue facing those in L2 writing (Bitchener & Ferris, 2012; Bitchener & Storch, 2016; Carson, 2001; Ferris, 2010; Manchón, 2011; Polio, 2001) and that often dovetails with writing research. These two may or may not be related. It might be possible, in other words, for students to improve individual pieces of writing, with feedback and revision, without increasing their L2 proficiency at all. Students might also improve their overall control and linguistic knowledge of the L2 without improving their writing. This dilemma has not been solved in L2 writing research. However, L2 writing teachers who are concerned mainly with helping students improve the quality of their writing will make certain kinds of decisions in their writing classrooms, and those concerned primarily with L2 acquisition will make others. Likewise, writing researchers who study written corrective feedback, a topic I will cover in some depth in this chapter, might not actually be investigating writing alone, but SLA, assuming that these can be separated. As is the case for students of SLA (Larsen-Freeman, 2009), L2 writers need to improve the complexity, accuracy, and fluency of their writing.

It is not the purpose of this chapter to try to characterize good writing definitively but to alert L2 writing teachers to the need to consider carefully what their own localized criteria for good writing are as they design activities to help students improve their writing. They will no doubt discover multiple criteria at many layers of attention and may find that they do not in fact need a stable and unambiguous characterization of good writing in order to help students along the path to improvement. They can attend to different criteria selectively, according to who the students are, why they are writing, what they are writing, and who they are writing for. Indeed, if criteria for good writing change according to who readers are, we may be doing students a favor by convincing them that there are no universal standards for good writing, and that their job is to learn as much as they can about what their readers (and realistically this usually means individual teachers) expect. The point is that teachers need to reflect on their criteria in conjunction with their goals and contexts for teaching and need to realize they cannot, and need not, do everything at once.

Now let me turn to the main issues in this chapter. I first introduce the tensions between the two different but equally desired goals for L2 writers: that of developing fluent writing (with attendant loss of fear of taking risks and making mistakes) and that of developing writing that is grammatically accurate, formally acceptable, and sufficiently complex to satisfy evaluators. Some of the arguments for and against attention to fluency and accuracy are revisited in the process-product debate, the second issue I discuss. I also touch on questions about genre in this section. The last section of the literature discussion concerns the topic of response to writing, with a main focus on the error correction debate as feedback and correction studies continue to proliferate. After the section on classroom perspectives, I end with many ongoing questions for teachers and researchers to ponder.

Discussions in the Literature

Fluency, Accuracy, and Complexity

It is probably safe to say that every L2 writing teacher hopes that all students develop both fluency and accuracy in their writing, even though neither one can be linked clearly to improvement in writing quality (Polio, 2001). *Fluency* can be seen as writers' ability to produce a lot of language without excessive hesitations, blocks, and interruptions. Fluent writers write without fear of making mistakes, knowing that they can go back to their writing at any time to make changes and corrections. They write smoothly, even if in small bursts, especially if they know their topics well and have something to say. They produce more language in a given time period than nonfluent writers, in most views. Although not much research has focused on fluency (Polio, 2001; van Waes & Leijten, 2015), in the past it was usually measured by the total number of words a writer can produce within a specified time limit (Wolfe-Quintero, Inagaki, & Kim, 1998). This view of fluency continues to be used (Hartshorn & Evans, 2015) but, more recently, it has also been depicted as writing with short pausing times, a lot of words produced between pauses (measured as mean length of "translating episodes" by Abdel Latif, 2009), high output, and few revisions (van Waes & Leijten, 2015, especially the table showing multiple perspectives on fluency in their study of L1 and L2 writers in Belgium).

Accuracy, on the other hand, usually refers to a writer's ability to produce language that is free of language errors at the word and sentence level. In this meaning it does not refer to a writer's accurate reporting of content. Accuracy in research is usually measured by error counts, such as the number of error-free T-units (a "minimal terminable unit" consisting of an independent clause and any attached dependent clauses or phrases, as defined by Hunt, 1977), analytic rating scales (Polio, 2001), or counts of individual linguistic features such as articles, prepositions, or past tense markers (Bitchener, Young, & Cameron, 2005), or even just articles themselves (Bitchener & Knoch, 2010a, 2010b; Ellis, Sheen, Murakami, & Takashima, 2008). These studies often find that subsequent student writing (on revised writing and new pieces of writing) shows improvement in the linguistic accuracy of the selected features. The problem for students and their writing teachers, however, is that fluency and accuracy are inversely related: As attention to one goes up, attention to the other goes down. This means that students may see more errors in writing that they do as part of fluency exercises than in writing that is done more slowly and deliberately, where they can either attend more systematically to errors or consciously avoid taking risks that might produce them. Both researchers and teachers continue to ponder the relationship between these two aspects of writing on the one hand and improvement in writing on the other.

Complexity is another area in which students' writing and their SLA in general is thought to improve if it becomes more complex, as well as more fluent and accurate (Larsen-Freeman, 2009; Norris & Ortega, 2009). In at least one automated essay rating system, one measure of complexity was the number of words before the main verb (McNamara, Crossley, & McCarthy, 2010). More commonly, complexity is measured by T-unit length, number of clauses per T-unit, and the amount and length of clausal subordination or phrasal elaboration (Norris & Ortega, 2009). Such studies are difficult to conduct because complexity in writing and speaking develops only slowly over time (Ortega, 2003, said it takes a year or more), in a nonlinear and individually variable way (Larsen-Freeman, 2009; Ortega, 2003). It is also linked in interesting ways to writers' topic knowledge (Yang, Lu, & Weigle, 2015). Writing that is more globally complex and syntactically diverse scored higher, in the Yang, Lu, and Weigle study; features in the higher-scored essays seemed linked in part to the kinds of reasoning demanded from each topic.

However, complexity in writing turns out to be a complex topic. Because academic writing that is complex is thought to be better (or at least more mature) than writing that is simple, writing teachers and scholars have often tried to help students learn how to construct subordinate or embedded clauses, for example, that will allow writers to connect more ideas in one sentence and to show their relationships. But the stereotype of academic writing as structurally complex in this way might not reflect clearly the nature of academic writing. Corpus studies on large databases of academic writing have found that professional academic writing achieves its complexity by means of nominalization and grammatical metaphor: the process of turning verbs into nouns and using phrasal elaborations within noun clauses to condense multiple ideas in a sentence (Biber & Gray, 2010; Biber, Gray, & Poonpon, 2011; Byrnes, 2009). In complex and condensed nominalizations, the relationships among ideas are likely not to be expressed as overtly as in longer sentences made of clearly connected clauses. Densely nominalized writing is therefore both harder to write and harder to read for both L1 and L2 students, but thought to be essential for students of academic writing to learn, as Byrnes (2009) showed in her study of how L2 students of German developed their uses of grammatical metaphor over time (see also Fang, Schleppegrell, & Cox, 2006; Schleppegrell, 2004).

It is also a style that is not universally praised. Academic writing needs to become linguistically simpler, not more complex, according to a number of critics who feel strongly that complex ideas do not need to be expressed in complex, heavily nominalized language (Billig, 2013). Complex noun phrases need to be unpacked and expressed with clear agents and actions and fewer passives and nominalizations (Billig, 2008; Pinker, 2014; Williams, 1997; Williams & Colomb, 2012). A dilemma for writing teachers therefore is whether to instruct students with models written in the heavily nominalized prose typical of academic writing or from models in which agents and actions are transparent. If we opt to help students develop a sophisticated yet simple prose style (this would certainly be my choice), we will probably still have to help them learn to read the denser nominalized styles that require readers to infer relations among ideas.

Product, Process, and Genre

In this section, I review the product-process debate, with attention to its history, followed by some comments on genre. This juxtaposition of process and product still has relevance in exam-centered writing instruction around the world, in discussions of how writing actually gets done, and in the debate on written corrective feedback, which I turn to in the final section of this chapter. Discussions of genre reflect interest in ways that writing can be seen not just as efforts made by a single individual to write according to a template, but as efforts made by writers to shape and situate their writing within social, cultural, and disciplinary communities.

For newcomers to the field of L2 writing, the history of the process-product debate is worth learning and reading about in some of the earlier incarnations. The basic concept remains the same today as many years ago: Do we ask students to compose one-shot drafts and evaluate them only on their finished writing (a product approach)? Or do we follow a process approach in which students work on a piece of writing multiple times, changing and revising it and attending to their strategies for composing? It is probably not controversial to say that both L1 and L2 writing scholars for many years have supported an approach that helps students understand their own composing processes and that helps them learn to revise.

This does not mean ignoring the final product of students' writing. All writing teachers no doubt hope to find balanced ways to help students improve the effectiveness of their writing processes on their way to producing a satisfactory written product. However, by the 1970s resistance began to arise to what Young (1978) called the "current-traditional paradigm" in L1 writing. According to Young, this traditional product-focused approach was tacit rather than set forth in a clear theoretical or pedagogical set of precepts. It included features that sound very familiar today:

> . . . emphasis on the composed product rather than the composing process; the analysis of discourse into words, sentences, and paragraphs; the classification of discourse into description, narration, exposition, and argument; the strong concern with usage (syntax, spelling, punctuation) and with style (economy, clarity, emphasis); the preoccupation with the informal essay and the research paper; and so on. (p. 31)

However, there probably has not been a time in which L1 and L2 writing educators have totally focused attention on the finished products of students' writing at the expense of attention to how they got there (see Matsuda's, 2003, historical review). Even so, there was a time when teachers paid little attention to writing processes. In a nutshell, when they focus on writing as a product, researchers and teachers look at the textual characteristics of writing samples and count various features, analyze rhetorical structures, and teach and evaluate grammatical, linguistic, and rhetorical forms that suit different genres (see the next section on feedback and response and Chapter 7 on Assessment). Their concerns do not lie with how writers got to the final stage of writing nor with how to help writers recognize the strategies they use before and during the act of writing, but with the form and evaluation of the resulting product. Improvement is signaled by changes in these features, often toward language that is more "native-like" or that fits criteria of high-stakes exams that are still common worldwide.

In contrast, when they focus on writing as a process, researchers and teachers define the act of writing as a non-linear, recursive activity of meaning-making, discovery, and problem-solving that may begin well before writers begin drafting. This view was made salient by an influential early article focusing on cognitive composing processes of competent L1 writers (Flower & Hayes, 1981). If students' writing processes become more similar to those used by experts, the argument went, we can expect the quality of the writing to improve.

Experts know that writing is social, strategic, and purposive, that it can be used to both generate and clarify ideas, and that it may require multiple revisions of ideas and content rather than just correction at the levels of word, sentence, and paragraph. In a process-oriented classroom, students work together, and the teacher is more of a collaborator than an evaluator. It was not clear then, nor is it certain now, how either of these approaches to writing instruction is linked to improvement over time in students' writing.

But in the early 1980s, a sense of change was in the air (Hairston, 1982), and the buzz word from the 1980s in first and second language writing and composition was "the process approach" (note definite article; not *a* process approach, or process *approaches*). Whether a foundational change actually happened that shifted attention away from written products to writing processes is debatable, given the historical diversity of the field of composition studies and a lack of evidence that the persuasive ideas of process pedagogies were ever fully turned into practice (Applebee, 1986; Matsuda, 2003; Susser, 1994). Part of the history of the debate, then, is a debate about perceptions and even misunderstandings rather than about realities of what writing educators actually did and said. Nevertheless, there was at the very least a perception among L1 and L2 writing educators that by the early 1980s things had indeed changed, and the "process" buzz word took hold.

Findings from the early work on writing processes found their way into L2 writing via review articles such as those by Zamel (1976, 1982). Case study research, such as that by Zamel (1983a), in which L2 writers talked and wrote about their writing processes, similarly concluded that experienced L2 writers use their writing to discover and explore ideas, and that their writing processes are not interrupted by language-level concerns. Process pedagogies that developed from this research were intended to help novice writers understand the roles of invention, planning, discovery, and revising, and of the inevitable place of errors and imperfections of language and thinking during the overall process of composing (Raimes, 1985, 1991, 1992; Spack, 1984; Zamel, 1982, 1987). Teaching writing as discrete skills or as a linear step-by-step process was severely criticized. An unproven assumption underlying this work was that novice writers, L1 or L2, would improve by learning how to write more like the experts (Casanave, 1988; Susser, 1994).

Another view of process writing links it with expressivist movements in which the act of expressive writing liberates student writers from the formal constraints of academic assignments and evaluations and helps them explore issues of personal importance. Perhaps the most influential liberator of all has been L1 writing educator Peter Elbow, who, as I discuss in Chapter 8, has been promoting the benefits of unevaluated personal writing for many years. Writers need to know themselves, Elbow has always argued, and writing can help them do that, but not the kind of tightly constrained, rule-bound writing that characterizes typical academic assignments. Student writers also need to satisfy themselves as readers of their own writing—to like their own writing and to have teachers like their writing and therefore respond more as interested readers than as evaluators (Elbow, 1993). Such a view of writing need not be harmful, Elbow has said to his critics; indeed, "self exploration usually increases people's ability to identify with others" (Elbow, 1999, p. 156). This kind of self-exploration, thought to lead to improvement in writers' confidence and fluency of expression, is not possible in a purely product-oriented approach to writing.

However, in the L2 writing literature, vocal critics to process writing surfaced as early as the mid-1980s. Some critics understood process gurus such as Zamel and Raimes to be saying that we do not need to concern ourselves with written products and that personal narratives will do (Barnes, 1983; Horowitz, 1986a, 1986b), and that writing as a discovery process refers to creative rather than academic writing (Reid, 1984a). Horowitz (1986b), for example, claimed that the bandwagon enthusiasm for process approaches neglected the kinds of writing that students needed to do to survive in academic settings, such as essay examinations—a concern that persists today worldwide. In criticizing Raimes for claiming that essay exams cannot be considered "real writing," Horowitz (1986b) argued that in a school setting nothing was quite so real for students as an essay exam. For Horowitz, then, improvement might be measured by passing rates on such exams.

Scholars who responded to these critiques tended to point out that paying attention to students' writing processes and exploration of self on the one hand and easing students into academic writing on the other are not mutually exclusive (Hamada & Izawa, 1998; Hamp-Lyons, 1986; Leibman-Kleine, 1986; Spack & Sadow, 1983; Vanett & Jurich, 1990). For example, Zamel (1983b, 1984) disagreed with the view that process writing of the personal expressive type dominated writing instruction, pointing out that her own students wrote academic essays. She further pointed out that because of their attention to revision, process pedagogies inevitably are intended to improve the products of students' writing (Zamel, 1983a). In other words, accuracy is not necessarily neglected. Furthermore, journal writing, often portrayed as personal memoir and reflection, can link personal, process-oriented writing to academic writing, particularly when journals consist of learning logs and responses to classes and readings (Carroll, 1994; Casanave, 2011; Cole, Raffier, Rogan, & Schleicher, 1998; Mlynarczyk, 1991, 1998; Vanett & Jurich, 1990; Weissberg, 1998). In my own work on journal writing, I found that my Japanese students could use personal and reflective topics in their journals to develop both fluency and depth of thinking, the latter characterized as detailed and thoughtful treatment of subject matter. Both fluency and depth of treatment can contribute to improved academic writing, which ultimately always requires accuracy (Casanave, 1994, 1995, 2011). We can thus counter the assumption that personal writing is not challenging, critical, or text-based, a view strongly held by the late L1 composition scholar, Wendy Bishop (1995).

The critiques and responses I have discussed above deal mainly with the typical subject matter (the self) and reflective nature of process writing approaches. Another kind of critique is aimed at the assumptions in process approaches of how writing actually gets done. Expert writers are thought to discover meaning through (rather than before) writing, to revise multiple times, to postpone attention to mechanics, to be personally engaged with their writing, and so on. However, there is little evidence to support such a uniform view of expert writers, particularly if we do not consider purpose, genre, and individual styles and strategies of writing. Reid (1984b), an expert writer by anyone's account, labeled herself a "radical outliner," unlike her husband, a "radical brainstormer." The outliner may not use writing as discovery, in other words, but employ discovery heuristics before beginning to draft. Such writers may also revise less than the brainstormers given that meticulous planning takes places in the first stages of writing rather than recursively, as predicted by process writing research. Moreover, some expert writers do not postpone attention to mechanics until all drafting gets done (I am one of them), but either weave attention to mechanics into every stage of writing, or (rarer?) attempt to perfect each sentence before moving on to the next, as Annie Dillard (1989) described in her writing autobiography. Likewise, being personally involved with one's topics sounds wonderful. However, it is probable that most of the required writing we do throughout all our years of schooling does not engage us personally in the ways that process advocates would wish, and is evaluated only in its finished form as a product. Such realities do not necessarily damage the quality of our writing. It is therefore important in this debate, indeed in any debate, to lay out and examine the assumptions that underlie the various positions. The assumptions may not be based on accurate depictions of writers and their diverse writing processes.

In spite of critiques, the writing process movement has had a great impact on how writing scholars and teachers from around the world think about writing, including well into the 21st century. We recognize that writing is often a lengthy, messy process involving multiple revisions where feasible, and that one-shot exam and essay writing that produces a single product to be evaluated can never represent the best a writer can do or tell us anything about how writing gets done. We also recognize that effective writing teachers help students develop their writing from the earliest stages through to the final product, whatever the interim processes and strategies and whatever the final product might be. Of course, essay exam writing continues to cause problems for instructors and students who are interested in strategies of planning, drafting, and revising because exams are one-shot products. Perhaps the best we can hope for is to provide students with practice in writing exam-style essays, such as frequent timed writings, when revision is not possible.

How does genre fit into these discussions? Genres, after all, can be considered a kind of socially based product, identified by typified forms and functions. In recent years, we are paying more attention to the social nature of writing, and how products of writing are situated within and evolve out of genres. Proponents of genre-based pedagogies (Cope & Kalantzis, 1993; Devitt, 2004; Hyland, 2002, 2003, 2004; Johns, 2002) and scholars of genre theory (Swales, 1990, 2004; Tardy, 2009, 2016) have thus found ways to incorporate earlier cognitive views of writing processes into more socially situated discussions of how writing gets done and how it might be taught. Genre scholars acknowledge that a written product does not derive from a fixed and formal template, given that genres themselves are dynamic, but from a writer's contextualized and conventionalized responses to local purposes and requirements. Writers with genre awareness and knowledge are also able to recontextualize their genre knowledge on new pieces of writing (Cheng, 2007) and to innovate within and beyond genre conventions (Tardy, 2016), thus improving their writing in ways not expected by a template-view of genre. Part of students' and scholars' improvement in writing therefore involves their recognizing and responding appropriately to local genre conventions. These conventions represent a social, not just linguistic, response to writing demands. (For more on some of the influential work on genre, see Bawarshi, 2003; Bazerman, 1994; Berkenkotter & Huckin, 1995; Berkenkotter & Ravotas, 1997; Bhatia, 1993; Cheng, 2007; Dressen-Hammouda, 2008; Freedman & Medway, 1994; Gentil, 2011; Hyland, 2015;

Hyland & Guinda, 2012; Hyon, 1996; Johns, 2008, 2011; Miller, 1984; Paltridge, 1997, 2014; Tardy, 2009, 2016).

To conclude this section, let me say that fortunate students in what some have called a socially oriented post-process era (Atkinson, 2003; Casanave, 2003; Kent, 1999; Trimbur, 1994) will learn writing process techniques that guide them toward appropriate linguistic and cultural goals in a way that does not pit writing processes against writing products or fluency against accuracy and complexity. They will also learn that by becoming aware of different genres of writing, they will be able to situate their own writing appropriately and even innovatively within social, ideological, disciplinary, and cultural contexts to ensure a receptive readership (Tardy, 2016). Such efforts and awareness are fundamental in improving the writing that all of us engage in.

Response (with Special Attention to the Error Correction Debate)

Teachers' responding activities to student writing are considered to be the most burdensome and time-consuming part of their jobs. We feel compelled to mark errors in particular, believing that our feedback will contribute to improvement in students' writing. Even when we are not sure if it helps, some of us seem genetically endowed to mark errors and simply cannot help ourselves. I am one of these and have pretty much given up fighting my impulses; I often edit students' work without worrying overly about future improvements in their writing. In this final section of the chapter, I concentrate on the unresolved debate about the value of written corrective feedback (WCF) (Bitchener & Storch, 2016; Bitchener & Ferris, 2012; Ferris, 2010, 2011; Truscott, 2007; Truscott & Hsu, 2008) because it has generated abundant research and controversies about its role in improvement. One of the findings of this research for teachers is that "WCF is an area of research where serious mismatches exist between research findings and classroom applications" (Lee, 2013, p. 117). (With regret I do not cover the important topic of peer feedback; see Ferris, 2011, pp. 147–150; Ferris & Hedgcock, 2014, pp. 254–262; Liu & Hansen Edwards, in press; Lundstrom & Baker, 2009; Min, 2006; Suzuki, 2008; Villamil & Guerrerro, 2006; Zhao, 2010).

A central controversy in the L2 writing literature on teacher response concerns this question of error treatment: Does it help students improve their writing? Are teachers wasting their time marking students' errors, as Truscott (1996) strongly asserted they are? All teachers who mark students' work hope that written corrective feedback can actually lead to long-term improvement on new pieces of writing, not just on revisions of the same piece, either from the perspective of SLA or L2 writing (Ferris, 2010), but evidence is not conclusive that it does. It is also evident that what positive research findings there are have not always been implemented in writing classes (Lee, 2013). But we keep at it, slipping into mindless routines of marking, believing that we are doing our jobs, regardless of inconclusive evidence that our efforts pay off in the long term. Let me start with earlier work on feedback to writing and then move to a discussion of Truscott, the responses to his assertions, and work on written corrective feedback that followed.

It may surprise teachers who are new to the field of writing that little evidence exists in either L1 and L2 writing research that teacher or peer feedback on students' writing has the positive effects that are intended, in spite of efforts in the past to establish such evidence (Leki, 1992; Robb, Ross, & Shortreed, 1986; Truscott, 1996). Based on her review of some of the earlier literature, Leki (1992) explained this failure from several angles. She noted the following: Students have no reason to pay attention to feedback on final drafts if they are not required to revise; they may not be developmentally (cognitively, linguistically) ready for the kinds of responses they receive from teachers; they may not understand teachers' comments clearly enough to be able to take action on them; they may reject comments on content as a way to maintain ownership of their texts; they may know more about the content and form of certain professional genres than their teachers and so reject comments because they see their teachers primarily as English experts;

and students who accept a teachers' feedback too readily do not learn to take responsibility for their own writing and so do not improve over time (Leki, 1992, pp. 122–123). Truscott's similar assertions a few years later (1996) were more direct and also narrower in his focus on grammar correction to the exclusion of other kinds of feedback on writing.

Truscott made three major points about correction, points he continued to make in the years that followed (e.g., Truscott, 2007; Truscott & Hsu, 2008). He first provided evidence from previous studies to show that grammar correction does not work to improve the grammatical accuracy of students' writing, either in L1 or in L2. He argued that even in the case of studies that claimed to find positive effects of grammar correction, such as Fathman and Whalley (1990), there is no evidence that "grammar correction in writing classes make[s] students better writers in any sense" beyond revisions on the same piece of writing (Truscott, 1996, p. 338). Truscott argued secondly that these findings can be explained by recognizing that L2 learners' grammatical accuracy improves mainly through a process of interlanguage development rather than through one of noticing and conscious self-correction. Truscott's third point was that grammar correction can actually harm students: "Even students who believe that correction is a necessary part of learning do not enjoy the sight of red ink all over their writing and probably find the experience extremely discouraging" (p. 354). Truscott's position has been that there is no reason to correct grammatical errors in students' writing until evidence conclusively demonstrates the effectiveness of correction (Truscott, 1996, 1999). He concluded that until that time, "grammar correction should be abandoned" (Truscott, 1996, p. 360). We need to note that in making these arguments, Truscott did not reject the importance of grammatical accuracy in writing or of the value of other kinds of feedback on the "content, organization, and clarity of a composition." The issue, he asserted, "is whether or not grammar correction can contribute to [the] development [of grammatical accuracy]" (Truscott, 1996, p. 329).

Writing scholars ever since have been trying to disprove Truscott's bold assertions by conducting studies that demonstrate some kind of improvement in students' writing, in linguistic accuracy in particular, as a result of written error correction. Studies have compared types of feedback practices such the following: whether it uses direct correction or simple underlining or circling of errors (Bitchener & Knoch, 2010b; Chandler, 2003); whether explicit feedback is or is not accompanied by teacher conferences or by oral or written explanation (Bitchener & Knoch, 2010a; Bitchener, Young, & Cameron, 2005); whether direct correction leads to better results on new pieces of writing than does explanation (Shintani, Ellis, & Suzuki, 2014); whether it is focused or unfocused, selective or comprehensive, as in Lee's work (2011, 2013, 2017); and whether feedback is provided on treatable or untreatable (i.e., resistant to change by instruction) errors (Ferris, 2006, 2011). More general issues such timing of feedback, feedback on the same writing and on new pieces of writing, short-term changes, and longer-term changes have also been investigated (Ferris, 2006). The links between written corrective feedback and language development have also been explored, with some explanations for inconsistent findings attributed to cognitive versus sociocultural perspectives. A sociocultural perspective depends more on the vagaries of individual interactions, diverse contexts, and particularities in how writers process feedback (Bitchener & Storch, 2016; Storch & Wigglesworth, 2010). In later work, Ferris and her colleagues continued to seek evidence in favour of error correction, noting not only that teachers seem to feel strongly about the need for clearly structured and focused feedback (Ferris, 2014), but also that students' accuracy improves when errors are selective, focused, discussed one-on-one with teachers in conferences, and addressed in revisions and new pieces of writing (Bitchener & Ferris, 2012; Ferris, 2006, 2011; Ferris, Liu, Sinha, & Senna, 2013). The findings however remain inconclusive in part because disputes over methods, evidence, and findings have never been fully resolved (Chandler, 2009; Ferris, 1999; Truscott, 1999, 2009, 2010).

Even when findings show positive effects of certain kinds of error treatment, changes are difficult to make in teachers' practices, especially when teachers feel pressured to mark all errors in students' writing. It is not surprising that they end up feeling frustrated and burned out and see little benefit from their efforts. This is what Lee found in her extensive work in Hong Kong on feedback that teachers provide L2 university students (Lee, 2011, 2013, 2017). In this work, she argued that teachers need to resist the compulsion to mark every error and instead provide students with "smarter" feedback selectively rather trying to respond to everything (Lee, 2011, 2017). She nevertheless admitted that her attempts to provide her pre-service teachers with innovative and less burdensome feedback techniques that were focused and selective did not succeed well because students and the institution resisted (Lee, 2016). Pressures to provide full and comprehensive feedback seemed required as part of the job, regardless of whether these practices led to improvements in students' writing.

Not only institutional pressures, but practicality of feedback practices conflicts with the findings of some research. Some studies have found that students can indeed improve a small number of linguistic errors over time, such as articles (e.g., Bitchener, Young, & Cameron, 2005; Bitchener & Knoch, 2010a, 2010b; Ellis, Sheen, Murakami, & Takashima, 2008). These findings are encouraging to some teachers and scholars, but as Lee (2016) pointed out, impractical for most teachers to apply to their classrooms. There simply are too many things to do in an L2 writing class for most teachers to focus selectively on just a few linguistic items. Equally impractical might be recommendations that "dynamic written corrective feedback" be provided to students immediately and frequently (Hartshorn & Evans, 2015). When class size is manageable, as it was in the numerous studies in the United States by Hartshorn, Evans, and colleagues, the technique of having students do repeated 10-minute writing exercises in every class, followed by quick feedback from teachers, supposedly worked to help students improve the accuracy of new writing (Evans, Hartshorn, & McCollum, 2010; Hartshorn & Evans, 2015).

However, many teachers in Japan and other East Asian countries, for example, meet their students only once a week, in English classes that are not dedicated only to writing. Moreover, teachers worldwide often have several hundred students during a single term, making most kinds of frequent and regular feedback impossible. Where teachers are expected to provided comprehensive (rather than selective and focused) feedback to students because of exam-centered pressures or institutional and parental expectations, teachers are lucky to be able to hastily mark a student's paper once. Multiple drafts might not be possible or even considered important in a one-shot essay, product-oriented system (Lee, 2008, 2011, 2013, 2016). Underlining an error rather than correcting it directly or explaining it might help save time (Chandler, 2003; Ferris & Roberts, 2001), but again there seems to be little evidence of long-term learning (Truscott & Hsu, 2008). In other words, even if teachers understand the benefits to students of regularly receiving focused feedback and then revising, there simply may be no feasible way to practice this type of responding and justify it as effective for improvement.

Finally, we need to continually remind ourselves that continued inconclusive and discouraging results on written error treatment studies could be due in part to methodological flaws in different kinds of research on written response, not to the effectiveness of feedback practices themselves. Such flaws have been pointed out in particular on research that promotes automated writing evaluation, a technique to which busy writing teachers and programs seem to be turning (Stevenson & Phakiti, 2014). But similar methodological problems apply to other research on teacher feedback as well. For example, in an overview of methods in 32 articles and 12 dissertations, Liu and Brown (2015) found numerous methodological problems. Clear conclusions about the effectiveness of corrective feedback cannot be made if designs do not include follow up or analysis of new pieces of writing, if studies are done with groups that are too heterogeneous to rule out other factors, if they look only at group averages rather than individual differences, or if outcome measures are too disparate to compare studies with each other.

Arguments, however, can be persuasive even without conclusive evidence (hard-core researchers will disagree). As part of the pro-correction debate, Ferris (2002, 2011) made several compelling points. First, even if there is no evidence of long-term improvement, long-term development surely follows from short-term improvement. Moreover, students like feedback, and they believe it helps them and so continue to be motivated to improve. And because accuracy in writing is important in the real world, students need to learn how to edit their own work. Teachers, she said, have a responsibility for helping students learn to do this (Ferris, 2011, pp. 130–141). Certainly learning how to self-edit can be seen as an important kind of improvement, as can other activities in self-regulated learning in L2 writing, such as developing effective writing strategies, managing time, and attending to the social and physical environments for writing (Andrade & Evans, 2013).

In all of this work, the presumption (hope?) continues that written corrective feedback leads to improvement in both writing and language development. But even if studies are well designed, feedback does not automatically result in improvement on students' writing, whether done by a teacher or a computer. Improvement in writing, in other words, is not the result of feedback alone because too many other factors intervene to influence how students improve, as well as how they respond to each kind of feedback (see the discussion in Bitchener and Storch, 2016, on sociocultural perspectives on error treatment). The processing, uptake, and retention of feedback, whether direct or indirect, whether done by teachers, peers, or computer, depends on unmeasurable multiple personal and affective factors and beliefs that differ with each individual according to their interest and engagement, as Storch and Wigglesworth (2010) pointed out. Moreover, we tend not to examine closely what McMartin-Miller (2014, p. 33) discovered, namely that "many students (1) do not know why their instructors mark errors as they do; (2) do not—as instructors feared—closely examine feedback; and (3) misunderstand what their own role is in the error treatment process." Such studies require time and a more complex design than many researchers and teacher-researchers can manage. The "one-off" experimental or descriptive studies of written corrective feedback tend not to include these messy factors, given the pressure to investigate a small number of errors or other factors that can be analyzed relatively quickly. The pendulum has swung too far, asserted Storch (2010), who wants writing scholars to engage in more ecologically valid projects, and as some scholars are doing, in more longitudinal studies of change.

I wish I could conclude this section with some clear answers to many of the questions we have about the effectiveness of responding in various ways to students' writing, but I cannot. I am not alone. Brown (2012) believes that teachers cannot solve the noisiest part of the debate about responses to writing, that of written corrective feedback, and that they should therefore proceed based on their intuition, experience, and student expectations. For my part, I can only recommend that teachers consider carefully how they wish to spend the short time they have with students in the L2 writing class. This will mean reflecting on what they mean by improvement, linking their beliefs about improvement to their responding practices, and, importantly, following up with students to see what they do with the feedback they receive (Ferris, 2014). These reflections need to include as well attention to the many other possible sources of improvement in writing, such as practice, reading, noticing, development of awareness through instruction and interaction, development of topic knowledge, and strong internally-motivated purposes for learning to write. Our goals for improvement, even in our own writing, need to be realistic as well as to reach beyond surface level correctness. Although all of us need to keep studying these questions, we are compelled in the meantime to make decisions locally, reflectively, and as knowledgeably as possible.

Classroom Perspectives

It is difficult to provide useful examples of how classroom writing teachers help their students improve their writing because each teacher, group of students, class goals, and practical constraints differ so greatly. Furthermore, many of the past and recent studies of feedback and revision in classroom settings concern rather superficial changes in students' writing, often on the same writing task rather than on new pieces of writing. Of course we will see improvement from Draft A to Draft B, but we often have no idea if these changes reflect real improvement over time. I provide one brief example from my own experiences teaching in Japan simply as a demonstration of the kinds of decisions I faced in helping my students improve their English, and their writing in particular (see also Casanave, 1994). My feedback had less to do with error correction than with other kinds of responses designed to help students improve fluency, revision skills, and depth of thought.

For several years, I taught what might be called intermediate-level undergraduate students at a Japanese university (TOEFL® PBT about 400–450). The students were required to take three semesters of intensive foreign language classes, defined as four 90-minute classes a week. I taught several classes of about 35 students each (considered a "small" class at the time) two times a week for at least two consecutive semesters. A number of us at that time taught content/project-based courses, centered around some general theme such as Human Relationships, Education, or Culture, allowing us great flexibility with specific lessons and projects and allowing students to contribute much of their own knowledge of these topics while also expanding their existing knowledge. We did not use textbooks. Students watched films, did short readings, discussed issues, and did some kind of semester-long project that would involve them in a variety of English skills.

I had to decide what I meant by improvement for a group of students that had never before been taught in English as the language of instruction and for the most part had written no extended discourse in English. Many students were also reticent to speak out in class (common in Japan; Harumi, 2011; King, 2013; Talandis & Stout, 2014) or to write much for fear of making mistakes (identified by Truscott, 1996, as part of the error correction debate). Because my students had studied grammar and translation for up to six years and taken many tests in English where there was always a right answer, I decided to define improvement as the development of fluency and expression of their own ideas, increased willingness to take risks without fear of making mistakes, and the ability to write and revise one or more pieces of writing for a class "book" of their own work. I therefore asked the students to write personal journals once a week on topics of their choice, double-spaced and typed, and to form small groups of five or six students that would work on a separate "book" project. These groups discussed their ideas together during the semester, primarily in Japanese.

I responded each week to the ideas in the journals, without making more than a few language corrections (a bit of grammar and vocabulary if the problem seemed to interfere with meaning), but did not ask students to revise their journals (see more on journals in Casanave, 2011). Rather, they collected them week by week, until by the end of the semester they had a collection of 30 or more pages of journal entries, much to their amazement. As for the separate "book" project, each group of students designed its own "book" (title, cover, author bios, contents). I set a schedule, helped them correct and revise their short essays or poems and to write bio-statements, and copied the final products for group members. These projects, by the way, were primarily text-based, not the type of multimedia online compositions and video projects being discussed these days (e.g., Hafner, 2013; Gunsberg, 2015; see Chapter 3). Were I to do a project like this today, much of the work and distribution of final copies would be done online.

Did these students improve their writing? According to the criteria I established at the beginning of the semester, they did, although as a practicing classroom teacher I had no irrefutable proof, especially in the short span of one or two semesters. By the end of the term, most of the students reported that they wrote more in the their journals in less time than at the beginning; they showed no signs of being afraid of making mistakes (e.g., no more apologies for bad grammar or lack of vocabulary and plenty of evidence that they did not proofread their journals!); and they expressed pride in and enthusiasm about their final book products and their 30-pages of journal entries. These aspects of their improvement carried over into the second semester, which I also had with them. In short, many students had gone from fearing or disliking English to showing confidence in and engagement with their written tasks. In a separate study of journal writing, I also showed specific changes in the writing of some students in several intermediate classes, such as greater detail, depth, and maturity in their journal writing (always difficult to define, of course). Additionally, I documented improvements in grammatical accuracy in some cases and drops in accuracy in others, the latter of which I took to be a possible sign of more risk-taking (Casanave, 1994).

However, I believe that if my only definition of improvement had been tied to specific linguistic and rhetorical changes that I could have specified beforehand and then taught, I might have been disappointed. My written corrections to some of the errors in students' journals seemed to have little effect on later journals, whereas the regular weekly practice did. It may have been that students improved the language of their journals through means other than my teaching and explicit feedback. For example, they could have used my feedback as a model of syntax and vocabulary, and readings and class discussion as a source of input waiting to be absorbed when they were developmentally ready. I also did not know what these students were doing in other classes that might have used English or in any out-of-class activities with English. In other words, improvement in students' writing is not dependent exclusively on our teaching, and certainly not only on corrective feedback. Links between students' improvement and our teaching might be quite tenuous. Such questions about improvement, and many others, remain to be investigated.

Ongoing Questions

It is frustrating for L2 writing teachers to have so few answers to important questions such as how to characterize good writing and improvement and how to and facilitate improvement in students' writing once we have a sense of what we mean by these. Of all the dilemmas in L2 writing pedagogy, perhaps this is the largest, most important, and the most problematic.

We recognize the essential role that a great deal of practice in reading, writing, and revision plays in helping students improve, and probably most teachers and researchers agree that real improvement refers to positive changes in new writing tasks. However, we seem stuck for now with local characterizations and solutions that fit the needs, purposes, and beliefs of particular teachers and students. This is fine, as long as teachers are reflective about the sometimes tenuous connections between their labor-intensive work and real improvement in their students' writing and as long as we resist becoming obsessed with error correction and concrete evidence of long-term improvement. We can rarely see real and lasting improvements within a semester or even a year.

Can we assume that our instruction and feedback help, even in the short time that most of us have with our students? What is our evidence, and to what extent do we or others need to see "proof"? Or, lacking evidence, are we assuming and hoping that various kinds of instruction (in fluency, accuracy, complexity, writing processes, topic knowledge, genre structure and purpose, response, correction of language errors…) help our students—if not now, then in the long run? Where does the burden of proof lie, with doubters or believers? And a point on which Truscott (1996) and Ferris (1999, 2001, 2011) disagree, do we provide students with what they think they need (e.g., error correction) even if we have little evidence from research or from our own teaching that it helps? What do individual differences in teacher and student attitudes and practices toward error treatment tell us about what we might learn in our own classrooms (McMartin-Miller, 2014)? What is the role of a positive and motivated attitude—of committed engagement in a writing task—in helping students improve? Importantly, how can we help shift the obsession that teachers and researchers have with corrective feedback and native-like standards (a concern of interest to SLA) to greater attention to rhetorical and stylistic issues of interest to writing teachers (Ferris, 2010)? And what about the profound role of topic knowledge in improving writing, even though the uncountable factors are more difficult to research and to teach? L2 writing teachers can begin to sort out some of the answers to these questions for themselves by reflecting on how they themselves learned to write. They can also pursue tentative answers by looking at and attending to the decisions they make in their own classrooms and the consequences of those decisions about how to help their students down (up? along?) the path to improvement.

Beliefs and Practices

Beliefs

1. In the context of your own teaching and/or learning of L2 writing, how do you characterize "improvement" in writing? Try to define what you believe each of the following improvements consists of, adding your own. Then rank order them from most important (1) to least important at two different points in a class term, early and late.

Area	Importance (early)	Importance (late)
Increase in fluency		
Increase in grammatical accuracy		
Clearer expression of personal involvement and voice		
More detail and depth of content		
More effective use of "expert" writing processes		
More confidence and motivation		
Increased knowledge of genre conventions of writing		
Better ability to revise in response to teacher's feedback		
Increased ability to self-edit		
Other_____		
Other_____		
Other_____		

2. Look at this list of beliefs. Explain why you agree or disagree with them.

a. Adult (child) L2 writing students benefit greatly from explicit instruction and feedback from a teacher.

b. Adult (child) L2 writing students improve primarily through a process of natural development that occurs as a result of practice.

c. The best way for writers to improve their writing is to read models of good writing.

d. Teachers should provide L2 writing students with the kinds of feedback they want even if there is little evidence that it leads to improved writing.

e. A "fluency first" approach makes a lot of sense with beginning writers.

f. L2 writing students can and should be taught explicit writing processes and strategies, including the processes and strategies used by expert writers.

g. Personal and expressive writing, focusing on fluency and depth of expression, benefits students, even in academic contexts.

h. In school settings, L2 writing students should be taught the formal structures and conventions for the kinds of writing they will probably need, including explicit instruction in genre; time should not be wasted on other kinds of writing.

i. Students' writing and images of themselves as writers will improve if students become aware of the complex social nature of writing.

j. Even if it does not reflect the complex realities of writing, L2 students improve most from a pattern-governed, "keep-it-simple" approach.

k. Writing cannot improve without corrective feedback.

l. Complexity (syntactic, in particular) in writing is not necessarily a sign of good writing.

m. Well-developed topic knowledge and interest are not essential for students to improve their writing.

Practices

1. If you or your colleagues have used or designed any writing assessment rubrics, what do those rubrics tell you about your conceptualizations of what good writing is and what improvement in writing consists of?

2. Describe some fluency exercises you have done/could do with particular L2 writing students (specify who). Then design some new fluency exercises.

3. In your own teaching or belief system, how concerned are you with the grammatical accuracy of L2 students' writing? In what kinds of writing situations are you most and least concerned with accuracy? What examples do you have from your own L2 writing experiences?

4. Describe how you demonstrate to students your concern (or lack of) for fluency. Describe how you demonstrate to students your concern (or lack of) for accuracy. Describe how you demonstrate to students your concern (or lack of) for complexity.

5. What aspects of process approaches have you used or do you plan to use, if any, with your L2 writing students? Why and how?

6. What kinds of finished products have you asked or do you plan to ask students to complete? Why? What steps do you take to help your students finish a piece of writing? Who is the audience for a finished piece of writing?

7. Examine several samples of your own written responses to some L2 students' writing. What do you notice about the patterns, emphases, gaps, inconsistencies, and in general the choices that you make in your responses? What kinds of improvements do you hope will result from your responses?

8. Putting yourself in your students' shoes, what effects do you believe your particular kinds of feedback have on students' attitudes toward writing? On their

improvement? What have been the effects on you of different kinds of responses to L2 (or L1) writing that you yourself have done?

9. Experiment in your own class(es) with two kinds of writing, one in which students have good knowledge of and interest in their topics and another in which topic knowledge and interest are low. What do you notice about the two kinds of writing and the possible influence of topic knowledge? Do you see any differences in the potential for improvement in these two kinds of writing?

References

Abdel Latif, M. M. (2009). Toward a new process-based indicator for measuring writing fluency: Evidence from L2 writers' think-aloud protocols. *The Canadian Modern Language Review, 65*(4), 531–558.

Andrade, M. S., & Evans, N. W. (2013). *Principles and practices for response in second language writing: Developing self-regulated learners.* New York: Routledge/Taylor & Francis.

Applebee, A. (1986). Problems in process approaches: Toward a reconceptualization of process instruction. In A. R. Petrosky & D. Bartholomae (Eds.), *The teaching of writing: Eighty-fifth yearbook of the National Society for the Study of Education, Part II* (pp. 95–113). Chicago: National Society for the Study of Education.

Atkinson, D. (2003). L2 writing in the post-process era: Introduction. *Journal of Second Language Writing, 12*(1), 3–15.

Barnes, G. A. (1983). Comments on Vivian Zamel, "Writing: The process of discovering meaning." *TESOL Quarterly, 17*, 137–138.

Bawarshi, A. (2003). *Genre and the invention of the writer: Reconsidering the place of invention in composition.* Logan: Utah State University Press.

Bazerman, C. (1994). Systems of genres and the enactment of social intentions. In A. Freedman & P. Medway (Eds.), *Genre and the new rhetoric* (pp. 79–101). London: Taylor & Francis.

Belcher, D., & Hirvela, A. (Eds.). (2001). *Linking literacies: Perspectives on L2 reading-writing connections.* Ann Arbor: University of Michigan Press.

Berkenkotter, C., & Huckin, T. N. (1995). *Genre knowledge in disciplinary communities: Cognition/culture/power.* Hillsdale, NJ: Lawrence Erlbaum.

Berkenkotter, C., & Ravotas, D. (1997). Genre as tool in the transmission of practice over time and across professional boundaries. *Mind, Culture, and Activity, 4,* 256–274.

Bhatia, V. K. (1993). *Analysing genre: Language use in professional settings.* London: Longman.

Biber, D., & Gray, B. (2010). Challenging stereotypes about academic writing: Complexity, elaboration, explicitness. *Journal of English for Academic Purposes, 9*(1), 2–20.

Biber, D., Gray, B., & Poonpon, K. (2011). Should we use characteristics of conversation to measure grammatical complexity in L2 writing development? *TESOL Quarterly, 45*(1), 5–35.

Billig, M. (2008). The language of critical discourse analysis: The case of nominalization. *Discourse & Society, 19*(6), 783–800.

Billig, M. (2013). *Learn to write badly: How to succeed in the social sciences.* Cambridge, U.K.: Cambridge University Press.

Bishop, W. (1995). Responses to Bartholomae and Elbow: If Winston Weathers would just write me on e-mail. *College Composition and Communication, 46*(1), 97–103.

Bitchener, J., & Ferris, D. R. (2012). *Written corrective feedback in second language acquisition.* New York: Routledge/Taylor & Francis.

Bitchener, J., & Knoch, U. (2010a). The contribution of written corrective feedback to language development: A ten month investigation. *Applied Linguistics, 31*(2), 193–214.

Bitchener, J., & Knoch, U. (2010b). Raising the linguistic accuracy level of advanced L2 learners with written corrective feedback. *Journal of Second Language Writing, 19*(4), 207–217.

Bitchener, J., & Storch, N. (2016). *Written corrective feedback for L2 development.* Bristol, U.K.: Multilingual Matters.

Bitchener, J., Young, S., & Cameron, D. (2005). The effect of different types of corrective feedback on ESL student writing. *Journal of Second Language Writing, 14*(3), 191–205.

Brown, D. (2012). The written corrective feedback debate: Next steps for classroom teachers and practitioners. *TESOL Quarterly, 46*(4), 861–867.

Byrnes, H. (2009). Emergent L2 German writing ability in a curricular context: A longitudinal study of grammatical metaphor. *Linguistics and Education, 20*, 50–66.

Carroll, M. (1994). Journal writing as a learning and research tool in the adult classroom. *TESOL Journal, 4*(1), 19–22.

Carson, J. (2001). Second language acquisition and second language writing. In T. Silva & P. K. Matsuda (Eds.), *On second language writing* (pp. 191–199). Mahwah, NJ: Lawrence Erlbaum.

Carson, J., & Leki. I. (Eds.). (1993). *Reading in the composition classroom: Second language perspectives.* Boston: Heinle and Heinle.

Casanave, C. P. (1988). The process approach to writing instruction: An examination of issues. *The CATESOL Journal, 1*, 29–39.

Casanave, C. P. (1994). Language development in students' journals. *Journal of Second Language Writing, 3*, 179–201.

Casanave, C. P. (1995). Journal writing in college English classes in Japan: Shifting the focus from language to education. *JALT Journal, 17*, 95–111.

Casanave, C. P. (2003). Looking ahead to more sociopolitically-oriented case study research in L2 writing scholarship: (But should it be called "Post-process"?). *Journal of Second Language Writing, 12*(1), 85–102.

Casanave, C. P. (2011). *Journal writing in second language education.* Ann Arbor: University of Michigan Press.

Chandler, J. (2003). The efficacy of various kinds of error feedback for improvement in the accuracy and fluency of L2 student writing. *Journal of Second Language Writing, 12*, 267–296.

Chandler, J. (2009). Dialogue: Response to Truscott. *Journal of Second Language Writing, 18*(1), 57–58.

Cheng, A. (2007). Transferring generic features and recontextualizing genre awareness: Understanding writing performance in the ESP genre-based literacy framework. *English for Specific Purposes, 26*, 287–307.

Cole, R., Raffier, L. M., Rogan, P., & Schleicher, L. (1998). Interactive group journals: Learning as a dialogue among learners. *TESOL Quarterly, 32*(3), 556–568.

Cope, B., & Kalantzis, M. (Eds.). (1993). *The powers of literacy: A genre approach to teaching writing.* London: The Falmer Press.

Crusan, D. (2010). *Assessment in the second language writing classroom.* Ann Arbor: University of Michigan Press.

Crusan, D. (2015). Dance ten: looks three: Why rubrics matter (editorial). *Assessing Writing, 16,* 1–4.

Currie, P. (1994). What counts as good writing? Enculturation and writing assessment. In A. Freedman & P. Medway (Eds.), *Teaching and learning genre* (pp. 63–79). Portsmouth, NH: Boynton/Cook.

Devitt, A. J. (2004). *Writing genres.* Carbondale: Southern Illinois University Press.

Dillard, A. (1989). *The writing life.* New York: Harper & Row.

Dressen-Hammouda, D. (2008). From novice to disciplinary expert: Disciplinary identity and genre mastery. *English for Specific Purposes, 27*(2), 233–252.

Elbow, P. (1993). Ranking, evaluating, and liking: Sorting out three forms of judgment. *College English, 55,* 187–206.

Elbow, P. (1999). In defense of private writing: Consequences for theory and research. *Written Communication, 16,* 139–170.

Ellis, R., Sheen, Y., Murakami, M., & Takashima, H. (2008). The effects of focused and unfocused written corrective feedback in an English as a foreign language context. *System, 36*(3), 353–371.

Evans, N. W., Hartshorn, K. J., McCollum, R. M., & Wolfersberger, M. (2010). Contextualizing corrective feedback in second language writing pedagogy. *Language Teaching Research, 14*(4), 445–463.

Fang, Z., Schleppegrell, M. J., & Cox, B. E. (2006). Understanding the language demands of schooling: Nouns in academic registers. *Journal of Literacy Research, 38*(3), 247–273.

Fathman, A., & Whalley, E. (1990). Teacher response to student writing: Focus on form versus content. In B. Kroll (Ed.), *Second language writing: Research insights for the classroom* (pp. 178–190). Cambridge, U.K.: Cambridge University Press.

Ferris, D. R. (1999). The case for grammar correction in L2 writing classes: A response to Truscott (1996). *Journal of Second Language Writing, 8,* 1–11.

Ferris, D. R. (2002). *Treatment of error in second language student writing.* Ann Arbor: University of Michigan Press.

Ferris, D. (2006). Does error feedback help student writers? New evidence on the short and long term effects of written error correction. In K. Hyland & F. Hyland (Eds.), *Feedback in second language writing: Contexts and issues* (pp. 81–104). Cambridge, U.K.: Cambridge University Press.

Ferris, D. (2010). Second language writing research and written corrective feedback in SLA: Intersections and practical applications. *Studies in Second Language Acquisition, 32*(2), 181–201.

Ferris, D. R. (2011). *Treatment of error in second language student writing* (2nd ed.). Ann Arbor: University of Michigan Press.

Ferris, D. R. (2014). Responding to student writing: Teachers' philosophies and practices. *Assessing Writing, 19*, 6–23.

Ferris, D., & Hedgcock, J. (2014). *Teaching L2 composition: Purpose, process, and practice* (3rd ed.). New York: Routledge/Taylor & Francis.

Ferris, D. R., Liu, H., Sinha, A., & Senna, M. (2013). Written correction feedback for individual L2 writers. *Journal of Second Language Writing, 22*(3), 307–329.

Ferris, D. R., & Roberts, B. (2001). Error feedback in L2 writing classes: How explicit does it need to be? *Journal of Second Language Writing, 10*, 161–184.

Flower, L., & Hayes, J. R. (1981). A cognitive process theory of writing. *College Composition and Communication, 32*(4), 365–387.

Frankfurt, H. (2005). *On bullshit*. Princeton, NJ: Princeton University Press.

Freedman, A., & Medway, P. (Eds.). (1994). *Learning and teaching genre*. Portsmouth, NH: Boynton/Cook.

Gentil, G. (2011). A biliteracy agenda for genre research. *Journal of Second Language Writing, 20*(1), 6–23.

Gunsberg, B. (2015). The evaluative dynamics of multimodal composing. *Computers and Composition, 38*, 1–15.

Hafner, C. A. (2013). Digital composition in a second or foreign language. *TESOL Quarterly, 47*(4), 830–834.

Hairston, M. (1982). The winds of change: Thomas Kuhn and the revolution in the teaching of writing. *College Composition and Communication, 33*(1), 76–88.

Hamada, M., & Izawa, H. (1998). Students' journal work. *Journal of the University of Marketing and Distribution Sciences, 10*(2), 93–116.

Hamp-Lyons, L. (1986). No new lamps for old yet, please. *TESOL Quarterly, 20*(4), 790–796.

Hartshorn, K. J., & Evans, N. W. (2015). The effects of dynamic written corrective feedback: A 30-week study. *Journal of Response to Writing, 1*(2), 6–24.

Harumi, S. (2011). Classroom silence: Voices from Japanese EFL learners. *ELT Journal, 65*(3), 260–269.

Haswell, J. H. (2006). Automatons and automated scoring: Drudges, black boxes, and dei ex machina. In P. F. Ericsson & R. H. Haswell (Eds.), *Machine scoring of student essays: Truth and consequences* (pp. 57–78). Logan: Utah State University Press.

Hirvela, A. R. (2016). *Connecting reading & writing in second language writing instruction* (2nd ed.). Ann Arbor: University of Michigan Press.

Horowitz, D. (1986a). The author responds to Liebman-Kleine. *TESOL Quarterly, 20*(4), 788–790.

Horowitz, D. (1986b). Process, not product: Less than meets the eye. *TESOL Quarterly, 20*, 141–144.

Hunt, K. W. (1977). Early blooming and late blooming syntactic structures. In C. R. Cooper & L. Odell (Eds.), *Evaluating writing: Describing, measuring, judging* (pp. 91–104). Buffalo: SUNY Press.

Hyland, K. (2002). Genre: Language, context, and literacy. *Annual Review of Applied Linguistics, 22*, 113–135.

Hyland, K. (2003). Genre-based pedagogies: A social response to process. *Journal of Second Language Writing, 12*, 17–29.

Hyland, K. (2004). *Genre and second language writing.* Ann Arbor: University of Michigan Press.

Hyland, K. (2013). Faculty feedback: Perceptions and practices in L2 disciplinary writing. *Journal of Second Language Writing, 22*(3), 240–253.

Hyland, K. (2015). Genre, discipline and identity. *Journal of English for Academic Purposes, 20*, 1–12.

Hyland, K., & Guinda, C. S. (Eds.). (2012). *Stance and voice in written academic genres.* Basingstoke, U.K.: Palgrave Macmillan.

Hyland, K., & Hyland, F. (Eds.). (2006). *Feedback in second language writing: Contexts and issues.* Cambridge, U.K.: Cambridge University Press.

Hyon, S. (1996). Genre in three traditions: Implications for ESL. *TESOL Quarterly, 30*(4), 693–722.

Johns, A. M. (Ed.). (2002). *Genre in the classroom.* Mahwah, NJ: Lawrence Erlbaum.

Johns, A. M. (2008). Genre awareness for the novice academic student: An ongoing quest. *Language Teaching, 41*, 237–252.

Johns, A. M. (2011). The future of genre in L2 writing: Fundamental, but contested, instructional decisions. *Journal of Second Language Writing, 20*(1), 56–68.

Kent, T. (Ed.). (1999). *Post-process theory: Beyond the writing process paradigm.* Carbondale: Southern Illinois University Press.

King, J. (2013). Silence in the second language classrooms of Japanese universities. *Applied Linguistics, 34*(3), 325–343.

Langer, J. A. (1984). The effects of available information on responses to school writing tasks. *Research in the Teaching of English, 18*(1), 27–44.

Larsen-Freeman, D. (2009). Adjusting expectations: The study of complexity, accuracy, and fluency in second language acquisition. *Applied Linguistics, 30*(4), 579–589.

Lee, I. (2008). Understanding teachers' written feedback practices in Hong Kong secondary classrooms. *Journal of Second Language Writing, 17*(2), 69–85.

Lee, I. (2011). Working smarter, not working harder: Revisiting teacher feedback in the L2 writing classroom. *The Canadian Modern Language Review, 67*(3), 377–399.

Lee, I. (2013). Research into practice: Written corrective feedback. *Language Teaching, 46*(1), 108–119.

Lee, I. (2016). Teacher education on feedback in EFL writing: Issues, challenges and future directions. *TESOL Quarterly, 50*(2), 518–527.

Lee, I. (2017). Working hard or working smart: Comprehensive versus focused written corrective feedback in L2 contexts. In J. Bitchener, N. Storch, & Wette R. (Eds.), *Learning to write for academic purposes.* London: Routledge/Taylor & Francis.

Leki, I. (1992). *Understanding ESL writers: A guide for teachers.* Portsmouth, NH: Boynton/Cook Heinemann.

Leki, I. (1995). Good writing: I know it when I see it. In D. Belcher & G. Braine (Eds.), *Academic writing in a second language: Essays on research and pedagogy* (pp. 23–46). Norwood, NJ: Ablex.

Li, X. M. (1996). *"Good writing" in cross-cultural context.* Albany: SUNY Press.

Liebman-Kleine, J. (1986). In defense of teaching process in ESL composition. *TESOL Quarterly, 20*(4), 783–788.

Liu, J., & Hansen Edwards, J. (in press). *Peer response in second language writing classrooms* (2nd ed.). Ann Arbor: University of Michigan Press.

Liu, Q., & Brown, D. (2015). Methodological synthesis of research on the effectiveness of corrective feedback in L2 writing. *Journal of Second Language Writing, 30,* 66–81.

Lundstrom, K., & Baker, W. (2009). To give is better than to receive: The benefits of peer review to the reviewer's own writing. *Journal of Second Language Writing, 18,* 30–43.

Manchón, R. M. (Ed.). (2011). *Learning-to-write and writing-to-learn in an additional language.* Amsterdam: John Benjamins.

Matsuda, P. K. (2003). Process and post-process: A discursive history. *Journal of Second Language Writing, 12*(1), 65–83.

Matsuno, S. (2009). Self-, peer-, and teacher-assessments in Japanese university EFL writing classrooms. *Language Testing, 26*(1), 75–100.

McMartin-Miller, C. (2014). How much feedback is enough? Instructor practices and student attitudes toward error treatment in second language writing. *Assessing Writing, 19,* 24–35.

McNamara, D. S., Crossley, S. A., & McCarthy, P. M. (2010). Linguistic features of writing quality. *Written Communication, 27*(1), 57–86.

Miller, C. R. (1984). Genre as social action. *Quarterly Journal of Speech, 70,* 151–167.

Min, H.-T. (2006). The effects of trained peer review on EFL students' revision types and quality. *Journal of Second Language Writing, 15*(2), 118–141.

Mlynarczyk, R. W. (1998). *Conversations of the mind: The uses of journal writing for second-language learners.* Mahwah, NJ: Lawrence Erlbaum.

Mlynarczyk, R. W. (1991). Is there a difference between personal and academic writing? *TESOL Journal, 1*(1), 17–20.

Newell, G. E., & MacAdam, P. (1987). Examining the source of writing problems: An instrument for measuring writers' topic-specific knowledge. *Written Communication, 4*(2), 155–174.

Norris, N., & Ortega, L. (2009). Towards and organic approach to investigating CAF in instructed SLA: The case of complexity. *Applied Linguistics, 30*(4), 555–578.

Ortega, L. (2003). Syntactic complexity measures and their relationship to L2 proficiency: A research synthesis of college-level L2 writing. *Applied Linguistics, 24*(4), 492–518.

Paltridge, B. (1997). *Genre, frames, and writing in research settings.* Amsterdam: John Benjamins.

Paltridge, B. (2014). Genre and second-language academic writing. *Language Teaching, 47,* 303–318.

Pennington, M. C. (2014). Feedback in writing. *Writing & Pedagogy, 6*(2), 175–186.

Pinker, S. (Sept. 26, 2014). Why academics stink at writing . *The Chronicle of Higher Education.* http://chronicle.com/article/Why-Academics-Writing-Stinks/148989/

Polio, C. (2001). Research methodology in second language writing research: The case of text-based studies. In T. Silva & P. K. Matsuda (Eds.), *On second language writing* (pp. 91–199). Mahwah, NJ: Lawrence Erlbaum.

Raimes, A. (1985). What unskilled ESL students do as they write: A classroom study of composing. *TESOL Quarterly, 19,* 229–258.

Raimes, A. (1991). Out of the woods: Emerging traditions in the teaching of writing. *TESOL Quarterly, 25*(4), 407–430.

Raimes, A. (1992). *Exploring through writing: A process approach to ESL composition* (2nd ed.). Boston: Allyn & Bacon.

Reid, J. (1984a). Comments on Vivian Zamel's "The composing processes of advanced ESL students: Six case studies." *TESOL Quarterly, 18,* 149–153.

Reid, J. (1984b). The radical outliner and the radical brainstormer. *TESOL Quarterly, 18,* 529–533.

Robb, T., Ross, S., & Shortreed, I. (1986). Salience of feedback on error and its effect on EFL writing quality. *TESOL Quarterly, 20,* 83–93.

Rogers, P. M., Zawacki, T. M., & Baker, S. E. (2016). Uncovering challenges and pedagogical complications in dissertation writing and supervisory practices: A multimethod study of doctoral students and advisors. In S. Simpson, M. Cox, N. Caplan, & T. Phillips (Eds.), *Supporting graduate student writers: Research, curriculum, and program design* (pp. 52–77). Ann Arbor: University of Michigan Press.

Schleppegrell, M. J. (2004). *The language of schooling: A functional linguistics perspective.* Mahwah, NJ: Lawrence Erlbaum.

Shintani, N., Ellis, R., & Suzuki, W. (2014). Effects of written feedback and revision on learners' accuracy in using two English grammatical structures. *Language Learning, 64*(1), 103–131.

Spack, R. (1984). Invention strategies and the ESL composition student. *TESOL Quarterly, 18*(4), 649–670.

Spack, R., & Sadow, C. (1983). Student-teacher working journals in ESL freshman composition. *TESOL Quarterly, 17*(4), 575–593.

Stevenson, M., & Phakiti, A. (2014). The effects of computer-generated feedback on the quality of writing. *Assessing Writing, 19*, 51–65.

Storch, N. (2010). Critical feedback on written corrective feedback research. *International Journal of English Studies, 10*(2), 29–46.

Storch, N., & Wigglesworth, G. (2010). Learners' processing, uptake, and retention of corrective feedback on writing: Case studies. *Studies in Second Language Acquisition, 32*, 303–334.

Strunk, W., Jr., & White, E. B. (1959). *The elements of style.* New York: The Macmillan Company.

Susser, B. (1994). Process approaches in ESL/EFL writing. *Journal of Second Language Writing, 3*(1), 31–47.

Suzuki, M. (2008). Japanese learners' self revisions and peer revisions of their written compositions in English. *TESOL Quarterly, 42*(2), 209–233.

Swales, J. M. (1990). *Genre analysis: English in academic and research settings.* New York: Cambridge University Press.

Swales, J. M. (2004). *Research genres. Explorations and applications.* Cambridge, U.K.: Cambridge University Press.

Sword, H. (2012). *Stylish academic writing.* Cambridge, MA: Harvard University Press.

Talandis, G., & Stout, M. (2014). Getting EFL students to speak: An action research approach. *ELT Journal, 69*(1), 11–25.

Tardy, C. (2009). *Building genre knowledge.* West Lafayette, IN: Parlor Press.

Tardy, C. M. (2016). *Beyond convention: Genre innovation in academic writing.* Ann Arbor: University of Michigan Press.

Trimbur, J. (1994). Taking the social turn: Teaching writing post-process. *College Composition and Communication, 45*, 108–118.

Truscott, J. (1996). The case against grammar correction in L2 writing classes. *Language Learning, 46*, 327–369.

Truscott, J. (1999). The case for "The case against grammar correction in L2 writing classes": A response to Ferris. *Journal of Second Language Writing, 8*, 111–122.

Truscott, J. (2007). The effect of error correction on learners' ability to write accurately. *Journal of Second Language Writing, 16*(4), 255–272.

Truscott, J. (2009). Dialogue: Arguments and appearances: A response to Chandler. *Journal of Second Language Writing, 18*(1), 59–60.

Truscott, J. (2010). Some thoughts on Anthony Bruton's critique of the correction debate. *System, 38,* 329–335.

Truscott, J., & Hsu, A. Y. (2008). Error correction, revision, and learning. *Journal of Second Language Writing, 17*(4), 292–305.

Vanett, L., & Jurich, D. (1990). The missing link: Connecting journal writing to academic writing. In J. K. Peyton (Ed.), *Students and teachers writing together: Perspectives on journal writing* (pp. 21–33). Alexandria, VA: TESOL.

van Waes, L., & Leijten, M. (2015). Fluency in writing: A multidimensional perspective on writing fluency applied to L1 and L2. *Computers and Composition, 38,* 79–95.

Villamil, O. S., & de Guerrero, M. C. (2006). Sociocultural theory: A framework for understanding the social-cognitive dimensions of peer feedback. In K. Hyland & F. Hyland (Eds.), *Feedback in second language writing: Contexts and issues* (pp. 23–41). New York: Cambridge University Press.

Weigle, S. C. (2002). *Assessing writing.* Cambridge: Cambridge University Press.

Weissberg, R. (1998). Acquiring English syntax through journal writing. *College ESL, 8*(1), 1–22.

Williams, J. M. (1997). *Style: Ten lessons in clarity and grace* (5th ed.). New York: Longman.

Williams, J. M., & Colomb, G. G. (2012). *Style: The basics of clarity and grace.* London: Longman.

Wolfe-Quintero, K., Inagaki, S., & Kim, H. (1998). *Second language development in writing: Measures of fluency, accuracy, and complexity* (Tech. Rep. No. 17). Honolulu, HI: National Foreign Language Resource Center.

Yang, W., Lu, X., & Weigle, S. C. (2015). Different topics, different discourse: Relationships among writing topic, measures of syntactic complexity, and judgments of writing quality. *Journal of Second Language Writing, 28,* 53–67.

Young, R. (1978). Paradigms and problems: Needed research in rhetorical invention. In C. R. Cooper & L. Odell (Eds.), *Research on composing: Points of departure* (pp. 29–47). Urbana, IL: National Council of Teachers of English.

Zamel, V. (1976). Teaching composition in the ESL classroom: What we can learn from the research in the teaching of English. *TESOL Quarterly, 10*(1), 67–76.

Zamel, V. (1982). Writing: The process of discovering meaning. *TESOL Quarterly, 10*, 67–76.

Zamel, V. (1983a). The composing process of advanced ESL students: Six case studies. *TESOL Quarterly, 17*, 165–187.

Zamel, V. (1983b). Reply to Barnes. *TESOL Quarterly, 17*, 138–139.

Zamel, V. (1984). The author responds. *TESOL Quarterly, 18*, 154–158.

Zamel, V. (1985). Responding to student writing. *TESOL Quarterly, 19*, 79–102.

Zamel, V. (1987). Recent research on writing pedagogy. *TESOL Quarterly, 21*, 697–715.

Zhao, H. (2010). Investigating learners' use and understanding of peer and teacher feedback on writing: A comparative study in a Chinese English writing classroom. *Assessing Writing, 15*(1), 3–17.

Zinsser, W. (2005). *On writing well: The classic guide to writing nonfiction* (25th Anniversary Edition). New York: Collins Reference.

Chapter 6

Writing from Sources and the Dilemma of Plagiarism

"Teachers, especially of composition and foreign languages, must do more to inform themselves about the cultural differences between themselves and their students—differences that left unexamined can give rise to charges of 'plagiarism' and 'intellectual dishonesty,' when the disagreements usually arise from different theories of knowledge, patterns of discourse, and cultural values." (Dryden, 1999, p. 84)

"I received all my education, with the exception of my graduate study, in China, and I never recall any of my teachers telling us it was acceptable to copy others' writing and turn it in as one's own, be it a paragraph or a couple of sentences." (Liu, 2005, p. 235)

"Plagiarism is not a violation of an absolute standard: it is the product of a particular context and cannot be judged without reference to the context in which it occurs." (Pecorari, 2008, p. 12)

"A sense of impending doom hangs over the academy as the specter of 'Internet plagiarism' threatens to undo the entire educational enterprise." (Howard, 2007, p. 3)

"A potentially punitive and insensitive detection tool [like Turnitin] is unlikely to encourage learning, and the power of detection does not compensate for the breaking of the pedagogical relationship between student and teacher." (Emerson, 2008, p.193)

LEADING QUESTIONS

- What is involved in learning to write from sources?
- How do institutions and individuals define and apply the concept of plagiarism?
- Why do writers plagiarize?
- How can we distinguish between unintentional and intentional plagiarizing in an academic context?
- What are some of the cultural issues surrounding the Western concept of plagiarism?
- How does the concept of plagiarism apply to the many different kinds of sources found on the internet?
- What does so-called "plagiarism detection software" do? What issues face institutions, writing teachers, and students who use this software?

Introduction to the Issues

In many school settings, students need to write from sources for certain kinds of essay exams and for various kinds of assignments. In the case of essay exams, the students might be given one or more sources along with the exam prompt that they are expected to incorporate in their writing (Weigle & Parker, 2012). For classroom assignments, sources might be ones they have been given by instructors or ones they need to locate themselves in libraries and increasingly from internet sources. In all cases, writing from sources poses challenges for all writers, including L1 and L2 authors who write and publish, not just L2 students. As Campbell (1990, p. 211) noted long ago, using background material in our own writing requires "reading, understanding, learning, relating, planning, writing, revising, editing, and orchestrating." Whether sources are print or digital, word-based or multimedia, writers need to be able to read with comprehension, select sources or parts of sources in a way that suits their writing tasks, integrate source material into their own writing directly and verbatim or through paraphrase and summary, and acknowledge sources in ways accepted by institutional convention (Sutherland-Smith, 2008). It is quite a staggering multi-faceted task, actually, one that does not come naturally or quickly to anyone, and one that is plagued by controversies about plagiarism—what it is, how to detect it, and how to avoid it. In an academic setting, students, faculty, and staff alike are obligated to understand the complexities of plagiarism, because they cannot write from sources without facing the challenges of knowing both how to integrate and acknowledge their sources in their own writing.

One area of controversy when we consider how people write from sources deals with how writers interact with the words and ideas of others, namely those from authors of print or digital texts whose words or ideas a writer wishes to incorporate into his or her own texts. Novice writers tend not to see that they are interacting with other authors when they write from sources, but instead to see sources as authoritative funds of information that just need to be transferred into their own writing. It takes many years of practice and reflection to understand that to write from sources is to have a conversation with another author, not just to adopt their words and ideas as "information."

If a writer uses the words of others as though they were his or her own (i.e., does not acknowledge the source), academic regulations in many English-medium contexts call this plagiarism—metaphorically referred to as "theft," "stealing," "cheating," or an academic "crime." But plagiarism and ownership of words are relatively recent concepts in Western countries, and may have no clear parallel in other cultures (Bloch, 2012; Pennycook, 1996). Even in the West, the concept of plagiarism itself has never been defined in a way that all teachers and authors (and lawyers) agree on. Moreover, all academic writers practice "textual borrowing" (Pennycook, 1996) or "language re-use" (Flowerdew & Li, 2007a), but very few of them intentionally plagiarize. Determining intention turns out to be one of the most difficult challenges of plagiarism hunters who wish to punish perpetrators, particularly if teachers or institutions use controversial so-called plagiarism detection software (or anti-plagiarism systems) such as Turnitin. Such software cannot detect intention; it can only match textual patterns.

In order to make fair and ethical decisions in their writing classes about how to teach writing from sources and treat textual borrowing as conversations writers have with authors, L2 writing teachers need to understand these issues and to recognize that what they call plagiarism is neither easily defined nor taught, may not exist in the cultures of some of their students in the same way it does in the West, and may occur unintentionally without a (developing) writer's intention to deceive. In the next sections I discuss some of these issues in more detail.

Discussions in the Literature

Using background reading sources as a foundation for writing is an inherent and essential activity in academic writing (Belcher & Hirvela, 2001; Campbell, 1990; Hirvela, 2016; Pecorari & Shaw, 2012). If not in high school, at least in early years of college or university, students are expected to learn how to make the sources their own (to integrate them smoothly into their own writing) and to paraphrase, summarize, and reference appropriately (Pecorari, 2013; Spatt, 2011; Swales & Feak, 2012). Universities may or may not teach L1 and L2 students explicitly how to write from sources and about the concept of plagiarism and techniques for avoiding it, but policy statements about the "crime" of plagiarism and its consequences at particular institutions are common. However, defining plagiarism in ways that are clear for both students and writing teachers turns out to be tricky.

Defining Plagiarism

Despite the simplistic definition of plagiarism as using the unattributed words of another person as if they were one's own, defining plagiarism in a straightforward unambiguous way has never been possible. The concept developed over hundreds of years, in conjunction with notions of intellectual property and copyright (Bloch, 2012; Marsh, 2007), spurred by the invention of the printing press by Gutenberg in the mid-1400s when questions of originality and ownership arose. Confusions flourished in the centuries that followed as to what was considered creative and original and what was a copy, and whether words could ever be original and owned, in the form of intellectual property. It is not possible to plagiarize in the absence of the idea of intellectual property and the legal notion of copyright, which developed in England in the late 1600s and early 1700s (see Bloch, 2012; Marsh, 2007). These questions have not been resolved in the last 300 years, but have only gotten more vexed as digital media and possibilities of cutting, pasting, copying, mixing, and altering have proliferated.

However, in academic settings, both individual faculty and the institution itself need to have an idea of what they mean by plagiarism in order to advise, decide how to instruct, and perhaps punish, students. The concept of plagiarism presumes that people can own words and ideas, that words and ideas can be original—that they can be authored— and that "stealing" someone else's words is both a moral and a legal offense. This presumption, on the surface, seems straightforward, as the statements on plagiarism commonly communicated in departmental handbooks reveal. A familiar example can be seen in Angélil-Carter's (2000, p. 58) departmental handbook from a South African university, which begins with these familiar words: "Plagiarism means that another writer's words and/or opinions have been used without being acknowledged. This occurs when someone else's work has been copied word for word, or in a slightly altered form, and there are no quotation marks and/or references to show that these words have been borrowed."

This definition is common in universities and in writing guidebooks (although we might find the notion of "borrowing" words a bit odd). As Pecorari and Petric (2014, p. 270) noted in their extensive review of work on plagiarism, "University definitions tend to be quite consistent." In her interview study, for example, Roy (1999) found that faculty tended to define plagiarism either as stealing or taking someone else's work without giving credit, or misrepresenting someone else's ideas as one's own. Plagiarism, in other words, consisted either of stealing or of deceiving. In her international survey of 54 universities, Pecorari (2001), too, found a great deal of consistency in how documents in Australia, the United States, and Great Britain characterized and punished plagiarism. Although details differed, it was generally described as unattributed use of the work of others, through copying or paraphrase, in work that was submitted for assessment. Most universities in her survey treated plagiarism as an academic crime that is punishable. But do these simple definitions encompass more than inappropriate use of print sources? In this digital age, it is likely that most students (and teachers) will draw mainly on digital sources for academic writing projects. How do we define plagiarism in such an age, when even guidelines from the past print era were unclear (Howard, 2007)? Because we still lack clear guidelines as to whether digital and print texts should be treated similarly in copyright and plagiarism cases, educators face difficult decisions in providing clear definitions of plagiarism for students and in guiding them to use internet sources in ways that fit existing legal and ethical notions of writing in academic settings.

Writing instructors worldwide thus have had problems understanding and consistently applying the criteria stated in university policies to student work (Angélil-Carter, 2000; Pecorari, 2013; Pecorari & Petric, 2014; Pecorari & Shaw, 2012; Pennington, 2010). As Polio and Shi (2012, p. 95) noted, lack of consensus as to "what is acceptable textual appropriation in student writing," particularly in the cases of L2 and developing writers, is widespread. Lei and Hu (2015) for example, surveyed 112 Chinese university teachers about their knowledge of and attitudes toward plagiarism and found great diversity and complexity of responses. Lei and Hu (2014, 2015) similarly found varying degrees of knowledge about and ability to identify plagiarized text, even though the teachers had fairly consistent punitive attitudes to its use. The tutors that Angélil-

Carter (2000) interviewed in South Africa about particular comments they had made on students' writing showed similar inconsistencies in how they defined and treated plagiarism, as did the teachers interviewed by Pecorari (2008).

It is not surprising, then, that students themselves, both L1 and L2, at undergraduate and graduate levels, may have diverse or confused ideas about what plagiarism consists of (Abasi, Akbari, & Graves, 2006; Abasi & Graves, 2008; Angélil-Carter, 2000; Deckert, 1993; Hu & Lei, 2012; Kroll, 1988; Pecorari & Petric, 2014). This difficulty includes the apparently simple problem of distinguishing common knowledge (no need to cite) from authors' particular ideas that require citations (Shi, 2011). In an interesting study of peer writing groups, for example, Spigelman (1999) found that L1 students' ideas and values about appropriating ideas, words, and phrases from their peers differed from student to student, a common finding in research that followed. One student distinguished between ideas that peers gave him in peer discussion groups and ideas that were taken without someone's knowledge or permission. Another student defined plagiarism as direct copying, word for word, but considered it legitimate appropriation if he reshaped the words and ideas from the original. Students disagreed as well as to whether it was possible to own ideas. Still, all the students in her study considered plagiarism to be a form of "personal misrepresentation," including the "unacknowledged appropriation of student texts" (Spigelman, 1999, pp. 234–235).

In other settings, students from non–English dominant contexts also understand plagiarism in a variety of ways that indicate lack of consensus of definitions and applications. Even when students understand that direct copying is not condoned, they might accept it as an imitation or memorization technique for learning as has been documented in cases of Chinese students' and professionals' writing (Bloch, 2008b, 2008c; Bloch & Chi, 1995; Liu, 2005; Matalene, 1985; Pennycook, 1996; see further discussion in the section on Cultural Issues in Textual Appropriation). Students in many parts of the world might also define and apply their ideas of plagiarism in individual ways (Abasi, Akbari, & Graves, 2006; Abasi & Graves, 2008; Ahmadi, 2014; Angélil-Carter, 2000). Confusion has also increased in recent years as to whether material cut and pasted from the internet is open and free to be used in any way an author wishes, as some students believe. In short, both teachers and students seem to have inconsistently defined and applied views of plagiarism even when a university policy seems straightforward.

Some helpful distinctions when we try to define plagiarism consist of distinguishing moral and ethical definitions of plagiarism (as a crime, as cheating) from its textual or linguistic manifestations (Pecorari, 2008). Pecorari's study of plagiarism as a textual (i.e., linguistic) phenomenon further separates what she calls "prototypical plagiarism"—committed with intention to deceive—from patchwriting, a useful concept taken from Howard (1995, 1999) that Pecorari considers unintentional textual plagiarism. Patchwriting includes textual appropriation techniques that would technically be labeled plagiarism, such as substituting synonyms into unchanged syntax, paraphrasing without attribution, and copying short phrases taken from a source into a piece of writing. These patchwriting techniques can be found in the writing of most novice writers and even of experienced writers. Howard and others (e.g., Pecorari, 2008) consider patchwriting to be part of a developmental stage as students learn to write from sources. However, deciding whether to define patchwriting as an instance of plagiarism is tricky (Li & Casanave, 2012), and opinions differ as to how to handle such instances, even when intention to deceive is not present. I discuss this issue in more detail in the section on Intentional and Unintentional Plagiarizing.

Unable (with apologies to frustrated readers) to define plagiarism in an unambiguous, uncontextualized way, I urge writing teachers and their students to study plagiarism policies at their own schools and to analyze, critique, and consider how to apply them in their own local contexts.

How Widespread Is Plagiarism?

We do not actually know how widespread plagiarism was in the past or is today because so much of it has gone, and continues to go, unnoticed (see Pecorari's, 2008, study), and we have little basis on which to make comparisons (Howard, 2007, p. 7). However, many teachers in English-medium colleges and universities have suspected that plagiarism has always been widespread, particularly if writing assignments are not carefully designed to discourage copying, cutting, and pasting. Some evidence exists as to widespread plagiarism across universities (see some survey results reported in Bloch, 2012, pp. 1–2). Other evidence is anecdotal (Pecorari, 2001) and historical. In her historical look at plagiarism in U.S. colleges in the 19th century, Simmons (1999, p. 41) claimed that "[w]ith the requirement to write papers came student plagiarism," particularly with canned paper topics. Even though there were admonitions against cheating, students who felt little ownership of their papers and whose primary goal was just to get through school saw no reason not to copy, use "fraternity files," or purchase papers (p. 50). This motivation from the past still resonates today, in an era when student papers can be bought and downloaded from websites.

In other work done in the 1990s from a faculty perspective in the United States, Buranen (1999, p. 64) noted that instructors in a teleconference reported that "cheating was more widespread among students than we would like to believe." Buranen herself had had "occasional" experiences of L1 and L2 students turning in plagiarized papers. On the other hand, in a telephone interview study of 20 faculty members at her U.S. university, Roy (1999) was told by only two of the interviewees that plagiarism was a large problem in their classes. Several more said that the problem was moderate.

L2 writing scholars, on the other hand, have had particular interest in the writing problems of their students from countries like Japan and China, both in ESL and EFL contexts. In a focused study of attitudes toward and practices of plagiarism in Japan, LoCastro and Masuko (1997) examined several senior theses written in Japanese and English and 30 other student papers, and found that the theses and over half the student papers contained large quantities of unattributed material from other sources. My own undergraduate students in Japan revealed to me in class discussions about their writing in other courses that cutting and pasting from internet sources was routine at report time. Also in Japan, Dryden (1999) noted that there is a great deal of unattributed translation from English to Japanese in the writing of graduate students and faculty (the issue of translating one's article for a dual publication is itself an interesting controversy; Wen & Gao, 2007). In addition, faculty mentors routinely list their names on work produced solely by their students. I observed both these practices while I was in Japan. Perhaps also widespread is the unattributed use by students of well-known texts, as has been reported in Hong Kong and China (Bloch, 2008b; Bloch & Chi, 1995). In one familiar example, Pennycook (1996) reported on a student from Hong Kong who wrote a memorized essay about Abraham Lincoln, a story that one of my own students from China also had to memorize, prompting Pennycook to ask whether this should be considered plagiarism. However, recognizing instances of plagiarism in order to determine how widespread it is requires that we define plagiarism (including self-plagiarism) in an unambiguous way, a task that has proved challenging, as I discussed in the previous section.

When we ask if plagiarism is widespread, we tend to think about the inappropriate use of source texts in students' writing. However, scandals have surfaced in the work of scientists, politicians, and journalists as well (see Bloch, 2012; Marsh, 2007; Pecorari, 2008), and perhaps most surprising in the work of professional academics who publish their work in journals and books. Pennycook (1996), in his important article on the links among textual ownership, textual borrowing, and memory, found numerous examples in the published writing of Western scholars that could be considered plagiarized if we do not apply nuanced definitions to the concept. Roig (2001) too found in study of paraphrasing that up to 30 percent of L1 university faculty who participated had appropriated text without acknowledgment when they were asked to write a paraphrase from a difficult source text; the percent was much lower when the professors read an easier source text. In a large study of 600 journal articles in two broad disciplines (sciences and social sciences), Sun (2013) found that all texts had instances of text use matched to sources in the Turnitin "plagiarism detection" database, with higher scores in the sciences than in the social sciences. Thus, the practice of appropriating text from sources for one's own purposes without full acknowledgement does indeed seem widespread. Do we call the practice plagiarism? Patchwriting? Textual borrowing, re-use, or appropriation? Do we label it transgressive (intentional) or nontransgressive (unintentional)? And most importantly, do we punish it, and if so how? If not, how can we use this widespread practice as learning tool to help all writers learn to integrate and interact with source texts in acceptable ways?

Cultural Issues in Textual Appropriation

Related to how we define and identify plagiarism in its many widespread uses is the thorny issue of cultural differences in how writers treat source material and conceptualize the idea of authorship. In the late 1980s and into the 1990s, possibly as a result of large increases in populations of L2 students in English-dominant settings, the search for cultural influences on plagiarism in student writing expanded greatly (Barks & Watts, 2001; Bloch, 2001, 2008a; Bloch & Chi, 1995; Buranen, 1999; Deckert, 1993; Dryden, 1999; Pecorari, 2001; Pennycook, 1996, 2001; Scollon, 1995; Swearingen, 1999). Much of the work in this area in the past concerned the writing of Chinese students.

For example, following Kroll's (1988) survey of L1 college students on their views of plagiarism, Deckert (1993) conducted a survey of 170 first-year and 41 third-year students at his university in Hong Kong. He found that the first-year students had little ability to detect plagiarism or sense why it was wrong except that it hampered their learning. Their attitudes differed from Kroll's (1988) L1 students, who showed awareness of the idea that writers can own words and that they need to be able to do independent work. Deckert's third-year students, on the other hand, showed more concern for the original author, leading Deckert to conclude that his students' educational experiences were influential. His experience in Hong Kong and the results of his survey led him to claim that "most Chinese students overuse source material through an innocent and ingrained habit of giving back information exactly as they find it" (Deckert, 1993, p. 133).

Not only were inexperienced Chinese writers thought to view source material in different ways from Western writers, but differences were also found at the professional level. Bloch and Chi (1995) studied how Chinese and English-speaking academic writers use citations when they write in their own languages. They analyzed 60 articles each in Chinese and English from the physical and social sciences and found that the Chinese writers used older citations more often than did the English language writers. The authors explained that this difference could be due to the Chinese writers' reliance on older texts, as part of a Confucian respect for tradition, or that the Chinese writers simply had less access to newer texts. They found as well that the writers used citations somewhat differently, both across languages, and within Chinese texts in different disciplinary areas: English language writers used more citation strategies than did the Chinese writers, but the Chinese writers, unlike the stereotype suggesting that they are not good at making critical commentary, used critical citations in both the physical and social science articles. However, they tended not to place them in the introduction. Bloch and Chi also discussed at length the possible influences of cultural and rhetorical traditions from Chinese history, with the intention of dismantling the myth that Chinese culture and rhetoric are based on simple collectivist ideas of social harmony: "Chinese rhetoric, rather than being monolithic, encompasse[s] a variety of forms of thought, often reflecting the divergence of philosophical inquiry in Chinese society" (Bloch & Chi, 1995, p. 267).

Others have explained the problem as stemming from Chinese students' reliance on literary traditions based on imitation of authorities (Matalene, 1985), on the influence of Confucian and neo-Confucian rhetoric, and on the historical influence of the Chinese civil service exams, which emphasized memorization (Bloch & Chi, 1995). However, it is not necessarily the case that L2 students from Asia are relying on ancient cultural traditions. Instead, they may simply not be fully socialized into ways of thinking about academic writing in an English-dominant context that differ from their educational experiences at home. Students may also be employing developmental and compensatory strategies due to their low English language proficiency (Bloch & Chi, 1995), an argument that has been made in more recent studies of plagiarism that take a developmental perspective (discussed further later). Case studies of ESL writers have shown that what might be labeled plagiarism served as a successful survival strategy for the undergraduate L2 writers who lacked confidence in their language ability and had little time to prepare their written work in more acceptable ways (Currie, 1998; Spack, 1997). Students who are new to Western academia also clearly lack specific training in how to write and cite from sources in ways that suit Western norms and probably do not view sources as material for having conversations with authors rather than as information to be learned. More surprising is the later finding by Pecorari (2008) that some L2 graduate students who were writing theses and dissertations, and who supposedly were proficient in English, incorporated source material into their work in ways that, if it had been discovered by faculty, would be labeled as clear instances of both plagiarism and patchwriting.

However, novice L1 writers as well use techniques to construct pieces of academic writing that Howard (1995) has labeled patchwriting, as more recent work has also found. Graduate students in particular are under extra pressure to write "original" work (a concept that Pennycook, 1996, reminded us is difficult to define) as well as to incorporate the words and ideas of others in their writing. The need to situate work within a disciplinary community, particularly in literature review sections of their work (Feak & Swales, 2009; Ridley, 2008; Swales, 1987, 1990), is quite basic to graduate-level academic writing. Beginning some time ago, there was at least some evidence suggesting that graduate ESL students' conceptions of textual borrowing do not differ greatly from those of L1 students, leading Barks and Watts (2001) to ask whether ignorance and lack of experience, rather than culture, lead to unorthodox textual borrowing. It is likely, too, that writing tasks that are perceived as meaningless to students encourage plagiarizing, as do high-stakes writing tasks such as theses and dissertations that require that students take on the authoritative voices of experts (Pecorari, 2008). This authoritative voice comes more easily from external sources than from students themselves.

As research evidence builds, in other words, it has become increasingly difficult to attribute L2 students' plagiaristic practices to cultural traditions alone. Numerous studies have found that cultural arguments about plagiarism have simplified and stereotyped an extremely complex topic, namely why students (or others) plagiarize. Explanations are numerous, including lack of understanding and absence of explicit instruction and practice in some educational traditions, insufficient language proficiency, unfamiliarity with a discipline's conventions, insufficient content knowledge, cultural respect for the "expert," influence from type of task (e.g., summary or opinion), and unclear guidance from particular instructors who themselves might be confused about specific incidences of possible plagiarism (Angélil-Carter, 2000; Le Ha, 2006; Liu, 2005; Martin, 2011; Pecorari & Petric, 2014; Shi, 2004, 2006, 2012; Song-Turner, 2008; Sutherland-Smith, 2008; Tang, 2012; Wheeler, 2009). One interesting study from the management field (Martin, 2011) found that, contrary to stereotypes of Western and Asian cultures (e.g., Sowden, 2005), the individualists in their study plagiarized more than the collectivists, and that basically no significant differences could be found between Caucasian and Asian students (see further discussion on individualism and collectivism in Chapter 8). Likewise, in her work with native English-speaking and multilingual students, Shi (2006) found that the majority of participants regardless of background were unsure about what words and ideas they needed to cite and attribute to sources. Therefore, given that source-based academic writing does not come naturally to anyone, and that all novice writers tend to rely more on source texts than do experienced writers (Keck, 2014), both L1 and

L2 students need to understand and develop skills in source-based writing over time. This is a developmental issue that any of us who has tried to learn to write from sources without plagiarizing can relate to.

Moreover, if students are simultaneously learning the content and discourse conventions of their disciplines, both L1 and L2 students will no doubt struggle mightily to integrate their print and electronic sources appropriately into their writing (see the review in Pecorari & Petric, 2014). Disciplinary language is a kind of second language for everyone, with its own sets of conventions and expectations (Hyland, 2009, 2011). In the case of L2 students who are continuing to develop their language proficiency, and who may not have been provided with previous instruction or much practice in writing from sources, the difficulties are exacerbated (Angélil-Carter, 2000; Gu & Brooks, 2008; Shi, 2006; see also Ouellette's, 2008, case study of "Annie"). In other words, differences between novice L1 and L2 writers in their tendencies to plagiarize and patchwrite have been overstated in the view of some scholars (Keck, 2014; Pecorari & Petric, 2014; Weigle & Parker, 2012). That said, the cultural argument has not disappeared (see, for example, Chien, 2014, who discusses traditions of memorization and repetition in Taiwan that might influence students' plagiarism), and still plays a role—even if reduced—in the complex views of scholars in the 2000s.

In short, from the mid-1990s and early 2000s, our understanding of plagiarism and of cultural influences on how L2 writers interact with the work of others became more complex as L1 and L2 scholars provided us with historical, cultural, and disciplinary information about authorship, the ambiguities in the Western notion of plagiarism, and about other possible reasons why students plagiarize (Angélil-Carter, 2000; Bloch, 2001, 2012; Bloch & Chi, 1995; Eisner & Vicinus, 2008; Howard, 1995, 1999; Marsh, 2007; Pecorari, 2008; Pennycook, 1996; Stearns, 1999). The result of our more complex understanding of writing from sources, plagiarizing, and patchwriting is that strong arguments are being made that educational institutions and faculty should not be too hasty in judging instances of inappropriate textual appropriation either as a cultural matter or as an academic crime. Certainly if there is clear evidence that a writer has intended to deceive and cheat (such as buying a paper from an online supplier or using someone else's data for a research report), then the writer deserves to be punished. But other cases need to be considered carefully as possible steps in a long and difficult learning process. By treating what looks like plagiarism by students as a crime, we are unfairly imposing an oversimplified and outdated Western notion of (original) authorship on a complex cross-cultural, developmental, and disciplinary phenomenon that is as ideological as it is textual.

Intentional and Unintentional Plagiarizing

It is likely that the distinction between intentional (transgressive or prototypical) and unintentional (nontransgressive) plagiarizing (Chandrasoma, Thompson, & Pennycook, 2004), also referred to as patchwriting (Howard, 1995; Pecorari, 2008), does not pose a serious controversy in the L2 writing field. Most L2 educators probably view instances of plagiarizing in students' writing as unintentional, in the sense that students are not intending to cheat, or that they do not understand that certain kinds of textual appropriation are considered unacceptable. Unlike some administrators and subject matter faculty, L2 educators tend to see such instances as opportunities for instruction and language development. I discuss the question of intention here because departments and institutions may not be so forgiving given strict plagiarism policies that threaten students with severe consequences including expulsion. This unforgiving attitude is common even though studies have shown that it a challenge for any of us to determine intent on the part of student writers.

Given the stated policies at many schools and universities about the "crime" of plagiarism, it may be difficult to defend students who have appropriated text in ways that do not meet the policies. But L2 writing instructors want to treat student writers fairly and justly, and to understand that learning to write is a developmental process requiring a great deal of time and practice. Scholars and writing instructors have ample evidence that learning to write from sources is even more challenging than learning non-source based writing for both L1 and L2 students, and that simply handing students a plagiarism policy at the beginning of a school term will not ensure that that students (or their teachers!) know what plagiarism is and how to avoid it (Angélil-Carter, 2000; Pecorari, 2008; Russell-Pinson, personal communication, July 2016). Guidebooks (e.g., Pecorari, 2013; Spatt, 2011; Swales & Feak, 2012) and classroom instruction stress that novice writers need to learn the rules and then to paraphrase, summarize, and cite sources according to accepted conventions, but even then, students may fail to grasp the complexities of how to integrate sources with their own voices (Wette, 2010). Beyond being able to state plagiarism policies, both L1 and L2 students who are novice writers need to understand many other things, particularly if they need to write literature reviews for undergraduate or graduate work. These include learning how to comprehend what they read; how to appropriately select the words (and increasingly images) of others from print and digital sources; how to decide if the words of others are common knowledge or instead are "owned" by an author (Bloch, 2012, p. 82; Shi, 2006, 2011); how to recognize when a source they are using is itself using the words and ideas of another source (making this a secondary source for our student writer) (Pecorari, 2008); and how to use the words of others in ways expected by an assignment (e.g., as straight reporting and summarizing, or more likely as integrated into an argument, conversation with an author, or point the student writer wishes to make). These decisions are a normal part of a student's development as a writer and cannot be learned from a set of rules. But does failure to follow the rules signify an intent to cheat?

"Intention is difficult to get at," Pecorari (2008, p. 98) pointed out; "only the writers can provide direct evidence as to whether they intended to deceive." Conferring with individual students in the presence of their writing can thus sometimes reveal that they truly did not know they were committing an academic offense or did not know how to avoid doing so. For example,

Pecorari (2008) found that in her study of graduate student thesis writing both plagiarism and patchwriting happened without students' intending to cheat (some of her examples at the graduate level are quite shocking in the extent of copied material). The students did intend to use the words and ideas of others, as this is what writing from sources is all about and what they believed they were required to do. In interviews with these students, Pecorari justified their extensive copying and lack of appropriate citation in ways that convinced her that they did not intend to deceive. But writing instructors and subject matter instructors might not know for certain if an accused student is telling the truth.

The burden on teachers seems heavy. When students, intentionally or not, misuse source texts in their own writing, it is up to faculty readers to detect inappropriate use of source material and to consult with students about their intentions. But another disturbing find in Pecorari's (2008) study was that the faculty supervisors that she interviewed across numerous disciplines had not identified any problems of source use in the students' writing. They did not recognize odd shifts in style, or recognize passages copied inappropriately from sources they might have been familiar with, or find serious problems with students' failure to use quotation marks or page numbers for cited sources, or failure to cite altogether. The faculty readers seemed to feel that occasional copied passages in background sections of a thesis were not a serious problem, particularly in the sciences, although in some of the interview data provided by Pecorari they seem surprised at the extent of students' plagiarizing and patchwriting. It might be common that instructors do not notice instances of plagiarism or patchwriting in students' work, or do not know why they marked certain passages as plagiarized and others not, as Angélil-Carter (2000) found in her interviews with teachers at a South African university. The depressing reality is that neither writing teachers nor subject matter teachers have time to do the laborious work of checking all possible infractions of source use in their students' work. Both Pecorari and Angélil-Carter did this detailed checking as part of major research projects, but it is impossible for practicing teachers to do so. So-called plagiarism detection software has promised to ease teachers' burdens, but controversies abound about the use of such software. Among many other problems, it cannot detect intention. It is to this messy controversy that I turn next.

"Plagiarism Detection Software"

First, let me stress a point I made in the introduction: "Plagiarism detection software" (also called anti-plagiarism software) is a misnomer because no matter which program is used, it can only detect matching patterns between a submitted document and one in its database or on the internet. It does nothing more than compare texts (Pecorari & Petric, 2014). It cannot detect intention, and without knowing a writer's intention, we cannot know if plagiarism, as an intentional act of deception, has occurred. It is not sufficient to presume intentionality on the part of a graduate student who plagiarizes or of a student who has been given a plagiarism policy, just because at the graduate level or with a plagiarism policy in hand they "should know better." The result of such simplistic attitudes is that a rhetoric of fear rather than pedagogy has conspired to keep the phrase "plagiarism detection" in common use. With this in mind, I will from this point use a different phrase, such as *text-matching software,* except when I refer to the work of others who use the term *plagiarism detection software.*

Text-matching software systems that are developed and then sold at great expense to universities are not necessarily needed. Searches to check the presumed originality of selected passages can be made by entering passages into search engines like Google, which have some success at locating matching passages between submitted and published work. But for-profit websites specifically targeted at academic writing have proliferated in recent years (see some examples in Flowerdew & Li, 2007b, pp. 174–175). Many schools have adopted corporate systems such as Turnitin. The Turnitin corporation (http://turnitin.com/), launched as a for-profit company in the mid

1990s, advertises that it offers online plagiarism detection and prevention as well as automated feedback on student writing. The website claims to help students improve their writing, creativity, originality, and critical thinking. This system and others like it depend on algorithms programmed to match the language in students' writing with existing password-free texts in the database and on the internet. Their services are designed to detect "unoriginal" writing, provide "originality reports" and instant feedback and even grades to students, and so act as a deterrent to plagiarism and a quick way for teachers and students themselves to check written work for possible infractions. In the case of Turnitin, all work that students submit to this site and its many subsidiary text-matching tools becomes the property of the company, a feature that has raised questions about privacy, copyright, and intellectual property. A useful introduction to Turnitin could be found at the time I drafted this chapter on Wikipedia at https://en.wikipedia.org/wiki/Turnitin, but readers should search other sources (and investigate other text-comparison software in use at readers' own institutions) as needed. Turnitin has also been analyzed and critiqued by Marsh (2004) and some of its services described by Vie (2013). In what follows I describe a few of the discussions in the literature that comment on issues that arise for writing scholars and students who use text-matching software such as Turnitin.

In the first and second language writing literature, critiques of systems like Turnitin are common. For example, such systems presume an outdated view of the author as a lone and creative individual, and according to Marsh (2004, p. 433), "a digital reformulation of rather old pedagogical formulae." Plagiarism detection technologies also presume an individualist view of writing, which Vie (2013) encouraged composition teachers to resist because this view does not account for the communal writing that takes place these days in wikis, blogs, and other social media. It is still not clear how plagiarism policies apply to diverse social media and multi-media constructions and compilations from print and especially internet sources. Second, the issue of privacy and intellectual property rights of students' work has not been resolved. If all students have to submit their work to the system, then the system functions like a digital archive (Purdy, 2009), compiled without full knowledge and permission of the student writers. A third concern also raised by Purdy and others is that such systems risk disengaging teachers from students and their writing, with authority passed to a numerical system. Purdy (2009, p. 73) cautioned that "… we risk losing the critical engagement with texts that we work so hard to teach our students. With these services," he said, "saving time comes at the expense of more thoughtful and less punitive approaches to writing pedagogy." From the writers' perspective, novice writers who do not understand the complexities and sophistication of how to integrate sources smoothly and appropriately into their own writing might also risk losing the essential engagement with ideas, language, and readers that is so essential to learning to write. Instead, they might shift their attention to the mechanics of how to avoid a damaging report (i.e., how to trick the system), as did the undergraduate students in the U.K. studied by Lea and Jones (2011). Similar arguments about loss of engagement have been made against automated essay scoring (see Chapter 7, Assessment). Fourth, at least one study found that Turnitin did not act as a deterrent for student plagiarism, but that students actually increased the extent of their plagiarizing over the four years of their studies (Walker, 2010). Another study concluded that "the deterrent effect of plagiarism detection systems remains anecdotal" (Emerson, 2008, p. 189). Finally, some people worry that the scores provided by such systems will be taken as proof of plagiarism, even when corporate caveats say that the system cannot provide such proof. Even though such systems cannot prove intent to cheat, many people worry that students will be accused too hastily, resulting in unfair and mistaken assumptions about guilt and intention (Introna & Hayes, 2008; Pecorari, 2008)

Other studies of systems like Turnitin have made limited and cautious conclusions about the usefulness of such systems. If in fact teachers miss many instances of inappropriate source text use in their students' writing, then text-matching detection systems seem like a good starting place for busy teachers. But follow up by teachers is essential. When scores and numerical reports are used and interpreted carefully by teachers rather than accepted uncritically, they can alert teachers to potential problems that students might be having writing from sources. Once alert to potential problems, teachers can identify areas that require further pedagogical instruction and intervention. Likewise, students who know their work must be submitted to Turnitin are likely to be more careful in how they use source material in their own work. Even though in some cases, for unclear reasons, Turnitin was found to have no deterrent effect at all (see Walker, 2010), this deterrent effect has been touted as a benefit, as long as students do not use all their time and energy to construct their writing in ways to trick the system. Benefits have been documented, for example, for undergraduate students in Ireland (Ledwith, & Rísquez, 2008) and graduate students in Hong Kong (Stapleton, 2012). Sutherland-Smith and Carr (2005) also found that the Turnitin system helped undergraduate students in Australia find instances of matching text. However, no studies could prove intent to deceive from the text-matching patterns found in students' work. Only teacher engagement and consultation can do that. In short, supporters of text-matching systems urge teachers to use them for educational rather than policing purposes (Ledwith, & Rísquez, 2008, p. 383). Whatever our views, debates about the value and appropriateness of text-matching software such as Turnitin have engendered many important discussions that might not have otherwise occurred (Stapleton, 2012).

Concluding Thoughts

To conclude this discussion of plagiarism, I refer briefly to the growing dilemma facing educators in developed and developing countries—that of the proliferation of opportunities for students of all kinds to construct their writing from sources drawn from the internet. As Howard (2007, p. 4) pointed out, "Indisputably, the Internet makes texts readily available for plagiarizing." Because we still do not have clear guidelines as to whether electronic and print texts should be treated similarly in copyright and plagiarism cases (Bloch, 2001, 2012), educators face difficult decisions in guiding students to use internet sources in ways that fit existing legal and ethical notions of writing in academic settings. Confusion thus grows as to what we should consider authorship in an era of writing from internet sources. Has the traditional view of an author as someone who creates his or her own ideas and words disappeared (Lunsford & West, 1996; Woodmansee & Jaszi, 1995)?

The main point to be taken from these discussions of plagiarism is that the concept is both complex, even within Western cultures, and culturally loaded. L2 writing teachers may not easily be able to answer the many questions that surround the practice of textual borrowing, except in clear cases of intentional deception when large amounts of text are copied or data are appropriated in work that is submitted for evaluation. However, before assigning writing tasks that require students to write from sources, teachers are advised first to think through some of the issues described in this chapter; learn something about the historical, cultural, and legal complexities and ambiguities of plagiarism; discuss them with colleagues and students; learn what institutional regulations exist; and plan how to approach the issue from a positive, educational perspective with students. Part of a positive educational approach is to recognize that all novice writers can benefit from patchwriting: At early points in writing instruction, copying words, phrases, and even passages can contribute to students' linguistic and rhetorical development (see phrasebanks such as www.phrasebank.manchester.ac.uk/). Moreover, teachers can try to design meaningful source-based writing activities for their students—ones that help students understand what they read and ones that go beyond the kinds of canned topics that are easily plagiarized. In general, I think it is not controversial to say that issues of plagiarism in writing from sources are best treated pedagogically, not punitively.

Classroom Perspectives

Whatever attitudes we take toward writing from sources and the dilemma of plagiarism, all of us hope for good pedagogy in our writing classes, and not punitive policies. Some guides can help students learn to write from sources and document their work appropriately so as to avoid accusations of plagiarism (e.g., Pecorari, 2013; Spatt, 2011; Sutherland-Smith, 2008; Swales & Feak, 2012). In this section, I provide two examples of classroom activities that are designed to helps students understand textual borrowing practices (Barks & Watts, 2001) and to critically analyze text-matching and paper mill websites (Vie, 2013).

In this first example, two writing teachers discuss a variety of ways to familiarize L2 graduate students with textual borrowing practices (Barks & Watts, 2001). They first critiqued the limited ways that textbooks tend to address this issue. Textbooks, they asserted, tend to present black and white definitions of plagiarism, warn students about how serious the "crime" of plagiarism is in Western contexts, and finally introduce exercises in paraphrase, summary, and quotation (p. 252). Barks and Watts believe that such a simplistic approach is both pedagogically unsound and (following Pennycook, 1996) intellectually arrogant (Barks & Watts, 2001, p. 253).

The authors then present a variety of instructional strategies culled from the literature and from their own teaching materials for developing students' understanding of and skill at textual borrowing. First, they suggest ways to discuss with students the complexities of authorship, notions of originality and plagiarism, and cross-cultural practices of textual borrowing. Noting that students and teachers are easily attracted to simple explanations and unambiguous definitions, they encourage teachers not to settle for the easy way out, but to engage students in lively if difficult discussion—the kind of interaction and intellectual engagement "that ultimately lead to greater understanding" (p. 254). To spur this discussion, Barks and Watts present a list of true-false statements to be responded to twice, once for the context of students' home countries and once for the United States (the context of the authors' teaching), such as "It is acceptable to copy passages from a source text and use them in your paper without attribution" (p. 255). In a second discussion activity, the authors pose open-ended questions about students' practices of using source texts and their own definitions of terms such as *author* and *intellectual property*. A third example borrowed from Swales and Feak (1994; see also Feak and Swales, 2009, and Swales and Feak, 2012) asks students to consider the purposes of citation practices in English language academic contexts and to compare these practices with their own understandings. With exercises like these, the authors raise students' awareness of the issues surrounding textual borrowing and build a foundation for instruction in the practices themselves.

Students who write in academic contexts need to learn how to integrate the voices of the authors they read into their own work. In the next set of exercises adapted from ideas in Howard (1995), Barks and Watts recommend helping students with the intermediary step of textual borrowing, which Howard calls patchwriting. (As discussed in previous sections, patchwriting includes textual borrowing techniques that would technically be labeled plagiarism, such as copying, paraphrasing without attribution, and using short phrases from sources to compose a paragraph.) Students then need to cross the line from patchwriting to acceptable borrowing techniques. Swales and Feak (1994, 2012) showed how students can paraphrase appropriately by retaining all technical terms from their sources, relieving students of the worry of not knowing how to find synonyms for technical vocabulary. Barks and Watts then cite an example from the early 1984 book on academic writing by Arnaudet and Barrett on how to simplify detailed definitions of technical words in short summaries. Finally, they mention how students can appropriate stock phrases used in academic writing without fear of plagiarizing, a technique I also discussed in an earlier article (Casanave, 2003). Formulaic phrases that express a function such as framing a paper, introducing results or findings, and signaling arguments can all be used directly in students' writing (see Hyland, 2009, and academic phrasebanks on websites). The examples from Barks and Watts (2001, p. 260) include: *The data show that...; One explanation for this may be...;* and *It should be noted that....* "Stealing" formulaic and functional phrases like these is not considered plagiarism according to most scholars.

Barks and Watts then ask students to take an "ethnographic approach," recommended by Hirvela (1997), Johns (1997), and others. In this approach, students examine the interactive literacy practices in their chosen fields by analyzing various features of published articles. They examine, for example, how and why citations are used, interview faculty about their practices of textual borrowing, and analyze how they themselves, their peers, and their own teachers use citations. These investigations then feed into students own writing and their reflections on their writing.

Barks and Watts conclude with an important dilemma, one that has plagued my own teaching for many years, and that is the separation of courses for L2 students into reading and writing courses. Both reading and writing are considered closely linked interactive practices in academic writing (Hirvela, 2016) but are still often considered separate skills. For example, in Japan I was assigned to teach "professional English" courses to graduate students who wished to improve their reading and writing in English. The reading and writing courses were listed separately, and most students had no time to take both of these labor-intensive courses at the same time. In some cases, separating reading and writing courses may be justified, but in graduate-level EAP instruction, reading and writing are two aspects of the same interactive practice. We cannot teach L2 students about writing from sources and textual borrowing without involving them deeply in reading activities. In making decisions about how to help students with academic writing, administrators, curriculum developers, and teachers themselves are advised to merge reading and writing courses whenever possible.

In a second example of possible classroom activities, I turn to an article by Vie (2013) in which she described how she has helped her students analyze text-matching websites and paper mills. I hope readers will seek out this article and study it in detail. She begins by noting that increasing numbers of institutions are now requiring students to submit their writing to sites like Turnitin, in spite of widespread critiques and calls for more focus on pedagogy rather than fear. In such cases, Vie has called for a "pedagogy of resistance" that encourages composition teachers to resist plagiarism detection technologies, as I mentioned earlier in this chapter. However, in addition to fostering fear, "...plagiarism detective services [have] become seductively sweet..." (p. 4) in their claims to save teachers time and so are hard to resist.

As a classroom activity of resistance, Vie suggests that students compare two websites, one a "plagiarism detection site" and one a paper mill (e.g. Turnitin and SchoolSucks) to critically analyze the sites for underlying assumptions, methods of use, types of artifacts, audiences, and purposes. She believes that "asking students to examine online paper mill sites alongside plagiarism detection sites equips them to better understand the limitations of doing all of their research online rather than relying on a mixture of sources" (p. 8). Students who do such an analysis will also become aware of how systems like these work and so take greater control of their own understanding of the complexities of plagiarism as well as of their complicity in perpetuating such systems. Even asking students to analyze only the main page of these sites can lead to an informative discussion.

Vie's lessons with students are in great part visual. She points out that students can even learn a great deal just by examining each site's cover pages, asking what the images, colors, and messages imply and speculating about the truth of the claims that each site makes. Students can also critically discuss paper topics and sample essays on the websites, noting, for example, the irony of paper topics on the subject of "honesty" on the School Sucks site. Vie also comments that her students "are often surprised at the shoddy work that is presented on most of these sites," with papers that seem intentionally substandard (p. 9). Students are apparently expected to fix the problems, and so make the papers their own.

The Turnitin cover sheet, in contrast to the one for School Sucks, appeals more to institutions and instructors than to students (Vie, p. 10; Figure 3, p. 11). The colors, among other things are different, with red suggesting danger. Students who analyze this site will notice that much of the discourse emphasizes good writing pedagogy and downplays plagiarism detection. Other discourse sets up false binaries of good and bad practices (and so good and bad students?) (p. 11). The discourse of any such sites can be analyzed critically by students, as pointed out by Vie:

> Students can examine these sites or similar ones, considering how each site acts as a persuasive text rather than simply a space offering a commodity for sale. As well, students may be guided to discuss how the sites themselves position students and instructors: as adversaries pitted against one another in warlike montages? (p. 11)

The overall purpose of this classroom activity is to help students (and teachers, I might add) "embrace these controversies as evidence of the complicated nature of authorship, integrity, and plagiarism" (p. 12). Rather than being victims of such sites, students can become analysts and critics of the sites as part of classroom writing assignments. Vie concludes by insisting that all of us need to ask the difficult questions about the financial benefits for these for-profit corporations, benefits that accrue from the "intellectual work of others" (p. 13).

Ongoing Questions

Many L2 students need to learn to write academic essays, reports, and theses. In all of these cases, they will be asked to draw on print and internet sources to build and support ideas and arguments. In their disciplinary and subject matter classes, they are not likely to get specific instruction and practice in writing from sources, but may simply be given a plagiarism policy statement at the beginning of a class. If such students are not also enrolled in a writing class of some kind, I am not sure how they can best learn to write from sources except by trial and error. Will they get good (and sympathetic) feedback from disciplinary instructors? If on the other hand students are enrolled in a writing class in which teachers understand the complexities and ambiguities of plagiarism, will there be enough time for instructors to help students become aware of conventions for writing from both print and digital sources and to practice this complex skill? Can teachers resist the easy stereotypes of cultural explanations for students' plagiarizing and patchwriting? And if we insist that students strictly follow Western conventions for textual borrowing and citation, are we arrogantly imposing ethnocentric cultural norms, as Pennycook (1994, 1996) suggested long ago? How are cultural norms of textual borrowing in non-Western cultures changing as scholarship becomes increasingly international, multiliterate, and digital? What roles, if any, are there for copying and imitation in the L2 writing class? And how are practices and expectations for multivocalic and multimedia texts changing as a result of digital technology?

Finally, Pecorari (2015; see also the other short commentaries in this Disciplinary Dialogue in the *Journal of Second Language Writing*) has asked whether it is "time to close the case" on research on plagiarism. She asserted in a opinion piece that we do not need more research on plagiarism that covers ground we already know. Instead of investigating students', teachers', and gatekeepers' attitudes and practices by means of questionnaires and interviews, she would have us delve further into specific contexts and individual variability of understandings and practices within those contexts. She also urged L2 researchers to read widely, beyond our own disciplines, and to do what we can to disseminate findings to others outside the L2 writing field. This last goal will remain challenging as long as faculty in the disciplines (and even in L1 composition) continue to show as little interest in L2 writing scholarship as they have in the past. So the final questions in this section ask what kinds of research do we still need on the topic of plagiarism, textual re-use, and intertextual practices in order to push our understanding forward? And how can we do a better job at learning how that research translates into effective pedagogical practices in L2 writing classes at all levels?

Beliefs and Practices

Beliefs

1. Before reading this chapter, what were your beliefs about and definitions of plagiarism? If your beliefs have changed, describe the changes.
2. Do you believe that intentional and unintentional plagiarism should be handled similarly or differently at the institutional level? The classroom level? At the educational level?
3. Do you believe that intentional and unintentional plagiarism should be handled similarly or differently in Western ESL settings and in non-Western EFL settings?
4. Do you believe that writing from sources is a skill that can be taught, or must it be primarily learned through practice over time? To what extent are both essential?
5. Many possible reasons have been given for why both L1 and L2 students plagiarize. Which of the following reasons do you believe can be addressed through instruction? How would you do this? (Keep in mind that even writing instructors and legal scholars do not agree on what plagiarism is!)
   a. No knowledge of plagiarism or plagiarism policies.
   b. Knowledge about plagiarism but incomplete, and/or with misunderstandings and confusions.
   c. No awareness of distinctions between plagiarizing and patchwriting.
   d. Insufficient proficiency in English to write without plagiarizing.

e. Understanding of plagiarism and the need to cite sources but inadequate strategies for knowing how to do this.

f. No time to write an "original" paper.

g. Laziness.

h. Boredom with a topic.

i. Lack of knowledge about a topic.

j. Different expectations in the home educational culture about writing from sources.

k. Belief that the internet and other public sources are open to everyone without the need to acknowledge sources.

l. Lack of confidence in own writing.

m. No interest in writing; just in need of a grade.

n. Actual intent to knowingly cheat.

Practices

1. What stories, if any, have your students or colleagues told you about the practice of plagiarism at your school?

2. What written or unwritten institutional or departmental regulations exist to define and control plagiarism at your school? Locate a policy statement, and discuss in as much detail as you can how the policies might be applied to L2 writing students' work.

3. Examine several pieces of your own source-based writing in light of your current understanding of plagiarism and patchwriting. What techniques have you used to incorporate the words and ideas of others into your own writing?

4. If you have experiences dealing with a plagiarism problem in class, or if you provide guidelines for your students, describe these and compare them with those of your classmates or colleagues.

5. If you, your peers, or your students are from non-Western cultures, compare your views on copying, imitation, and memorization as (a) instructional techniques in the writing class and (b) practices that are or are not allowed in academic writing.

6. Try designing a (multi-step) source-based writing task for a group of L2 students that you are currently working with or hope to work with in which you decide about and specify the following: the authentic aspects of the task (if any); the real or imagined audience(s); and the means by which you will attempt to prevent intentional or unintentional plagiarism in part by the design of the assignment.

References

Abasi, A. R., Akbari, N. & Graves, B. (2006). Discourse appropriation, construction of identities, and the complex issue of plagiarism: ESL students writing in graduate school. *Journal of Second Language Writing, 15*(2), 102–117.

Abasi, A. R., & Graves, B. (2008). Academic literacy and plagiarism: Conversations with international graduate students and disciplinary professors. *Journal of English for Academic Purposes, 7*(4), 221–233.

Ahmadi, A. (2014). Plagiarism in the academic context: A study of Iranian EFL learners. *Research Ethics, 10*(3), 151–168.

Angélil-Carter, S. (2000/2014). *Stolen language? Plagiarism in writing.* New York: Routledge/Taylor & Francis.

Barks, D., & Watts, P. (2001). Textual borrowing strategies for graduate-level ESL writers. In D. Belcher & A. Hirvela (Eds.), *Linking literacies: Perspectives on L2 reading-writing connections* (pp. 246–267). Ann Arbor: University of Michigan Press.

Belcher, D., & Hirvela, A. (Eds.). (2001). *Linking literacies: Perspectives on L2 reading-writing connections.* Ann Arbor: University of Michigan Press.

Bloch, J. (2001). Plagiarism and the ESL student: From printed to electronic texts. In D. Belcher & A. Hirvela (Eds.), *Linking literacies: Perspectives on L2 reading-writing connections* (pp. 209–228). Ann Arbor: University of Michigan Press.

Bloch, J. (2008a). Blogging as a bridge between multiple forms of literacy: The use of blogs in an academic writing class. In D. Belcher & A. Hirvela, (Eds.), *The oral-literate connection* (pp. 288–309). Ann Arbor: University of Michigan Press.

Bloch, J. (2008b). Plagiarism across cultures: Is there a difference? In C. Eisner & M. Vicinus (Eds.), *Originality, imitation, and plagiarism: Teaching writing in the digital age* (pp. 219–230). Ann Arbor: University of Michigan Press.

Bloch, J. (2008c). *Technologies in the second language composition classroom.* Ann Arbor: University of Michigan Press.

Bloch, J. (2012). *Plagiarism, intellectual property and the teaching of writing.* Bristol, U.K.: Multilingual Matters.

Bloch, J., & Chi, L. (1995). A comparison of the use of citations in Chinese and English academic discourse. In D. Belcher & G. Braine (Eds.), *Academic writing in a second language: Essays on research and pedagogy* (pp. 231–274). Norwood, NJ: Ablex.

Buranen, L. (1999). "But I *wasn't* cheating": Plagiarism and cross-cultural mythology. In L. Buranen & A. M. Roy (Eds.), *Perspectives on plagiarism and intellectual property in a postmodern world* (pp. 63–74). Albany: SUNY Press.

Campbell, C. (1990). Writing with others' words: Using background reading text in academic compositions. In B. Kroll (Ed.), *Second language writing: Research insights for the classroom* (pp. 211–230). Cambridge, U.K.: Cambridge University Press.

Casanave, C. P. (2003). Multiple uses of applied linguistics literature in a multidisciplinary graduate EAP class. *ELT Journal, 57*(1), 43–50.

Chandrasoma, R., Thompson, C., & Pennycook, A. (2004). Beyond plagiarism: Transgressive and nontransgressive intertextuality. *Journal of Language, Identity, and Education, 3*(3), 171–193.

Chien, S.-C. (2014). Cultural constructions of plagiarism in student writing: Teachers' perceptions and responses. *Research in the Teaching of English, 49*(2), 120–140.

Currie, P. (1998). Staying out of trouble: Apparent plagiarism and academic survival. *Journal of Second Language Writing, 2*, 131–148.

Deckert, G. (1993). Perspectives on plagiarism from ESL students in Hong Kong. *Journal of Second Language Writing, 2*, 131–148.

Dryden, L. M. (1999). A distant mirror or through the looking glass? Plagiarism and intellectual property in Japanese education. In L. Buranen & A. M. Roy (Eds.), *Perspectives on plagiarism and intellectual property in a postmodern world* (pp. 75–95). Albany: SUNY Press.

Eisner, C., & Vicinus, M. (Eds.). (2008). *Originality, imitation, and plagiarism: Teaching writing in the digital age.* Ann Arbor: University of Michigan Press.

Emerson, L. (2008). Plagiarism, a Turnitin trial, and an experience of cultural disorientation. In C. Eisner & M. Vicinus (Eds.), *Originality, imitation, and plagiarism: Teaching writing in the digital age* (pp. 183–194). Ann Arbor: University of Michigan Press.

Feak, C. B., & Swales, J. M. (2009). *Telling a research story: Writing a literature review.* Ann Arbor: University of Michigan Press.

Flowerdew, J., & Li, Y. (2007a). Language re-use among apprentice scientists writing for publication. *Applied Linguistics, 28*(3), 440–465.

Flowerdew, J., & Li, Y. (2007b). Plagiarism and second language writing in an electronic age. *Annual Review of Applied Linguistics, 27,* 161–183.

Gu, Q., & Brooks, J. (2008). Beyond the accusation of plagiarism. *System, 36,* 337–352.

Hirvela, A. (1997). "Disciplinary portfolios" and EAP writing instruction. *English for Specific Purposes, 16*(2), 83–100.

Hirvela, A. (2016). *Connecting reading & writing in second language writing instruction* (2nd ed.). Ann Arbor: University of Michigan Press.

Howard, R. M. (1995). Plagiarisms, authorships, and the academic death penalty. *College English, 57*(1), 788–805.

Howard, R. M. (1999). *Standing in the shadow of giants: Plagiarists, authors, collaborators.* Stamford, CT: Ablex.

Howard, R. M. (2007). Understanding "internet plagiarism." *Computers and Composition, 24,* 3–15.

Hu, G., & Lei, J. (2012). Investigating Chinese university students' knowledge of and attitudes toward plagiarism from an integrated perspective. *Language Learning, 61*(3), 813–850.

Hyland, K. (2009). *Academic discourse.* London: Continuum.

Hyland, K. (2011). Disciplinary specificity: Discourse, context, and ESP. In D. Belcher, A. Johns, & B. Paltridge (Eds.), *New directions in English for specific purposes research* (pp. 6–24). Ann Arbor: University of Michigan Press.

Introna, L., & Hayes, N. (2008). Plagiarism detection systems and international students: Detecting plagiarism, copying or learning? In T. Roberts (Ed.), *Student plagiarism in an online world: Problems and solutions* (pp. 108–123). Hershey, PA: Information Science Reference.

Johns, A. M. (1997). *Text, role, and context: Developing academic literacies.* Cambridge, U.K.: Cambridge University Press.

Keck, C. (2014). Copying, paraphrasing, and academic writing development: A re-examination of L1 and L2 summarization practices. *Journal of Second Language Writing, 25,* 4–22.

Kroll, B. (1988). How college freshmen view plagiarism. *Written Communication, 5,* 203–221.

Lea, M. R., & Jones, S. (2011). Digital literacies in higher education: Exploring textual and technological practice. *Studies in Higher Education, 36*(4), 377–393.

Ledwith, A., & Rísquez, A. (2008). Using anti-plagiarism software to promote academic honesty in the context of peer reviewed assignments. *Studies in Higher Education, 33*(4), 371–384.

Le Ha, P. (2006). Plagiarism and overseas students: Stereotypes again? *ELT Journal, 60*(1), 76–78.

Lei, J., & Hu, G. (2014). Chinese university lecturers' stance on plagiarism: Does knowledge matter? *ELT Journal, 68*(1), 41–51.

Lei, J., & Hu, G. (2015). Chinese university EFL teachers' perceptions of plagiarism. *Higher Education, 70,* 551–565.

Li, Y., & Casanave, C. P. (2012). Two first year students' strategies for writing from sources: Patchwriting or plagiarism? *Journal of Second Language Writing, 21*(2), 165–180.

Liu, D. (2005). Plagiarism in ESOL students: Is cultural conditioning truly the major culprit? *ELT Journal, 59*(3), 234–241.

LoCastro, V., & Masuko, M. (1997). *Plagiarism and academic writing of NNS learners.* Paper presented at the 31st Annual meeting of the Teacher of English to Speakers of Other Languages, Orlando, FL, March 11–15.

Lunsford, A. A., & West, S. (1996). Intellectual property and composition studies. *College Composition and Communication, 47,* 383–411.

Marsh, B. (2004). Turnitin.com and the scriptural enterprise of plagiarism detection. *Computers and Composition, 21,* 427–438.

Marsh, B. (2007). *Plagiarism: Alchemy and remedy in higher education.* Albany: SUNY Press.

Martin, D. E. (2011). Culture and unethical conduct: Understanding the impact of individualism and collectivism on actual plagiarism. *Management Learning, 43*(3), 261–272.

Matalene, C. (1985). Contrastive rhetoric: An American writing teacher in China. *College English, 47*(8), 789–808.

Ouellette, M. (2008). Weaving strands of writer identity: Self as author and the NNES "plagiarist." *Journal of Second Language Writing, 17*(4), 255–273.

Pecorari, D. (2001). Plagiarism and international students: How the English-speaking university responds. In D. Belcher & A. Hirvela (Eds.), *Linking literacies: Perspectives on L2 reading-writing connections* (pp. 229–245). Ann Arbor: University of Michigan Press.

Pecorari, D. (2008). *Academic writing and plagiarism: A linguistic analysis.* London: Continuum.

Pecorari, D. (2013). *Teaching to avoid plagiarism: How to promote good source use.* Buckingham, U.K.: Open University Press.

Pecorari, D. (2015). Plagiarism in second language writing: Is it time to close the case? *Journal of Second Language Writing, 30*, 94–99.

Pecorari, D., & Petric, B. (2014). Plagiarism in second-language writing. *Language Teaching, 47*(3), 269–302.

Pecorari, D., & Shaw, P. (2012). Types of student intertexuality and faculty attitudes. *Journal of Second Language Writing, 21*(4), 317–345.

Pennington, M. C. (2010). Plagiarism in the academy: Towards a proactive pedagogy. *Writing & Pedagogy, 2*, 147–162.

Pennycook, A. (1994). The complex contexts of plagiarism: A reply to Deckert. *Journal of Second Language Writing, 3*, 277–284.

Pennycook, A. (1996). Borrowing others' words: Text, ownership, memory, and plagiarism. *TESOL Quarterly, 30*, 201–230.

Pennycook, A. (2001). *Critical applied linguistics: A critical introduction.* Mahwah, NJ: Lawrence Erlbaum.

Polio, C., & Shi, L. (2012). Perceptions and beliefs about textual appropriation and source use in second language writing. *Journal of Second Language Writing, 21*(2), 95–101.

Purdy, J. P. (2009). Anxiety and the archive: Understanding plagiarism detection. *Computers and Composition, 26*, 65–77.

Ridley, D. (2008). *The literature review: A step-by-step guide for students.* Thousand Oaks, CA: Sage Publications.

Roig, M. (2001). Plagiarism and paraphrasing criteria of college and university professors. *Ethics & Behavior, 11*(3), 307–323.

Roy, A. M. (1999). Whose words these are I think I know: Plagiarism, the postmodern, and faculty attitudes. In L. Buranen & A. M. Roy (Eds.), *Perspectives on plagiarism and intellectual property in a postmodern world* (pp. 55–61). Albany: SUNY Press.

Scollon, R. (1995). Plagiarism and ideology: Identity in intercultural discourse. *Language in Society, 24*, 1–28.

Shi, L. (2004). Textual borrowing in second language writing. *Written Communication, 21*(2), 171–200.

Shi, L. (2006). Cultural backgrounds and textual appropriation. *Language Awareness, 15*, 264–282.

Shi, L. (2011). Common knowledge, learning, and citation practices in university writing. *Research in the Teaching of English, 45*(3), 308–334.

Simmons, S. C. (1999). Competing notions of authorship: A historical look at students and textbooks on plagiarism and cheating. In L. Buranen & A. M. Roy (Eds.), *Perspectives on plagiarism and intellectual property in a postmodern world* (pp. 41–51). Albany: SUNY Press.

Song-Turner, H. (2008). Plagiarism: Academic dishonesty or 'blind spot' of multicultural education? *Australian Universities Review, 50*(2), 39–50.

Sowden, C. (2005). Plagiarism and the culture of multilingual students in higher education abroad. *ELT Journal, 59*(3), 226–233.

Spigelman, C. (1999). The ethics of appropriation in peer writing groups. In L. Buranen & A. M. Roy (Eds.), *Perspectives on plagiarism and intellectual property in a postmodern world* (pp. 231–240). Albany: SUNY Press.

Spack, R. (1997). The acquisition of academic literacy in a second language: A longitudinal case study. *Written Communication, 14*, 3–62.

Spatt, B. (2011). *Writing from sources* (8th ed.). New York: Bedford/St. Martin's.

Stapleton, P. (2012). Gauging the effectiveness of anti-plagiarism software: An empirical study of second language graduate writers. *Journal of English for Academic Purposes, 11*(2), 125–133.

Stearns, L. (1999). Copy wrong: Plagiarism, process, property, and the law. In L. Buranen & A. M. Roy (Eds.), *Perspectives on plagiarism and intellectual property in a postmodern world* (pp. 5–17). Albany: SUNY Press.

Sun, Y.-C. (2013). Do journal authors plagiarize? Using plagiarism detection software to uncover matching text across disciplines. *Journal of English for Academic Purposes, 12*, 264–272.

Sutherland-Smith, W. (2008). *Plagiarism, the internet and student learning: Improving academic integrity.* Abingdon, U.K.: Routledge.

Sutherland-Smith, W., & Carr, R. (2005). Turnitin.com: Teachers' perspectives of anti-plagiarism software in raising issues of educational integrity. *Journal of University Teaching and Learning Practice, 2*(3). Available at: http://ro.uow.edu.au/jutlp/vol2/iss3/10

Swales, J. (1987). Utilizing the literatures in teaching the research paper. *TESOL Quarterly, 21*(1), 41–68.

Swales, J. M. (1990). *Genre analysis: English in academic and research settings.* New York: Cambridge University Press.

Swales, J. M., & Feak, C. B. (1994). *Academic writing for graduate students: A course for nonnative speakers of English.* Ann Arbor: University of Michigan Press.

Swales, J. M. & Feak, C. B. (2012). *Academic writing for graduate students: Essential tasks and skills* (3rd ed.). Ann Arbor: University of Michigan Press.

Swearingen, C. J. (1999). Originality, authenticity, imitation, and plagiarism: Augustine's Chinese cousins. In L. Buranen & A. M. Roy (Eds.), *Perspectives on plagiarism and intellectual property in a postmodern world* (pp. 19–39). Albany: SUNY Press.

Tang, R. (2012). Two sides of the same coin: Challenges and opportunities for scholars from EFL backgrounds. In R. Tang (Ed.), *Academic writing in a second or foreign language* (pp. 204–232). London: Continuum.

Vie, S. (2013). A pedagogy of resistance toward plagiarism detection technologies. *Computers and Composition, 30*, 3–15.

Walker, J. (2010). Measuring plagiarism: Research what students do, not what they say they do. *Studies in Higher Education, 35*(1), 41–59.

Weigle, S., & Parker, K. (2012). Source-text borrowing in an integrated reading assignment. *Journal of Second Language Writing, 21*(2), 118–133.

Wen, Q., & Gao, Y. (2007). Viewpoint: Dual publication and academic inequality. *International Journal of Applied Linguistics, 17*(2), 221–225.

Wette, R. (2010). Evaluating student learning in a university-level EAP unit on writing using sources. *Journal of Second Language Writing, 19*(3), 158–177.

Wheeler, G. (2009). Plagiarism in the Japanese universities: Truly a cultural matter? *Journal of Second Language Writing 18*(1), 17–29.

Woodmansee, M., & Jaszi, P. (1995). The law of texts: Copyright in the academy. *College English, 57*, 769–787.

Chapter 7

Assessment

"Not everything that can be counted counts, and not everything that counts can be counted." (Cameron, 1963, p. 13, but used widely since by many others)

"No one can make a trustworthy judgment about a student's skill or ability in writing without seeing multiple pieces of writing, written on multiple occasions, in multiple genres, directed to different audiences, written in more or less realistic writing conditions." (Elbow, 1994, p. 44)

"Whether a 25-minute essay written on an unfamiliar topic is scored by a human or a computer—or by a human and a computer—it is still a poor representation of writing and can provide only severely limited information about the writer." (Condon, 2013. p. 100)

"Even if one had a perfect [machine scoring] system … that almost perfectly correlated with scoring by human readers, it would still be the case that NO ONE was actually reading the student's writing and attending to what he or she has to say and how it is said." (Ravitch, 2013, par. 7, caps in original)

"We have mistaken elevated uniformity and consistency for fairness, resulting in writing assessments that are inconsistent with many of the most fundamental values and best practices associated with the field." (Neal, 2011, p. 132)

LEADING QUESTIONS

- What distinctions are there between assessment and testing?
- What purposes does assessment of writing serve?
- What are some of the basic problems we face in making fair and accurate assessments of students' writing?
- What are some issues surrounding notions in writing assessment such as reliability, validity, objectivity, and subjectivity?
- What aspects of writing can and cannot be scored by a computer?
- What ethical issues are implicated in writing assessment, particularly of L2 students?
- What alternatives are there to traditional assessment in L2 writing classes?

Introduction to the Issues

Many of the decisions that writing teachers and their institutions make about both L1 and L2 students revolve around assessment of students' writing. Assessment activities and schemes pervade language and content classes and the broader system of schooling as well. Indeed, in most countries assessment of all kinds, not just of writing, is such an inherent part of the whole enterprise of schooling that it is difficult to imagine doing without it. Because a culture of assessment is built into the schooling enterprise, teachers rarely ask whether they need to assess their students. After all, the system often starts, continues, and ends with assessments of many kinds: for entrance, placement, progress, and exit purposes.

Not all teachers are happy about the culture of assessment they are immersed in. Moreover, a surprising number of teachers have had no training in assessing writing, particularly those who have been in the field for a while and missed out on more recent teacher education programs (Crusan, Plakans, & Gebril, 2016). But regardless of individual teachers' opinions and beliefs about assessment, if students are to be given a grade or admitted into or released from a class or program, their ability, performance, and progress usually need to be evaluated. Rather than recommending wholesale overthrow of assessment schemes, therefore, most teachers ask instead how their students can be assessed accurately and fairly. The issue of accurate and fair assessment of student writing probably constitutes the major dilemma in both the L1 and L2 writing fields, and I will discuss the specifics of some of the controversies later in this chapter. But first, let me highlight several key questions that L2 writing teachers need to consider as they reflect on their own beliefs about assessment and as they plan writing and assessment activities within their own classrooms.

Early in the decision-making process, writing teachers and administrators need to be clear about what they mean by assessment. Consider the following terms: *assessment, testing, measurement, grading, evaluating.* All are related but refer to different aspects of assessment (perhaps the broadest of the terms). By giving some kind of test, we can measure something and then assign a grade or a score. We can also evaluate students' writing in a variety of ways that may or may not result in a grade or a score, although informal judgments of some kind are always present in an evaluation. In the early days of the general language testing field, Bachman (1990) distinguished among the terms *measurement, test,* and *evaluation. Measurement* refers to "the process of quantifying the characteristics of persons according to explicit procedures and rules" (p. 18). A *test* is a measurement of a "specific sample of an individual's behavior" (p. 20). *Evaluation* refers to collection and perusal of information for the purpose of making decisions about people (p. 22). Later, Bachman and Palmer (2010) used the terms *testing* and *assessment* interchangeably, oddly defining assessment as "the process of collecting and recording information" (pp. 19–20) rather than as a judgment of some kind based on the information that has been collected. However, I will distinguish these terms in this chapter, referring to *assessment* as a broad term for a judgment (procedure and outcome) based on information and to *testing* as one of many techniques for making assessments. It is possible to assess for the purposes of evaluating without testing, just as it is possible to test without assessing and evaluating. Assessing for the purposes of evaluating may take the form of a test, but it requires some kind of judgment about the quality or characteristics of a piece of writing and some kind of connection to a decision about students or to instructional activities in the form of washback (the effects an assessment has on instruction and learning) (Bailey, 1996, 1998) and feedback. A simple score or grade is not enough.

In all cases, both low- and high-stakes writing assessments, writing teachers and administrators are also faced with concerns about what they understand the purpose(s) to be of assessing students' writing (see also Bailey's 1998 discussion of the dilemmas of conflicting purposes in language assessment). Is students' writing being assessed in order to see if the students are qualified to enter a particular school or program? In this case, writing assessment functions as a selection and sorting instrument. Is writing being assessed in order to place students in some kind of hierarchy, such as in a remedial writing class, a low-, mid-, or high-level ESL class, or an honors writing class? In this case, students are guaranteed some kind of placement, but the specifics of placement decisions may determine whether students can take other classes or get credit for their writing classes. Within writing classes, writing is assessed as well, but possibly without grades and scores. Ongoing assessment of writing (i.e., formative assessment) is common in process writing classes and in classes where students are asked to keep portfolios (print or electronic) of their writing. In other words, teachers and researchers often assess writing without formal testing as a way to get a sense of whether and how students develop writing skills over time (see also Chapter 5, this book, Paths to Improvement). A final portfolio or collection of writings may then be assessed sum-matively to indicate what students have learned or how their writing has changed during a term. Writing assessment may also take the form of an exit mechanism, as is the case on some university campuses. In some high-stakes writing assessment, students who do not pass a writing test are not allowed to graduate, in spite of passing grades in other classes.

Formal assessments of writing for purposes of deciding who enters and exits a school, class, or program are considered high-stakes in the sense that students' lives can be affected by the outcomes in major ways. Large-scale and standardized language assessments for L2 students such as those designed and sponsored by ETS (Educational Testing Service) (e.g., TOEFL®, TOEIC®) now often include a writing component and have been criticized for their lack of local relevance (Crusan, 2010a; Huot & Neal, 2006). Such huge, high-stakes international tests have also spurred controversies surrounding automated (electronic) essay scoring (referred to variously as automated essay scoring [AES], automated essay evaluation [AEE], e-scoring, e-rating, machine-scoring, or computerized scoring) to replace or dominate assessment by human readers. Less formal assessments that evaluate proficiency and progress in writing for purposes of ongoing evaluation and feedback to students are considered low-stakes in that they do not usually affect students' lives in major and irrevocable ways.

Teachers need to be aware as well that formal assessments of many kinds, not just of writing, may not really be designed to benefit students, but to provide evidence to agencies and funders that a particular (writing) program is working well, to influence changes in curriculum, through the back door as it were, by virtue of washback effects on curriculum and pedagogy (Bailey, 1996; Hamp-Lyons, 1997; Messick, 1996), to exert some kind of social or political control (Shohamy, 1997, 2001b; Spolsky, 1997), or to aim for social and political equality (Hamp-Lyons, 2014). In all cases, the intended uses of a writing assessment and its consequences need to be clear to everyone (Bachman & Palmer, 2010; McNamara, 2006).

In short, writing teachers and administrators need to clarify for themselves and for students what the purposes are for different kinds of assessments of students' writing, particularly those on which decisions about students are based, e.g., sorting before a class or program begins or ends (selective evaluation), demonstrating ongoing growth (formative evaluation), or showing achievement at the end of a course or program (summative evaluation) (Cumming, 2001). If there is a social or political agenda to writing assessment, this too needs to be made clear to all stakeholders (Bachman & Palmer, 2010; McNamara, 2006; Shohamy, 2001b).

Once the purposes for assessment are clarified, the question becomes what kinds of assessment instruments will best achieve those purposes. It is here that decisions become entangled in practical, institutional, and logistical constraints in addition to challenging our beliefs and knowledge of how students' writing ability or growth can be accurately assessed. In large-scale assessment (state- or nation-wide, or throughout an entire institution), how much time and money are required for teachers, students, and administrators to do a fair assessment? In such cases, a single essay written under constraints of time and place, such as TOEFL's Writing Test (formerly TWE®: Test of Written English), may be the only practical solution. Similarly, raters of student placement essays and writing teachers with large classes are constrained by the difficulties of finding time to read and assess possibly hundreds of student papers. Even though a single piece of writing is no longer thought to represent accurately a student's ability, it is often not feasible to assess multiple writings, particularly in large-scale assessments. One of the biggest dilemmas in writing assessment is therefore finding an accurate yet practical means of assessing. Computerized essay scoring programs continue to be developed to help alleviate the human burden (Shermis & Burstein, 2013), but these have sparked much controversy in the testing field, including the trade-offs between reliable computerized scores and loss of local validity (Elliot & Williamson, 2013; Ericcson & Haswell, 2006; Huot & Neal, 2006;

Ravitch, 2013). This controversy will be discussed further in the section on Computer Scoring of Essays.

Questions about fair and accurate assessments of writing have confronted us for many years. In many kinds of L1 and L2 writing assessment, particularly when a numerical score is needed for record keeping or accountability, assessment involves one or more readers' evaluating actual samples of writing. In the past, indirect measures of writing that did not involve any actual writing, such as multiple choice tests of grammar and style, were used as assessment instruments because they were considered objective and reliable and could be subjected to the psychometrician's statistical tools "proving" them to be so. Now, however, direct tests of writing, also called performance assessments, in which students actually write something, are much more widely used. Although direct assessments have face validity and authenticity to varying degrees, they have proved to be very difficult to score in ways that were traditionally considered valid and reliable. More recent e-scoring systems for direct tests of writing are considered reliable but are the subject of great controversy (see Huot & Neal's, 2006, "techno-history" of writing assessment and discussion later in this chapter). And as Messick (1994, p. 21) pointed out, the term *direct assessment* is a bit of a misnomer, given that it is mediated by people's judgment. The main dilemmas, which will be discussed in more detail, lie in the fact that different readers rate the same essay in different ways, and that students themselves do not write consistently. Writing teachers and scholars are thus hard pressed to define what they mean by a "fair and accurate" score.

Another major question asks what the assessments are assessing when we are not even certain if there is such a thing as "general writing ability." Is writing ability a general behavior made up of separable complex skills? If so, how do we describe those skills? Are they connected or not with particular domains and genres? And if we do not see writing as consisting of a complex of skills, how do we characterize the act of writing? Questions such as these pose dilemmas for all who evaluate writing and other complex performances in school settings, and discussions in both the L1 and the L2 literature demonstrate how thorny this issue is. (See the excellent discussion by Messick, 1994, in which he lays out many of the controversies in performance-based educational assessment, the thorough discussion of dilemmas in language testing by Fulcher, 2015, and Crusan's, 2013, review of issues in assessing writing.)

For instance, it is one thing to say that we wish to evaluate the quality of students' writing, and quite another to define in unambiguous terms what we mean by "quality." In the case of L2 student writing, evaluators look for evidence that students control the basic grammar and vocabulary of the language, yet every writing teacher and scholar knows that writing quality is not determined just by writers' control of the linguistic aspects of their writing. Cross-cultural research shows as well that standards for "good writing" may differ across cultures and disciplines (Cai, 1999; Currie, 1994; Hamp-Lyons & Zhang, 2001; Li, 1996; see also the literature on contrastive rhetoric, Chapter 2 of this volume and elsewhere, and Chapter 5 in this volume). Additionally, a debate in the EAP scholarship concerns whether assessment instruments (usually of reading and writing) need to deal with discipline- and domain-specific content and performance or with more general language proficiency (Clapham, 2000; Fulcher, 1999, 2000, 2015; Robinson & Ross, 1996). In all these cases major efforts by test designers and committees of teachers therefore go into constructing rubrics that try to encapsulate descriptively what constitutes a strong or weak essay, or more detailed rubrics in analytic scoring that describe different dimensions of writing (e.g., coherence, logical flow of ideas, mechanics) that are then assigned a number. (See, for example, the early composition profile in Jacobs, Zinkgraf, Wormuth, Hartfiel, and Hughey, 1981, and that same profile plus additional examples in Ferris and Hedgcock, 2014, and in Weigle, 2002; see also Crusan, 2010a, 2015 on rubrics). On the other hand, critics of the rubric system worry that such systems remove necessary ambiguity, flexibility, and informative descriptions in writing assessments (Neal, 2011, p. 95, citing Broad, 2003).

In general, many writing teachers and scholars believe that in order to understand what we are assessing, the criteria for our assessments need to be articulated, agreed upon by assessment designers and teachers, shared by raters, and made available to students. But even here arguments such as those made by Peter Elbow (1993, 1994) and others (e.g., Broad, 1994; Huot, 1996; Smit, 1994) state that it is unnatural for multiple raters to agree on the quality of a piece of writing. Rather than try to train or impose agreement, they argue, we should be seeking ways to assess writing that do not depend on agreement among raters (in psychometric terms, interrater reliability). They say that natural judgments of writing quality are inherently subjective and to try to force them into the psychometrician's conception of objectivity is to do an injustice to student writers. Bachman (1990, p. 37) and Fulcher (2015) have further pointed out that even carefully designed language tests are subjective in nearly every aspect, including development, scoring, and interpretation, in the sense that the judgments of people are represented at all stages. Even computer-scored essays are first developed and rated by human scorers before they are put into a computer model (Bachman & Palmer, 2010, p. 355).

Let us now look at a few of these dilemmas in more detail. The arguments flourish in L1 writing and are generally later picked up by L2 scholars, so some of the published debates I discuss will draw on L1 literature, much of which is familiar to L2 writing scholars (sadly, the reverse is not true).

Discussions in the Literature

Fairness

Perhaps the most general and hotly debated issue in both first and second language writing assessment (and other kinds of assessments as well), and an umbrella issue under which other controversies flourish, is that of fairness of assessment techniques and practices. As Neal (2011, p. 39) wisely reminded us, "Since writing assessments typically reflect the biases of the culture in which they operate, they rarely if ever advantage minority populations." What might a common sense view of a fair writing assessment be?

According to Bachman and Palmer (2010, p. 128), fairness in assessment involves equal treatment of all individuals and lack of bias in processes, records, and interpretation. A fair assessment of writing, above all, treats all students equally without bias against differences in culture, background knowledge of content, students' experience (or lack of) with particular assessment instruments, different conditions of writers at the time they write a piece for assessment (are they ill? fatigued?), or even different environments for writing (a stuffy or crowded classroom? a solitary cubicle or carrel?). Biases can also stem from teacher personality, different definitions of "good writing," different views of the place of grammar conventions in writing, different approaches to pedagogy, and administrative bias that favors standardized testing (Crusan, 2010a). A fair assessment is also authentic, in the sense that it examines performance in writing rather than (for example) multiple choice knowledge of grammar, style, or vocabulary, and in the sense that it asks student to write something that they have been taught or that they will actually need to write later. A fair assessment, furthermore, captures what it is that students can actually do in writing, so that each evaluation, whether a score or a description, describes students' abilities and writing quality in a meaningful and accurate way. This would be the case whether we believe that there is such a thing as general writing ability or that writing must be assessed within specific domains and disciplines. Fairness means as well that we acknowledge that writers are better at some kinds of writing than at others, and that writing improves if we are writing on a topic we know something about. We thus know that students should not be penalized for doing poorly on a single sample. A fair assessment is also ethical, in the sense that it does not harm writers. It seems obvious, therefore, that if we guard against different biases, we will be able to assess writing fairly.

The well-known problem with this common sense view of writing assessment is that by capturing the complex and multidimensional nature of the activity of writing, it practically assures that no assessment instrument can ever be totally fair or accurate (Horowitz, 1991; Skehan, 1984) and, like all assessments involving language, will certainly never provide a complete picture (Bachman & Palmer, 2010). Moreover, even if we acknowledge that all assessments are incomplete, a fair assessment will still require that writing teachers prepare specific evaluation criteria for each assignment, a point that Crusan (2010a, 2015) has made in her arguments in favor of using locally constructed rubrics, rather than one rating scale for all written work. Many of the dilemmas teachers face in deciding how to fairly assess their students' writing stem from our knowledge of this complexity and from a paucity of adequate assessment tools (Slomp, 2012), particularly in an era of multimodal writing (Davis & Yancey, 2014).

Objectivity and Subjectivity/Reliability and Validity

In debates about fairness in writing assessment, a very basic argument concerns whether assessments can or should be objective, or instead, whether what has traditionally been pejoratively labeled *subjectivity* is inevitable and even desirable, particularly when human raters of writing do not easily agree on their ratings (Huot & Neal, 2006). The arguments link to two other controversial concepts in assessment, those of reliability and validity, also the subject of debate in literature on educational measurement (e.g., Fulcher, 2015; Messick, 1989, 1994), and in language assessment literature as to what these terms mean (e.g., Bachman, 1990; Bachman & Palmer, 2010; Bailey, 1998; Cohen, 1994; Crusan, 2010a; McNamara, 1996, 2000) and how they should be applied to writing assessment (e.g., Ferris & Hedgcock, 2014; Hamp-Lyons, 1991a; Henning, 1991; Horowitz, 1991; Neal, 2011; Weigle, 2002; White, 1994). The proponents of objectivity in assessment have persuasive arguments on their side, including the weight of "science," the statistical tools of the powerful psychometricians who dominate traditional views of testing and evaluation, and the increasing evidence of reliable (i.e., consistent) scoring from computerized scoring systems (discussed further below). Fairness and accuracy in assessment must be protected from the vagaries of teachers' and raters' individual values, beliefs, and interpretations, the argument goes; we must find ways to interpret students' writing abilities consistently, according to criteria that lie outside the minds of individual raters (Ferris & Hedgcock, 2014). In his argument against subjectivity in portfolio assessment, for example, White (1994, p. 36) asserted that "[u]nreliable [i.e., inconsistent] measures are merely subjective impressions by disparate individuals...." Our judgments of writing, he claimed, must "stand up to outside scrutiny" (p. 30).

One reason that indirect tests of writing, such as multiple choice or fill-in tests, were so attractive over the years is that they did stand up to outside scrutiny by being scored easily and without disagreement among scorers (Crusan, 2013; Fulcher, 2015; Huot & Neal, 2006). Measuring the objective features in themselves was thought to provide a degree of fairness in evaluation not possible with fuzzier assessment instruments. The numbers are based on clear criteria of right and wrong answers, are not subject to multiple interpretations, and so are highly reliable, allowing for easy comparison of individuals and groups. The controversy arose, beginning in the late 1970s with the communicative language teaching movement, when critics complained that assessments of writing needed to be based on actual samples of writing, not on indirect, right-wrong measures. In addition, indirect measures of writing such as multiple choice tests were considered invalid because they lacked, at the very least, the face validity that makes an assessment of writing authentic. The problem with actual writing samples, which have high face validity, lay in how to make sure that the targeted aspects of writing were actually the ones being assessed, and how to generate stable scores.

Proponents of objectivity in assessment have continued to seek ways first to clarify and describe criteria by which writing samples are assessed, and in the absence of or in conjunction with an e-rating system, to train raters to evaluate essays according to the same criteria so as to meet traditional standards of reliability (consistency) and validity (simplistically defined as accuracy in measuring what an assessment instrument intends to measure; see Messick, 1989, 1994, and 1996, for a more nuanced view). Likewise, computerized essay scoring programs that count lexical, syntactic, and mechanical features of writing similarly continue to be improved so as to provide scores that are at the very least consistent, hence overcoming the problem of rater reliability. As consistent as this style of objective evaluation is, where words, clauses, errors, and length are counted as they are in e-scoring, it can be criticized for describing writing quality in terms of surface complexity and accuracy, and missing larger discourse features and the uncountable aspects of writing that have a social dimension and an impact on real readers (CCCC position statements, 2004, 2009; Hesse, 2012; Neal, 2011; Ravitch, 2013). But the search for objective ways to evaluate student writing persists as do beliefs by some scholars that a writing assessment needs to be reliable in order to be valid. Those who support the belief that writing assessment should be both reliable and valid speak in unhedged terms. Hamp-Lyons (1991b, p. 252) asserted strongly that "[n]o test can be valid without first being reliable. Only when we have stable score data to look at can we usefully go on to ask questions about validity." Her position was echoed many years later by Ferris and Hedgcock (2014) among others.

A different argument is made by people who feel that the psychometrician's metalanguage and goals (objectivity, reliability, validity, generalizability) need to be disposed of before we can let go of concepts that do not and cannot apply to the assessment of writing (or even to language ability in general). It will not do simply to try to fine-tune the same criteria, they claim. Validity, seen in more complex terms as an evaluative statement about a decision and its consequences and not as a property of a test, does not need to be linked to the psychometrician's view of reliability (Messick, 1989, 1994, 1996; Neal, 2011). Instead, we should be suspicious of a system that "reads" a piece of writing 100% consistently and ties such consistency to notions of validity (Neal, 2011, pp. 114–120). In the context of large-scale portfolio assessment, Broad (1994) asserted that we spend far too much time and money trying to achieve statistical reliability among raters and that we need to "let go of the quantification of writing ability" (p. 271) in order to learn more about the "positioned readings that 'produce' those numbers" (p. 269). According to Smit (1994), it is impossible to come up with general criteria of competence in writing because each writing sample is the product of particular assignments written in particular contexts and so must be assessed locally (Condon, 2013; Crusan, 2010a; Huot & Neal, 2006) with criteria being adjusted as well for students' proficiency levels (Banerjee, Yan, Chapman, & Elliott, 2015).

One of the strongest supporters of using more local and context-rich writing assessment as opposed to standardized assessments that follow the psychometrician's notions of objectivity, reliability, and validity is Huot (1990a, 1990b, 1996; Huot & Neal, 2006; Huot & Williamson, 1997). Criteria for making decisions about students' writing cannot be separated from local contexts, he argued; it thus makes little sense to "maintain [...] procedures based on a positivist epistemology..." (Huot, 1996, p. 563). Echoing Moss (1994), Huot and Williamson (1997) challenged the "traditional notion that assessment has to be reliable in order to be valid" (p. 45) and that "concepts like validity and reliability are unquestionable and theoretically necessary" (p. 44). What matters most in fair writing assessment are the very local and diverse practices that supporters of traditional "objective" assessment wish to downplay or to erase through mathematical juggling. As Elbow (1993, p. 188) put it, "Evaluation implies the recognition of different criteria or dimensions—and by implication different contexts and audiences for the same performance."

Some years later, Huot and Neal (2006) continued to support the need for locally driven assessment in response to the growing enchantment of the writing field with technology-driven digital tools, asserting that the reliability of such tools does not ensure (local) validity: "It is crucial that we understand the difference between reliability-driven writing assessment and those procedures driven by a need to make the best decisions for students (validity)" (Huot & Neal, 2006, p. 430). Similarly, a local assessment will need to account for a variety of different responses to students' writing by different readers, a point made by Elbow (1993) some years ago. Expressing this dilemma, Hamp-Lyons (2011, p. 4) commented that "… scholars still do not agree whether our goal is perfect reliability or the appreciation of the varied judgements of different readers, since it remains impossible to achieve both at once" (p. 4). If we adopt this view, it is likely we will consider large-scale assessment to be inherently unfair. Elbow, Huot, Condon, Crusan, Neal, and other critics of large-scale standardized assessment schemes believe that fair assessment can only be done locally, where the people, practices, and purposes involved in writing are well known.

Authenticity

Fairness of writing assessment seems necessarily linked to notions of authenticity of a writing task, but what we mean by authenticity is not always clear. A short timed writing on a topic that students have not prepared for, as is the case with many large- and small- scale writing tests, does not seem authentic at all, unless we think (perversely?) of the essay testing world as an authentic context for writing. As Hamp-Lyons (2016) has pointed out, big tests and big test agencies are here to stay. Discussions of authenticity thus need to consider whether we believe that only activities performed outside a school context or closely modeled on them, in the so-called "real world," are authentic, or whether the school and testing contexts themselves are their own authentic worlds, even if the activities there differ from those beyond classroom doors (Messick, 1994; Sternberg, 1990).

Messick's (1994) arguments about the validation of performance assessments can be helpful in laying out the issues for writing teachers. In the case of portfolio assessment, for instance, we can ask whether educational assessments should

be "authentic reflections of classroom work or authentic representations of real-world work" (Messick, 1994, p. 18). Writing
teachers and assessment designers may have strong beliefs
about what they consider to be authentic performances and
assessments of writing or even whether authenticity is important. In discussions of what "authentic writing" in a school
context might mean, teachers can get bogged down in false
dichotomies, of course, namely that a writing performance
that is not authentic is by definition bad. Or, as Messick (1994)
pointed out, if we believe that only direct, performance assessments are authentic and valid, we may be tempted to conclude
that other forms of assessment are unauthentic (p. 14).

In a broader argument concerning authenticity and performance assessment in educational contexts, Messick (1994,
pp. 14–15) asked us to consider whether a performance or a
product are the targets or the vehicles of an evaluation. In an
arts contest or athletic competition, what counts for an evaluation is only the quality of the product or the performance.
Evaluators do not need to worry about the replicability and
generalizability of the artist's or athlete's one-time performance, nor do they need to make inferences about or evaluate
underlying skills and interim processes. Does writing fit in
such a category, better characterized as a generic proficiency
rather than a composite of underlying skills and constructs? If
so, teachers may focus their assessment efforts on task development, and not concern themselves with scoring criteria. In this
view, every skill that contributes to the writing performance in
a task-centered approach is considered relevant, with the result
that judgments of qualities such as clarity of expression and
depth of understanding cannot be separated. These judgments
therefore "contaminate" each other (Messick, 1994, p. 17).

If, on the other hand, we view authentic writing performance
as made up of a complex array of different constructs, teachers
and assessment designers might wish to break down writing
performance into those different skills and constructs and
describe them as thoroughly as possible, as has been promoted
by supporters of analytic scoring and rubrics (Crusan, 2010a,
2015; Ferris & Hedgcock, 2014; Hamp-Lyons, 2016). The prob-

lem for teachers who believe in this approach to authenticity in writing assessment is that, as Messick (1994) reminded us, something will always be left out (what is referred to in the literature of educational assessment as "construct underrepresentation"). If we assess by task, in contrast, without breaking a writing performance into skills and constructs, we cannot know what a score means. As Messick (1994, p. 20) asked: "By what evidence can we be assured that the scoring criteria and rubrics used in holistic, primary trait, or analytic scoring of products or performances capture the fully functioning complex skill?" Separate skills are most difficult to untangle, he noted, from aspects of performance such as clarity and coherence (p. 20). He argued for a construct-centered approach in which scoring rubrics are designed that fall somewhere in between a task-specific description and a generic description. Is such an approach to assessment inherently more authentic than faster evaluation techniques such as holistic scoring and computerized scoring? It seems inevitable that no matter how we define authenticity, there will be trade-offs in our choices of how to assess a piece of writing.

Holistic, Analytic (Multi-Trait), and Portfolio Scoring by Human Raters

Holistic scores of writing consist of one score, usually a number, applied to an entire piece of writing. Trained and experienced raters can quickly assess writing holistically and for the most part reliably. Analytic or multi-trait scoring consists of separate scores for different facets of writing, such as organization, mechanics, grammar, and vocabulary, described carefully in rubrics (Brown & Bailey, 1984; Charney, 1984; Crusan, 2010a, 2015; Ferris & Hedgcock, 2014; Hamp-Lyons, 1991c; Jacobs et al., 1981; Sasaki & Hirose, 1999) and other multiple trait or analytic scoring schemes (Bachman & Palmer, 2010; Hamp-Lyons, 2016). Even the most complex and sophisticated of these methods, ones that take into account variability in writers, readers, and task, still aim for an objective, often numerically consistent and accurate assessment that is both reliable and valid (see, for example, Bachman & Palmer, 2010, for a discussion of multiple trait scoring and McNamara's, 1996, justification of mathematical Rasch models for this purpose). Clearly holistic scoring is much faster than analytic scoring, so evidence that the two systems are fairly well correlated in spite of some discrepancies is important (Zhang, Xiao, & Luo, 2015). Analytic scoring on the other hand, though slower than holistic one-score ratings, provides much more information about a writer's abilities in different categories. In her discussion of the complexity involved in trying to judge the many relevant influences on a piece of writing, such as a writer's knowledge of grammar, vocabulary, coherence, content, and writing processes, Hamp-Lyons—a supporter of multi-trait analytic scoring—stated that a single holistic score cannot capture the strengths and weaknesses of a writing sample (1995, pp. 760–761).

Still, for both holistic and analytic scoring, it is widely believed that the only fair way for writing to be assessed by readers is if all readers agree on the scoring criteria and then respond in ways that are similar to each other and that are consistent within their own readings. It is especially difficult to justify diverse readings in high-stakes large-scale assessments. If raters A and B disagree on how to rate an essay, how can the final score (e.g., an average or a total) be fair or meaningful to the writer? Similarly, if a rater scores one way when fresh and another when fatigued, how can a student whose paper is read when the reader is tired be rated fairly? These two kinds of consistency in responding are referred to in the general testing literature as interrater reliability (among raters) and intrarater reliability (within the same rater), and can be calculated mathematically (see Bailey, 1998 or other books on educational research or testing in applied linguistics).

In seeking ways to learn how raters respond and how to help them respond in similar ways, such as through training or norming sessions, writing researchers have conducted various studies in both L1 and L2, with results that are not as conclusive as we might wish. Discussions with raters themselves show a wide range of criteria used by them even if final scores are similar, with more agreement on lexical features and less on discourse features at different proficiency levels, suggesting a need to revise and "refresh" rating scales regularly (Banerjee, Yan, Chapman, & Elliott, 2015). Likewise, criteria for decisions on holistic and analytic ratings may differ among L1 and L2 raters, novice and experienced raters, and content instructors and language teachers. Still, in the assessment debate, many support the idea that we must fine-tune our criteria and find ways to train readers, in large- and small-scale assessment and in research on writing, to respond consistently to the same criteria in the papers they evaluate. Supporters of this argument, including politicians and school boards, who want some accountability for how their money on testing is being spent, believe that it is both possible and necessary to articulate criteria for assessment, and that it is therefore possible to train raters to use the criteria consistently and appropriately.

The other side of the argument, against large-scale testing and in favor of local assessment (Huot, 1996; Huot & Williamson, 1997), has been expressed most persuasively in the past by Peter Elbow in his defense of portfolio assessment and evaluation-free writing (1993, 1994). This stance has been taken by others from that era as well (e.g., Broad, 1994; Elbow & Belanoff, 1997; Smit, 1994). Elbow and others stated that when we get human readers to agree on essay scores through training and norming procedures, we are forcing them to read in ways that alter their normal responses to writing. If it is normal for readers to respond differently to the same writings, then "the reliability in holistic scoring is not a measure of how texts are valued by real readers in natural settings, but only of how they are valued in artificial settings with imposed agreements" (Elbow, 1993, p. 189). In the context of his own teaching, Elbow (1993; Elbow & Belanoff, 1997) argued that we need to identify only the very weakest and strongest writers in order to assess writing for pedagogical purposes, and that readers do in fact tend to agree on which writings lie at either end of this continuum. Furthermore, teachers should consider another form of judgment: liking. If we like a piece of writing, or something about a piece of writing, including our own writing, it is much easier to criticize it and improve it (Elbow, 1993). In short, educators like Elbow believe that too much emphasis on assessment and rater reliability undermines pedagogy in the classroom. Their arguments apply less convincingly to assessments at the level of institutions, states, or nations.

Possibly more important than rater reliability on a single piece of writing, a valid assessment of someone's writing must include more than a single sample from a writing test, given that students perform quite differently on different kinds of writings (Hayes, Hatch, & Silk, 2000). Elbow and others cautiously favor portfolio assessment for this very reason: Multiple kinds of writing, at different stages of completion, reveal much more validly than does a single essay what students' writing ability consists of (Black, Daiker, Sommers, & Stygall, 1994; Calfee & Perfumo, 1996; Ferris & Hedgcock, 2014; Hamp-Lyons & Condon, 1993, 2000; Huot & Williamson, 1997; Murphy, 1997, 1999; Murray, 1994; Yancey, 1992, 1996; Yancey & Weiser, 1997). A portfolio collection, increasingly compiled electronically and referred to as ePortfolios (Neal, 2011), is more ecologically valid than individual pieces of writing (Wardle & Roozen, 2012). However, with multiple pieces and multiple readers, the collection will probably not be scored reliably (consistently) (Elbow & Belanoff, 1997). Such a collection would require "coordinated assessment" across departments and people (Neal, 2011, p. 85; Wardle & Roozen, 2012, p. 107) rather than consensus. In fact Broad (1994) labeled "portfolio scoring" a contradiction in terms, noting that the push to reach consensus on evaluations of student writing does not allow raters to value variety, richness, and diversity (p. 273). Given that not all assessments need to lead to decision-making (Bachman, 1990), consistency and consensus are not always major issues. For this group of scholars, it is indeed possible to separate validity and reliability. They do not need or want stable scores to assess writing. On the contrary, they believe that stable, consensually produced scores undermine the validity of the writing assessment.

White (1994) disagreed. He has supported portfolio assessment as more valid than a single essay test but insisted we do not have to dispose of rater reliability in order to achieve validity. We should make every effort, he asserted, "to develop consistency in our judgments, not only so that our measures will be reasonably reliable (and hence support our claims for validity) but so that our students will be able to develop self-assessment by internalizing consistent criteria" (White, 1994, p. 36).

Multimodal assessments can be considered a kind of portfolio assessment, given the varied components of multimodal projects (visual, audio, textual, possibly performance). Davis and Yancey (2014, p. 13) argued against conventional assessment of such projects and favor instead "the preliminary question of how we encounter and interpret them." Others have supported the careful development of rubrics for multimodal projects that emphasize feedback more than rating and scoring (Burnett, Frazee, Hanggi, & Madden, 2014). Multimodal projects and multimodal design will continue increasing in the future (Hafner, 2013, 2015), not only as digital technology improves but as access to it becomes more widespread in less developed countries. (See further discussion in Chapter 3, Writing in a Digital Era).

Computer Scoring of Essays

Computer scoring of essays, which I will refer to here as e-scoring (note also the common use of AES—automated essay scoring and other terms) by definition does not involve human readers. Instead, essays are scored according to various algorithms that are able to identify and count certain features and patterns of writing. The most important thing to remember is that if a feature cannot be identified and counted, it cannot be scored by a digital system, in spite of increasing complexity and sophistication of software (Shermis & Bernstein, 2013; note that the majority of authors in this edited volume have links to corporate testing companies, as is often the case with research on automated essay evaluation; Warschauer & Ware, 2006). The growth of the commercial e-scoring industry thus forces us to reconsider our definitions of writing and of writing quality (see Chapter 3, this book).

Digital technology enthusiasts (whether or not they are being paid by ETS) will continue to be optimistic about the potential for e-scoring to make the lives of writing teachers and administrators easier by virtue of its speed and ability to generate reliable scores on student essays. The other side of this ongoing debate argues that e-scoring of writing is so fraught with problems that it should not be used for assessment purposes. Computer-generated feedback, on the other hand, when not used for grading, has more potential to assist writers (Ware, 2011). Still, as Warschauer and Ware (2006, p. 160) pointed out, computer-generated feedback "varies in quality, but none of it is remotely similar to what a trained writing instructor can provide, and the ability of students to make use of the feedback is also questionable." Assessment of writing, on the other hand, a fundamentally social and human activity, should be done by human readers and not by means of a machine (CCCC, 2004, 2009; Ericsson & Haswell, 2012; Herrington & Moran, 2012; Hesse, 2012; Neal, 2011; Ravitch, 2013). The Conference on College Communication and Composition organization made this position clear in its 2004 and 2009 position statements:

> As stated by the CCCC Position Statement on Teaching, Learning, and Assessing Writing in Digital Environments [2004], "We oppose the use of machine-scored writing in the assessment of writing." Automated assessment programs do not respond as human readers. While they may promise consistency, they distort the very nature of writing as a complex and context-rich interaction between people. (CCCC, 2009)

What E-Scoring Can and Cannot Do

E-scoring systems cannot read or understand anything that a student writes. They can only identify sentence- and word-level patterns and errors according to algorithms designed by human coders. Because such systems are good at some kinds of error identification and correction, in an era when error-free writing and good writing quality are often conflated, they are touted as beneficial to students at early stages of writing. If students submit an early draft to an e-rating system, and if the system identifies and corrects language-level errors according to algorithms of standard Anglo-American English (see Chapter 4 for the debate on standards of English), the burden on writing teachers is reduced, so the argument goes. Students and teachers are thus free to work on less quantifiable, and arguably more important, aspects of writing. However, only certain aspects of writing are assessed this way—those things that can be identified by an algorithm and counted, leading us to ask how strongly writing quality is really linked to error-free writing. Sometimes linguistic factors (e.g., grammar, usage, mechanics, lexical complexity, length of essay) are the only things that teachers and researchers seem interested in focusing on (Enright & Quinlan, 2010; McNamara, Crossley, & McCarthy, 2010) in part because these aspects of writing are easy to identify and fix both by humans and by machines.

In conjunction with their error-identification capabilities, e-rating systems are also widely accepted as promoting "speed, reliability, and efficiency" (Neal, 2011, p. 9). Faster and newer seems better. True, such systems are fast and reliable and perhaps the only way to efficiently assess large-scale tests of writing these days. However, outside artificial and timed testing conditions, good writing itself does not usually happen quickly, but slowly and laboriously. Likewise, as I have already discussed, human responses to writing are inherently and normally variable unless human raters are trained to read in the same way (Elbow, 1993, 1994; Neal, 2011). To reiterate, in considering what e-scoring systems can and cannot do, writing teachers need to define carefully what they mean by effective writing, including going beyond superficial language-level definitions, and spell out what their specific purposes are in having students write. It might be that speed, reliability, and efficiency fade in importance in light of their considerations. My own view is that teachers who want their workloads decreased by means of e-scoring systems probably shouldn't become writing teachers.

Reliability and Correlations of Human Raters and E-Scoring

In spite of strongly argued views on our need for local and diverse evaluations of students' writing, it is still widely believed that the major problem framing writing assessment is "the inability for raters to agree on scores for the same paper" (Huot & Neal, 2006, p. 428). Although not everyone sees this as a problem (e.g., Neal, 2011), this fundamental issue of lack of reliability of human readers, particularly ones who are not trained to read in similar ways, has spurred the turn to computerized scoring systems to solve this problem. Human raters will never score essays as consistently as does an e-scoring system; the same essay submitted multiple times to an e-scoring system will be scored 100 percent reliably, a feat not possible by human raters (Shermis, Burstein, & Bursky, 2013, p. 12). However, if human raters can be trained to agree with each other fairly consistently, and if e-scoring is shown to correlate well with human raters, even if only on superficial linguistic features of writing, some criticisms of e-scoring can be alleviated. The point is, proponents of the reliability argument need to be convinced that human raters and e-scoring correlate well enough to be considered reliable. Otherwise, one system cannot complement or substitute for the other, either on large- or small-scale scoring.

Numerous studies have indeed shown high reliability of e-scoring systems, demonstrating understandably greater consistency than human raters because of algorithmic calculations. But moderate to high correlations between human raters doing holistic or analytic scoring and e-scoring systems have also been found (Bridgeman, Trapani, & Attali, 2012; Enright & Quinlan, 2010; Lee, Gentile, & Kantor, 2010; many authors in Shermanis & Burstein, 2013; Weigle, 2010, 2013a, 2013b). Nevertheless, when different factors are compared, rather than just overall holistic scores, findings of correlation studies are less clear cut. In a study of TOEFL's® "e-rater" system and human raters, Lee, Gentile, and Kantor, (2010, p. 410) found adequate links between human raters and e-scores on mechanics, but less so on scores of grammar:

> ... the most clear-cut finding from the e-rater variable analysis was that it was possible to establish a link between the mechanical accuracy ratio computed by the automated scoring engine and the mechanics score assigned by human raters. [...] However, we were not able to confirm a similar link between the grammatical accuracy ratio variable and the grammar/usage scores assigned by human raters or between the usage accuracy ratio and the grammar/usage score.

Weigle (2010, 2013a, 2013b), moreover, found not surprisingly that e-scoring ratings missed some factors in the writing of L2 students that human raters picked up. Writing skills, she concluded, need to be distinguished from language proficiency. Similarly, in a small-scale study comparing e-scoring and human scoring in a university ESL classroom, Dikli and Bleye (2014) found that essays written by 37 students from three different prompts were scored quite differently by the e-scoring system and human raters, with the instructors providing more and better quality feedback.

However, in the case of large-scale testing, it is no longer feasible for two sets of human raters to score in an efficient or accurate manner all the standardized essays tests used worldwide, so the need arises for reliability between at least one human rater and an e-scoring system. As expressed by Weigle (2010, p. 350), "The use of automated scoring in conjunction with human scoring [can] make the process of assessing writing more efficient and potentially more reliable" particularly in the case of (large-scale) international testing of L2 writers (Weigle, 2013a, 2013b). Even with such reliability, as I have pointed out, automated scoring cannot assess writing beyond what can be programmed into an algorithm. A pointed critique of large-scale e-rater systems has been made by Condon (2013), who has not been convinced by the rater reliability argument. He pointed out that large-scale testing by corporations such as ETS is big business, and therefore difficult to resist. Human raters needed for the scale of testing done by ETS and other corporations are simply too expensive, too inefficient, and questionably reliable. But such realities do not dispel the main argument by Condon and others (Crusan, 2010a; Hesse, 2012; Ravitch, 2013): As the pressure to quantify increases, the validity of a test decreases (Condon, 2013, p. 104) partly because the kinds of writing that computers can score are short, timed, and "hopelessly inadequate" (p. 106). Even if we agree with Hamp-Lyons (2016, p. A2) that we cannot ignore big tests and powerful test agencies, and as reliable as e-scoring might be, such systems cannot ever read anything written by test takers with any understanding at all. It is unfortunate that the voices and assessments by teachers are silenced in the face of powerful automated systems supported by the authority of corporations, science, and statistics (Neal, 2011).

As Crusan (2010c) pointed out in her review of Ericsson and Haswell's edited collection, *Machine Scoring of Student Essays: Truth and Consequences* (2006), composition scholars understand meaning in different ways from proponents of e-scoring. As expressed by Condon (2013, p. 102), "No AES system can achieve the kind of understanding necessary to evaluate writing on the semantic level—on the level of mean-ing, let alone the level of awareness of occasion, purpose, and audience demanded by any form of real-world writing." The point is that teachers need to be clear by what criteria they and e-scoring systems evaluate writing and to resist attempts by their institutions to uncritically buy into the corporate argu-ments about efficiency and reliability.

Supporters of e-scoring can hope that the various automated assessment programs continue to improve not only their reli-ability, but their validity and their ability to identify more than superficial patterns of lexical, grammatical, and structural features of academic essays—one of the only genres that has enough of a predictable structure and style to be programmed by e-scoring algorithms. Assessing template-like structures and features of language, after all, is not the same as assessing writing. An accomplished writer of various genres must be able to do more than follow a template and write a grammatical sentence. Further, all student writers deserve to receive meaningful feedback on content, persuasive arguments, and style by a real reader. Some scholars, therefore, reject e-scoring as true writing assessment even while recognizing it might be needed for large-scale placement tests (Deane, 2013).

That said, it is becoming increasingly evident that e-scoring systems and human raters do not need to correlate highly in their ratings if we presume they should be rating different things. A "division of labor" approach may make more sense than trying to make e-scoring systems more and more like human raters. As Bridgeman (2013, p. 230–231) explained,

> In the future, the correlation of human and machine scores may become even less important as test users become more comfortable with the idea of letting machines do what they do best (e.g., counting objective grammatical and structural features) and letting people do what they do best (e.g., evaluating logic and persuasiveness of arguments), and not requiring that these separate functions be very highly correlated.

The problems associated with fairness, objectivity, rater reliability, validity, and authenticity in writing assessment will continue to be debated, and large testing corporations will continue to search for a refined digital assessment instrument rather than "looking at how and why decisions are made based on the results gathered by the assessment" (Neal, 2011, p. 19). However, it is important for teachers of writing to note that the dilemmas described above become most problematic when teachers themselves or administrators demand actual scores of some kind on students' writing in order to make decisions rather than to assess for other purposes, such as improvement in writing. Some of these problems diminish in importance if we do not need our assessments of students' writing to result in a score or a grade. In the third section of the chapter I describe some alternatives to traditional assessment that may help writing teachers escape the thorniest of these issues. But first, let me address a final set of issues that concern the ethics of assessment, some of which have been hinted at earlier.

Ethical Dilemmas

It has become increasingly common to hear arguments over the ethical uses of assessments (Bachman, 2000; Bachman & Palmer, 2010; McNamara, 2006; Neal, 2011). The arguments apply across the board to assessment of all kinds, of which writing assessment is just a small part. They concern how tests are developed, administered, scored, and interpreted, and—importantly for the discussion in this chapter—how formal tests and assessments are then used. In the next section I focus on the use of tests in the belief that even if classroom writing teachers are not involved in the development and administration of formal testing, they need to be aware of the issues related to how tests are developed and used (Crusan, 2010b). Particularly in the case of language and writing assessment of L2 speakers, ethical issues are especially touchy because they concern how fairly second language speakers are treated when they are being tested in a language that is not their own and often by means of digital input and e-scoring on material that is culturally unfamiliar (Weigle, 2013b).

How Tests Are Used

The language testing field, as described by McNamara (2001), has been the most positivist in orientation of all areas in applied linguistics, relying, as discussed earlier, on "scientific" notions of objectivity, reliability, and validity. Influenced in recent years by discussions of postmodernism and social constructionism, language testing is now seen as a social and political activity, inseparable from values and social consequences (McNamara & Roever, 2006). The work of Messick (1989, 1994, 1996), for example, has been recognized by some of the testing specialists in applied linguistics (e.g., Bachman,

2000) and incorporated into reconceptualizations of the traditional notion of validity. Messick, whose work spanned over 30 years, helped people in language testing to understand that an essential aspect of validity concerns the social consequences of how tests are used as well as the value-laden interpretive procedures by which we understand what tests mean. He noted:

> The consequential basis of test validity includes evidence and rationales for evaluating the intended and unintended consequences of test interpretations and use in both the short and the long term. Particularly prominent is the evaluation of any adverse consequences for individuals and groups that are associated with bias in test scoring and interpretation or with unfairness in test use. (Messick, 1994, p. 21)

Indeed, well-known voices in applied linguistics have been openly discussing for some time how important it is to consider the ethics and politics of how tests are used (Bachman, 2000; Bachman & Palmer, 2010; Hamp-Lyons, 1997; Lynch, 1997, 2001a, 2001b; McNamara, 2001; Norton & Starfield, 1997; Shohamy, 2001a, 2001b; Spolsky, 1997). In his review of modern language testing at the turn of the century, Bachman (2000) noted that testing issues had broadened greatly, to include among other things ethical issues related to how tests are used and the meaning of professionalism in language testing (p. 15). He noted that Messick contributed ideas on the social consequences of validity that make "validation research" a promising, and complex, area of investigation for the future (p. 22).

The strongest arguments on the dangers of unethical uses of tests come from Shohamy (1997, 2001a, 2001b). Part of a movement that supports a critical approach to language assessment (Lynch, 2001b), she has been worried that tests are used in many ways that have little to do with measuring knowledge or language proficiency. Rather, she sees how tests are used to manipulate and even control stakeholders. She has asked difficult questions, such as who makes tests, what the political motives are of test designers, how test results are used, and what the meaning of tests is for various stakeholders, such as teachers, students, parents, and school administrators (Sho-hamy, 2001b). In her research on tests of Arabic and of English in Israel, she found that tests were used to impose a politi-cally motivated curriculum, to force teachers to teach certain things and not others, and to "punish, exclude, gate-keep and perpetuate existing powers" (p. xii). Critical language testing, she asserted, challenges the power of tests and questions how they are used, works to involve those being tested in how tests are designed, and obligates test designers and administrators to take responsibility for ensuring that tests are used ethically (Shohamy, 2001a).

Ethics and Assessment of the L2 Writer

In L2 writing, ethical issues are closely tied to language and culture as well as to students' familiarity or not with the spe-cific technologies of testing. Digital technologies in particular are changing so rapidly that it is barely possible for students and educators in developed countries to keep up, to say noth-ing of developing countries. In the most obvious case, language proficiency and writing ability interact such that it is difficult to say anything meaningful about the writing ability or content knowledge of students whose proficiency in the L2 is quite low (Weigle, 2013b). Weigle (2013b, p. 89) reminded us that multiple kinds of assessments need to be distinguished: assess-ing writing, assessing content understanding through writing, assessing language proficiency through writing. A simple essay test that focuses on one aspect of writing is not sufficient.

Here are some common problems that can lead to ethi-cal dilemmas in assessing the writing of L2 writers. In one instance, Norton and Starfield (1997) documented a case in South Africa in which neither students nor faculty were clear about the extent to which language proficiency influenced the assessments made on students' academic writing. In other cases, L2 educators might be tempted to generalize about the writing and thinking abilities of L2 students, concluding from samples written in the L2 that students who do not write well cannot think well. Moreover, until recently, L2 writing researchers did not assess students' writing ability in L1, a problem that scholars such as Sasaki and Hirose (1999) tried to correct. It has also been pointed out by writing scholars interested in portfolio assessment (e.g., Murray, 1994; Neal, 2011; Wardle & Roozen, 2012) and journal writing (e.g., Casanave, 2011; Lucas, 1992) that students perform differently on different writing tasks because their cultural, experiential, and educational backgrounds differ greatly and might not prepare them for genres that are probably familiar to mainstream L1 English speakers. Personal writing in a school setting is a comfortable genre for many speakers of Japanese, for instance, but not for speakers of Arabic, who may do better at argumentative writing (Liebman, 1992).

There are further serious high-stakes ethical issues in assessing the writing of L2 students. The primary one concerns what to do with the student who seems to be passing his or her content classes but cannot pass an English writing exit exam or required ESL class (Johns, 1991; Schneider & Fujishima, 1995). If we believe that tests should benefit students and pedagogy, what are we to say about tests that prevent such students from continuing their studies or graduating?

Happily, ethical issues in language and writing assessment of L2 students are becoming increasingly salient to designers and users of assessment instruments (Bachman & Palmer, 2010; McNamara, 2006). These issues highlight aspects of assessment that simply were not considered in the past. Particularly when writing assessments are used to make evaluative high-stakes decisions about L2 students, these ethical issues need to be fronted, discussed, and shared with stakeholders as part of all decision making.

Classroom Perspectives

It is generally agreed that all assessment instruments provide only partial information about students' language and writing abilities. Nevertheless, in school settings, we cannot escape the realities and pressures of formal assessments, except perhaps occasionally in the privacy of our own classrooms. Many of the dilemmas I discussed in this chapter concern issues of assessment and testing beyond the individual classroom. Writing teachers may feel they have little control over decisions about assessment that are made or apply to writing done outside their own classes. Even in such cases, teachers have a responsibility to be aware of the issues and to the extent possible participate in and encourage ethical assessment practices (Crusan, 2010b; Lynch, 2001a). If they do not support their school's use of e-scoring, for instance, they need to know enough about e-scoring systems to understand what they are resisting. They also need to be aware that many calls are being made for alternatives to traditional assessment at the institutional level that may have repercussions in the local contexts of particular classrooms, such as by means of placement or exit assessments.

At the institutional level, one such attempt at alternative assessment was made some time ago at the University of Michigan, which developed a performance-based initial placement assessment for ESL students who were beginning university work (Feak & Dobson, 1996). Recognizing that the traditional single impromptu essay is unfair and invalid, in that it cannot represent what students can do in writing, and that portfolio assessment is too time-consuming and labor intensive to be used as a placement mechanism, the English Language Institute designed a "source-based assessment" for incoming freshman ESL students. This assessment activity involved examinees' reading and synthesizing quoted passages on a single general academic topic and generating two kinds of writing: sentence completions that asked students to compare and contrast views of different authors, and an essay in which students integrated their own ideas with those of the authors of the quoted passages. The assessment was designed to capture students' abilities to engage in the kinds of academic work that is typical at universities: reading, comparing and contrasting ideas, synthesizing, and commenting. These activities, moreover, paralleled those in the university's EAP classes. The problem of rater reliability remains, of course, and the authors regrettably did not comment on how they handled this problem, or what their beliefs were on this thorny issue.

Within their own classrooms, however, writing teachers are inevitably caught in the dilemma of being both supportive nonjudgmental readers and critical evaluators who ultimately must provide critical feedback and assign a grade to student performance. These roles conflict and in both cases require time on the part of instructors, who might otherwise be tempted to use e-scoring to lighten their workloads. Students know they will receive grades, even if individual papers are not marked, and so tend to write for grades (and in e-scoring contexts, to write to a machine) rather than to develop their writing. (This conflict is especially pronounced in required classes.) Teachers thus need to decide within the contexts of their own classes how to juggle their conflicting roles as readers and as evaluators. In this section, I consider project-based writing and assessment as a way to interweave instruction and assessment of students' writing without the need for scores, grades on papers, or inter-rater reliability. I will focus on one type of writing activity, with examples mainly from my own work.

The writing activity involves students in a project which results in a product of some kind. In my own work I compare this activity to the writing and research that teachers do in their professional lives—our ongoing project work that is not evaluated by grades and scores but by its acceptance by a professional community, for example in the form of a publica-tion (Casanave, 1998; Hyland, 2015; but note the perfidious influence of point systems for different kinds of publications in many university evaluation systems these days; Hyland, 2015). Similarly, we do not need to assess a student project with grades and scores, but instead can use descriptive feed-back on and evaluation of how students design and carry out the project and how well the final product meets their goals. As Sokolik and Tillyer (1992) pointed out long ago: "[S]ince the project has a clearly -defined goal—to complete the proj-ect—ambiguities of evaluation are frequently avoided: students either complete the task or they don't, and the decision is theirs" (p. 49).

In my own project assignments during my years of teaching in Japan, the project was "owned" by students in the sense that they designed something that was meaningful to them. I usually did not specify a word length, but tried to help students understand that if the project is designed and carried out well, the length will take care of itself. Importantly, I found it useful to "begin at the end" in my project work with Japanese university students, whether this was with undergraduates or with doctoral students planning a dissertation project. In order to design a meaningful project, one that involves many steps and activities during a semester, students need to have a vision of what they want to end up with. Much of the writing teacher's or thesis adviser's work occurs in these early design stages, which can last for many weeks (or months, in the case of doctoral students) as instructors help students formulate a vision and a plan for their projects. My students, undergraduates, masters, and doctoral students, often did not know exactly what they wanted to do or what topic or area they wished to investigate. They either began with ideas that were way too broad or way to narrow, and had little idea what they wanted their end product to look like. For the undergraduates, I resisted giving them the typical essay or report format, because such a format looks like just another paper written for a teacher rather than for themselves. What do you need or want to learn? I asked them. What might you need to do with writing this school year or the next? How can you use this project to accomplish your (not my) goals? In the case of doctoral students, a dissertation project that lasts over several years also needs to be interesting, feasible, and sustainable over time.

Even low and intermediate level L2 students, youngsters and college levels, can design and complete writing projects, including ones that last over a full school term. In the case of low level students who cannot do extensive reading in English, many interesting interview and observation projects can be created. An oral family history project can be designed to fit specific cases of each student. Students learn all they can about their families, drawing on photographs, phone, social media, or in-person interviews from questionnaires they have created, collections of family documents, or by written or electronic communication. The language used in gathering these data is not an issue, so in the case of low level students, the pressure is taken off to try to use English 100 percent of the time.

With teacher guidance, students then need to organize their data, transforming and selecting as needed to fit a particular format for their final product (including these days digital video projects; Christiansen & Koelzer, 2016; Hafner, 2013, 2015; see Chapter 3, this book). Designing an appropriate format, such as a booklet or a portfolio or a multimedia presentation or website, requires careful thought on the part of teacher and students, but should be done early so that data can be transformed in suitable ways. Time needs to be carefully managed; in my experience this is the most difficult aspect of project work, both at undergraduate and graduate levels and it is likely so at high school levels too. Whether done in print or electronic form, students need to produce drafts of different sections of their project, revise, rewrite, and perhaps even consider doing illustrations and a cover for print versions and audio and video portions for a web-based project. There is enough to do, in fact, to make the project the entire focus of a writing class. In Japan, my undergraduate classes usually met only once a week, so even spending an entire semester on a project required strict time management and even then some students could not finish a polished version of their project to their satisfaction.

Other examples of projects can be imagined by any writing teachers who know their students' interests, abilities, and special skills. Students can construct self-portraits and life histories, write and compile poems (e.g., Iida, 2008), and design school-based handbooks and guides about courses, professors, and resources for new students. More advanced academic students who need to write a thesis or paper for other classes can carry out a library research project that includes a reflective reading journal and an annotated bibliography. When students know that projects like these can be printed, bound, and copied for others, or presented online as an electronic multimedia project for anyone to see (e.g., Hafner, 2015), they invest in polishing and revising from pride of ownership rather than just to please a teacher. Whether or not such projects are ultimately given a letter or number grade, assessment of the instructional kind, including self-assessment, is built into them every step of the way as teachers and students work together to complete the projects. Assessment here is not done for traditional purposes, but from pride of ownership in a well-done project.

A final example is from an elective upper division and graduate level writing class that I offered each semester in my Japanese university. This small class met only once a week for a semester, for a total of 13 or 14 meetings. Students' English proficiency was mixed, but generally quite high (above 500 TOEFL®). I explained that I gave no tests, quizzes, or even grades on papers and drafts, but that any student who attended all classes and worked regularly on a writing project would easily pass with at least a B (cf. Peter Elbow's, 1993, similar grading scheme). Students were from different areas of study and at different places in their academic trajectories, so for them it made little sense for me to assign a uniform project or paper that I would then grade by uniform criteria. If they were to improve their writing in ways meaningful to them, they needed to design their own projects, and I needed to help guide them to do something that could reasonably be accomplished in a short time. (By the way, I myself am not able to write a paper in one semester, as I discovered over several semesters in which I tried to complete my own writing project along with students.) Some students worked on a literature review section of a masters thesis (some students wrote theses in English at my Japanese university); others did background literature searches and wrote summaries and responses to readings in preparation for doing a paper or thesis later. Other students wrote a conference proposal or a long self-introduction essay as part of an application for an English-medium graduate school. Assessment happened every week, as students did short free-writings and journals on their writing problems and progress, talked about their ideas and got feedback from me and from peers, and as they turned in ideas or drafts in writing and got written responses from me or shared drafts with peers. In my general assessment of the students I also considered the extent to which they demonstrated engagement in and commitment to the project through their attendance and participation in class.

The two most difficult aspects of project teaching for me were first that I could not, in good conscience, demand a final (i.e., finished) product if I were to be true to my word about having students work on a project that contributed to work they were doing outside my class. Students' deadlines outside my class differed from my schedule as a writing teacher. A few students who were heavily invested in their unfinished projects sometimes took the same class the following semester or followed up with me after the semester was over. Second, inevitably there were students in the class who were not ready to take on their own projects. These students probably belonged in a general academic writing class, and I encouraged such students to transfer into one, although not all took my advice. I was usually able, with some frustration, to accommodate students who did not want to transfer out, or who were seeking only a credit-bearing course in English or general writing practice. They too had to design their own projects even if they had no specific purpose for writing, and to participate in activities and discussions with the more focused students.

The point for this chapter on assessment is that with term-long in-class writing projects, assessment and instruction cannot really be separated, and that grades and scores diminish in importance as students gradually take control of the progress on their own projects. Assessment, importantly, eventually involves students' increasingly assessing their own work. The ultimate assessment lies in what happens with the final product: a print or online class publication that wins praise from outsiders, a master's thesis or doctoral dissertation in English, a conference paper accepted, a journal article published, an acceptance to an English-medium graduate school. Nevertheless, the project-writing alternative to assessment, no matter how satisfying as an assessment practice in the writing class, does not solve the continuing dilemmas associated with using L2 writing samples for admissions screening, placement, or exit mechanisms.

Ongoing Questions

It is likely that writing teachers hold strong beliefs about assessment. There are those who believe that assessment, and a lot
of it, benefits students and curricula greatly, e.g., via positive
washback, and that nothing is inherently harmful in assessment
practices. Even the strongest critics of unethical assessment
practices (e.g., Shohamy, 1997, 2001a, 2001b) believe that
assessment and testing can be conducted ethically and fairly
(Bachman & Palmer, 2010). There are other teachers who believe
that we do far too much assessment of our L2 students' language
growth and writing ability. These teachers ask: What would
change in my teaching and in my students' learning if I assessed
and tested less? What alternatives are there, they ask as well, to
traditional assessment? These teachers tend to reconceptualize
assessment as regular but informal interaction with students
as they write and as a central aspect of instruction rather than
of formal evaluation. In this view, "every assignment is an
assessment" of some kind (Crusan, personal communication,
July, 2016). Teachers who hold very different beliefs from one
another about assessment will not only assess their students
differently; they will also teach differently from one another,
given the natural washback effect of assessment on pedagogy.

It is also possible that those involved in assessment will
make different decisions according to the different beliefs
they have about assessment and the different purposes they
have for assessing students' writing. These decisions, as is
the case for all the decisions that teachers make, can only
be made in conjunction with the constraints and contexts of
particular settings, and in interaction with others, including
students. The central questions remain: In the context of my
particular setting, do I need to assess my L2 writing students
formally or informally? If yes, for what specific purposes? To
what extent are those purposes high-stakes or low-stakes for
students? To what extent do I need to test students as opposed
to integrate assessment and instruction? Who will design the
assessments and how will they be carried out fairly in my
particular setting? If I use any kind of e-scoring assessments,

what will such assessment instruments <u>not</u> be able to tell me about my students' writing? What will the assessments mean to students and how will the results be used? What influence will the assessments in my class and in my school have on my own teaching, my students' learning activities, a school or program curriculum, politicians, or someone or something else?

Hamp-Lyons (2001) some time ago noted that "third generation assessment" refers to portfolio assessment in writing research and pedagogy. Looking ahead, she predicted that "fourth generation assessment" would delve more deeply than at present into the role that digital technology might play in assessment, a prediction also made by Weigle (2002). This prediction has come true, beyond anyone's wildest imagination, and as evidenced by the enormous outpouring of literature on automated assessment and evaluation systems, will continue to develop and to pose controversies and dilemmas that teachers will need to decide about. It will also involve stakeholders—more than at present—in expanding their understanding of the humanistic, ethical, and political aspects of assessment, not just with accountability. These aspects will not go away. They await the responsible involvement of all who are engaged in assessment practices.

Beliefs and Practices

Beliefs

1. What distinctions do you believe need to be made, if any, between testing and assessment of L2 writing?
2. What do you believe the relationship is between validity and reliability in writing assessment?
3. Do you believe that L2 writers who are planning to study in English-medium universities should be required to achieve a certain score on a standardized test of writing (e.g., TOEFL Writing Test) as part of an admissions or exit requirement? What are your beliefs about the role of English language writing requirements in EFL as opposed to ESL contexts?

4. What are your beliefs about what a fair way to evaluate students' writing might be, for the purposes of grading, scoring, and accountability to an institution?

5. After considering the issues in this chapter, what do you currently believe that e-scoring systems can and cannot do to assess writing? Have your own definitions of writing changed at all in light of these beliefs?

6. What do you believe the purposes and effects are of giving your L2 writing students concrete scores or grades on some or all of their writing? What might the purposes and effects be of giving no grades at all?

Practices

1. What are your own experiences with different tests and assessments of L1 or L2 writing, as an L1 or L2 writer yourself? Describe these. In what ways were (or were not) these tests or assessments fair and accurate? What do you believe would be needed to establish a fair and accurate assessment of your own writing?

2. What are your experiences with different tests and assessments of L2 writing in your role as an L2 writing teacher? Describe these. In what ways were (or were not) these tests or assessments fair and accurate?

3. Have you ever assessed L2 students' writing without giving grades or scores of any kind? If so, describe what your assessment practices were and explain why you used them. If not, design a writing task that you can assess without needing to give a score or grade.

4. In your setting, are L2 students required to take any prerequisite writing classes or pass particular writing tests before they can take other classes, or before they can graduate later? Describe the requirements, and evaluate them in light of your beliefs and understandings about assessment.

5. What experiences have you had, if any, with large-scale assessment, e.g., as a writing test developer, reader of essays, or an interpreter of an e-score? Given your current beliefs about assessment practices, what are your reflections on those experiences?

6. In this three-part activity, first create a writing prompt for a group of students you are familiar with. Be sure to be able to justify the prompt for the particular group and purposes you intend. Second, create a rubric with which you can evaluate the writing that students produce. Third, discuss or create at least two alternative ways you could assess the piece of writing that results from students' responses to your prompt.

7. In this activity, take one of your own short essays (or any short academic essay) and prepare four versions of it. For the first, write in a way that you believe would be acceptable to be handed in as a writing assignment. For the second, put some intentional grammatical and lexical errors into the original, keeping it the same length. For the third, use version 2, with errors kept in place, but add several paragraphs to the essay, thus lengthening it. For the fourth use version 1, the "well-written" version, and rearrange the paragraphs in random order. Submit all four versions to an automated essay scoring system, and compare scores (and feedback, if there is any). What do you conclude about essay scoring software and its ability to assess written texts from this exercise? (Note: If your school does not have one of these systems that you can use, check Google (or other) websites for automated essay scoring resources.)

Alternatively, try to replicate McGee's (2006) experiment in trying to trick the Intelligent Essay Assessor (IEA is software that claims to assess "meaning"). McGee wrote three different responses to an IEA prompt, altering each in ways that would never be acceptable to a human reader, finding that scores were hardly affected.

References

Bachman, L. F. (1990). *Fundamental considerations in language testing.* Oxford, U.K.: Oxford University Press.

Bachman, L. F. (2000). Modern language testing at the turn of the century: Assuming that what we count counts. *Language Testing, 17*(1), 1–42.

Bachman, L. F., & Palmer, A. S. (2010). *Language assessment in practice: Developing language assessments and justifying their use in the real world.* Oxford, U.K.: Oxford University Press.

Bailey, K. M. (1996). Working for washback: A review of the washback concept in language testing. *Language Testing, 13*(3), 257–279.

Bailey, K. B. (1998). *Learning about language assessment: Dilemmas, decisions, and directions.* Pacific Grove, CA: Heinle & Heinle.

Banerjee, J., Yan, X., Chapman, M., & Elliott, H. (2015). Keeping up with the times: Revising and refreshing a rating scale. *Assessing Writing, 26*, 5–19.

Black, L., Daiker, D. A., Sommers, J., & Stygall, G. (Eds.) (1994). *New directions in portfolio assessment: Reflective practice, critical theory, and large-scale scoring.* Portsmouth, NH: Boynton/Cook.

Bridgeman, B. (2013). Human ratings and automated essay evaluation. In M. D. Shermis & J. Burstein (Eds.), *Handbook of automated essay evaluation: Current applications and new directions* (pp. 221–232). New York: Routledge/Taylor & Francis.

Bridgeman, B., Trapani, C. S., & Attali, Y. (2012). Comparison of human and machine scoring of essays: Differences by gender, ethnicity and country. *Applied Measurement in Education, 25*, 27–40.

Broad, R. L. (1994). "Portfolio scoring": A contradiction in terms. In L. Black, D. A. Daiker, J. Sommers, & G. Stygall (Eds.), *New directions in portfolio assessment: Reflective practice, critical theory, and large-scale scoring* (pp. 263–276). Portsmouth, NH: Boynton/Cook.

Brown, J. D., & Bailey, K. M. (1984). A categorical instrument for scoring second language writing skills. *Language Learning, 34*(4), 21–42.

Burnett, R. E., Frazee, A., Hanggi, K., & Madden, A. (2014). A programmatic ecology of assessment: Using a common rubric to evaluate multimodal processes and artifacts. *Computers and Composition, 31*, 53–66.

Cai, G. (1999). Texts in contexts: Understanding Chinese students' English compositions. In C. R. Cooper & L. Odell, L. (Eds.), *Evaluating writing: The role of teachers' knowledge about text, learning, and culture* (pp. 279–297). Urbana, IL: National Council of Teachers of English.

Calfee, R., & Perfumo, P. (Eds.) (1996). *Writing portfolios in the classroom: Policy and practice, promise and peril.* Mahwah, NJ: Lawrence Erlbaum.

Cameron, W. B. (1963). *Informal sociology: A casual introduction to sociological thinking.* New York: Random House.

Casanave, C. P. (1998). Procedural and conceptual parallels between student and teacher product-driven writing projects. *JALT Journal, 20*, 90–103.

Casanave, C. P. (2011). *Journal writing in second language education.* Ann Arbor: University of Michigan Press.

Charney, D. (1984). The validity of using holistic scoring to evaluate writing. *Research in the Teaching of English, 18*, 65–81.

Christiansen, M. S., & Koelzer, M.-L. (2016). Digital storytelling: Using different technologies for EFL. *MEXTESOL Journal, 40*(1), 1–14.

Clapham, C. (2000). Assessment for academic purposes: Where next? *System, 28*, 511–521.

Cohen, A. (1994). *Assessing language ability in the classroom* (2nd ed.). Boston: Heinle & Heinle.

Condon, W. (2013). Large-scale assessment, locally-developed measures, and automated scoring of essays: Fishing for red herrings? *Assessing Writing, 18*, 100–108.

Conference on College Composition and Communication. (2004). Position statement on teaching, learning, and assessing writing in a digital environment. http://www.ncte.org/cccc/resources/positions/digitalenvironments

Conference on College Composition and Communication. (2009). Writing assessment: A position statement. http://www.ncte.org/cccc/resources/positions/writingassessment

Crusan, D. (2010a). *Assessment in the second language writing classroom.* Ann Arbor: University of Michigan Press.

Crusan, D. (2010b). Assess thyself lest others assess thee. In T. Silva & P. Matsuda (Eds.), *Practicing theory in second language writing* (pp. 245–262). West Lafayette, IN: Parlor Press.

Crusan, D. (2010c). Review of Ericsson and Haswell (Eds.), Machine scoring of student essays: Truth and consequences. *Language Testing, 27*(3), 437–440.

Crusan, D. (2013). Assessing writing. In *The companion to language assessment, 1*(2), 201–215. Wiley Online Library.

Crusan, D. (2015). Dance ten: looks three: Why rubrics matter (editorial). *Assessing Writing, 16*, 1–4.

Crusan, D., Plakans, L., & Gebril, A. (2016). Writing assessment literacy: Surveying second language teachers' knowledge, beliefs, and practices. *Assessing Writing, 28*, 43–56.

Cumming, A. (2001). ESL/EFL instructors' practices for writing assessment: Specific purposes or general purposes? *Language Testing, 18*(2), 207–224.

Currie, P. (1994). What counts as good writing? Enculturation and writing assessment. In A. Freedman & P. Medway (Eds.), *Teaching and learning genre* (pp. 63–79). Portsmouth, NH: Boynton/Cook.

Davis, M., & Yancey, K. B. (2014). Notes toward the role of materiality in composing, reviewing, and assessing multimodal texts. *Computers and Composition, 31*, 13–28.

Deane, P. (2013). On the relation between automated essay scoring and modern views of the writing construct. *Assessing Writing, 18*, 7–24.

Dikli, S., & Bleye, S. (2014). Automated essay scoring feedback for second language writers: How does it compare to instructor feedback? *Assessing Writing, 22*, 1–17.

Elbow, P. (1993). Ranking, evaluating, and liking: Sorting out three forms of judgment. *College English, 55*, 187–206.

Elbow, P. (1994). Will the virtues of portfolios blind us to their potential dangers? In L. Black, D. A. Daiker, J. Sommers, & G. Stygall (Eds.), *New directions in portfolio assessment: Reflective practice, critical theory, and large-scale scoring* (pp. 40–55). Portsmouth, NH: Boynton/Cook.

Elbow, P., & Belanoff, P. (1997). Reflections on an explosion: Portfolios in the '90s and beyond. In K. B. Yancey & I. Weiser (Eds.), *Situating portfolios: Four perspectives* (pp. 21–33). Logan: Utah State University Press.

Elliot, N., & Williamson, D. M. (2013). Assessing Writing special issue: Assessing writing with automated scoring systems. *Assessing Writing, 18*, 1–6.

Enright, M. K., & Quinlan, T. (2010). Complementing human judgment of essays written by English language learners with e-rater® scoring. *Language Testing, 27*(3), 317–334.

Ericcson, P. F., & Haswell, R. (Eds.). (2006). *Machine scoring of student essays: Truth and consequences*. Logan: Utah University Press.

Feak, C., & Dobson, B. (1996). Building on the impromptu: A source-based academic writing assessment. *College ESL, 6*(1), 73–84.

Ferris, D., & Hedgcock, J. (2014). *Teaching L2 composition: Purpose, process, and practice* (3rd ed.). New York: Routledge/Taylor & Francis.

Fulcher, G. (1999). Assessment in English for academic purposes: Putting content validity in its place. *Applied Linguistics, 20*(2), 221–236.

Fulcher, G. (2000). The 'communicative' legacy in language testing. *System, 28*(4), 483–497.

Fulcher, G. (2015). *Re-examining language testing: A philosophical and social inquiry.* New York: Routledge/Taylor & Francis.

Hafner, C. A. (2013). Digital composition in a second or foreign language. *TESOL Quarterly, 47*(4), 830–834.

Hafner, C. A. (2015). Remix culture and English language teaching: The expression of learner voice in digital multimodal compositions. *TESOL Quarterly, 49*(3), 486–509.

Hamp-Lyons, L. (1991a). Basic concepts. In L. Hamp-Lyons (Ed.), *Assessing second language writing in academic contexts* (pp. 5–15). Norwood, NJ: Ablex.

Hamp-Lyons, L. (1991b). Reconstructing "academic writing proficiency." In L. Hamp-Lyons (Ed.), *Assessing second language writing in academic contexts* (pp. 241–276). Norwood, NJ: Ablex.

Hamp-Lyons, L. (1991c). Scoring procedures for ESL contexts. In L. Hamp-Lyons (Ed.), *Assessing second language writing in academic contexts* (pp. 87–107). Norwood, NJ: Ablex.

Hamp-Lyons, L. (1995). Rating nonnative writing: The trouble with holistic scoring. *TESOL Quarterly, 29*, 759–762.

Hamp-Lyons, L. (1997). Washback, impact and validity: Ethical concerns. *Language Testing, 14*(3), 295–303.

Hamp-Lyons, L. (2001). Fourth generation writing assessment. In T. Silva & P. K. Matsuda (Eds.), *On second language writing* (pp. 117–127). Mahwah, NJ: Lawrence Erlbaum.

Hamp-Lyons, L. (2011). Writing assessment: Shifting issues, new tools, enduring questions. *Assessing Writing, 16*, 3–5.

Hamp-Lyons, L. (2014). Writing assessment in global context. *Research in the Teaching of English, 48*(3), 353–362.

Hamp-Lyons, L. (2016). Farewell to holistic scoring? Editorial. *Assessing Writing, 27*, A1–A2.

Hamp-Lyons, L., & Condon, W. (1993). Questioning assumptions about portfolio-based assessment. *College Composition and Communication, 44*, 176–190.

Hamp-Lyons, L., & Condon, W. (2000). *Assessing the portfolio: Principles for practice, theory, and research.* Cresskill, NJ: Hampton Press.

Hamp-Lyons, L., & Zhang, B. W. (2001). World Englishes: Issues in and from academic writing assessment. In J. Flowerdew & M. Peacock (Eds.), *Research perspectives on English for academic purposes* (pp. 101–116). Cambridge, U.K.: Cambridge University Press.

Hayes, J. R., Hatch, J. A., & Silk, C. M. (2000). Does holistic assessment predict writing performance? Estimating the consistency of student performance on holistically scored writing assignments. *Written Communication, 17*(1), 3–26.

Henning, G., (1991). Issues in evaluating and maintaining an ESL writing assessment program. In L. Hamp-Lyons (Ed.), *Assessing second language writing in academic contexts* (pp. 279–291). Norwood, NJ: Ablex.

Herrington, A., & Moran, C. (2012). Writing to a machine is not writing at all. In N. Elliot & L. Perelman (Eds.), *Writing assessment in the 21st century: Essays in honor of Edward M. White* (pp. 219–232). New York: Hampton Press.

Hesse, D. D. (2012). Can computers grade writing? Should they? http://www.du.edu/writing/media/documents/hesse-can-computers-grade-writing.pdf

Horowitz, D. (1991). ESL writing assessments: Contradictions and resolutions. In L. Hamp-Lyons (Ed.), *Assessing second language writing in academic contexts* (pp. 71–85). Norwood, NJ: Ablex.

Huot, B. (1990a). The literature of direct writing assessment: Major concerns and prevailing trends. *Review of Educational Research, 60*(2), 237–263.

Huot, B. (1990b). Reliability, validity, and holistic scoring: What we know and what we need to know. *College Composition and Communication, 41*, 201–213.

Huot, B. (1996). Toward a new theory of writing assessment. *College Composition and Communication, 47*(4), 549–566.

Huot, B., & Neal, M. (2006). Writing assessment: A techno-history. In C. A. MacArthur, S. Graham, & J. Fitzgerald (Eds.), *Handbook of writing research* (pp. 417–432). New York: The Guilford Press.

Huot, B., & Williamson, M. M. (1997). Rethinking portfolios for evaluating writing: Issues of assessment. In K. B. Yancey & I. Weiser (Eds.), *Situating portfolios: Four perspectives* (pp. 43–56). Logan: Utah State University Press.

Hyland, K. (2015). *Academic publishing: Issues and challenges in the construction of knowledge.* Oxford, U.K.: Oxford University Press.

Iida, A. (2008). Poetry writing as expressive pedaogy in an EFL context: Identifying possible assessment tools for haiku poetry in EFL freshman college writing. *Assessing Writing, 13*(3), 171–179.

Jacobs, H. L., Zinkgraf, S. A., Wormuth, D. R., Hartfiel, V. F., & Hughey, J. B. (1981). *Testing ESL composition: A practical approach.* Rowley, MA: Newbury House.

Johns, A. (1991). Interpreting an English competency examination. *Written Communication, 8*(3), 379–401.

Lee, Y-W., Gentile, C., & Kantor, R. (2010). Toward automated multi-trait scoring of essays: Investigating links among holistic, analytic, and text feature scores. *Applied Linguistics, 31*(3), 391–417.

Liebman, J. D. (1992). Toward a new contrastive rhetoric: Differences between Arabic and Japanese rhetorical instruction. *Journal of Second Language Writing, 1*(2), 141–166.

Li, X. M. (1996). *"Good writing" in cross-cultural context.* Albany: SUNY Press.

Lucas, T. (1992). Diversity among individuals: Eight students making sense of classroom journal writing. In D. E. Murray (Ed.), *Diversity as resource: Redefining cultural literacy* (pp. 202–232). Alexandria, VA: TESOL.

Lynch, B. K. (1997). In search of the ethical test. *Language Testing, 14*(3), 315–327.

Lynch, B. K. (2001a). The ethical potential of alternative language assessment. In C. Elder, A. Brown, E. Grove, K. Hill, N. Iwashita, T. Lumley, T. McNamara, & K. O'Loughlin (Eds.), *Experimenting with uncertainty: Essays in honour of Alan Davies* (pp. 228–239). Cambridge, U.K.: Cambridge University Press.

Lynch, B. K. (2001b). Rethinking assessment from a critical perspective. *Language Testing, 18*(4), 351–372.

McGee, T. (2006). Taking a spin on the intelligent essay assessor. In P. F. Ericcson & R. Haswell (Eds.), *Machine scoring of students essays: Truth and consequences* (pp. 79–92). Logan: Utah University Press.

McNamara, D. S., Crossley, S. A., & McCarthy, P. M. (2010). Linguistic features of writing quality. *Written Communication, 27*(1), 57–86.

McNamara, T. F. (1996). *Measuring second language performance.* Harlow, U.K.: Addison Wesley Longman Ltd.

McNamara, T. (2000). *Language testing.* Oxford, U.K.: Oxford University Press.

McNamara, T. (2001). Language assessment as social practice: Challenges for research. *Language Testing, 18*(4), 333–349.

McNamara, T. (2006). Validity in language testing: The challenge of Sam Messick's legacy. *Language Assessment Quarterly, 3*(1), 31–51.

McNamara, T., & Roever, C. (2006). *Language testing: The social dimension.* Malden, MA: Blackwell Publishing.

Messick, S. (1989). Meaning and values in test validation: The science and ethics of assessment. *Educational Researcher, 18*(2), 5–11.

Messick, S. (1994). The interplay of evidence and consequences in the validation of performance assessments. *Educational Researcher, 23*(2), 13–23.

Messick, S. (1996). Validity and washback in language testing. *Language Testing, 13*(3), 241–256.

Moss, P. (1994). Can there be validity without reliability? *Educational Researcher, 23*(2), 5–12.

Murphy, S. (1997). Teachers and students: Reclaiming assessment via portfolios. In K. B. Yancey & I. Weiser (Eds.), *Situating portfolios: Four perspectives* (pp. 72–88). Logan: Utah State University Press.

Murphy, S. (1999). Assessing portfolios. In C. R. Cooper & L. Odell (Eds.), *Evaluating writing: The role of teachers' knowledge about text, learning, and culture* (pp. 114–135). Urbana, IL: National Council of Teachers of English.

Murray, D. E. (1994). Using portfolios to assess writing. *Prospect, 9*(2), 56–69.

Neal, M. R. (2011). *Writing assessment and the revolution in digital texts and technologies.* New York: Teachers College Press.

Norton, B., & Starfield, S. (1997). Covert language assessment in academic writing. *Language Testing, 14*(3), 278–294.

Ravitch, D. (2013). Can machines grades essays? Should they? http://diane ravitch.net/2013/05/16/can-machines-grade-essays-should-they/

Robinson, P., & Ross, S. (1996). The development of task-based assessment in English for academic purposes programs. *Applied Linguistics, 17*(4), 455–475.

Sasaki, M., & Hirose, K. (1999). Development of an analytical rating scale for Japanese L1 writing. *Language Testing, 16*(4), 457–478.

Shermis, M. D., & Burstein, J. (Eds.). (2013). *Handbook of automated essay evaluation: Current applications and new directions*. New York: Routledge/Taylor & Francis.

Shermis, M. D., Burstein, J., & Bursky, S. A. (2013). Introduction to automated essay evaluation. In M. D. Shermis & J. Burstein (Eds.), *Handbook of automated essay evaluation: Current applications and new directions* (pp. 1–15). New York: Routledge/Taylor & Francis.

Schneider, M., & Fujishima, N. K. (1995). When practice doesn't make perfect: The case of an ESL graduate student. In D. Belcher & G. Braine (Eds.), *Academic writing in a second language: Essays on research and pedagogy* (pp. 3–22). Norwood, NJ: Ablex.

Shohamy, E. (1997). Testing methods, testing consequences: Are they ethical? Are they fair? *Language Testing, 14*(3), 340–349.

Shohamy, E. (2001a). Democratic assessment as an alternative. *Language Testing, 18*(4), 373–391.

Shohamy, E. (2001b). *The power of tests: A critical perspective on the uses of language tests*. Harlow, U.K.: Pearson Education Ltd.

Skehan, P. (1984). Issues in the testing of English for specific purposes. *Language Testing, 1*(2), 202–220.

Slomp, D. (2012). Challenges in assessing the development of writing ability: Theories, constructs and methods. *Assessing Writing, 17*, 81–91.

Smit, D. W. (1994). A WPA's nightmare: Reflections on using portfolios as a course exit exam. In L. Black, D. A. Daiker, J. Sommers, & G. Stygall (Eds.), *New directions in portfolio assessment: Reflective practice, critical theory, and large-scale scoring* (pp. 303–313). Portsmouth, NH: Boynton/Cook.

Sokolik, M., & Tillyer, A. (1992). Beyond portfolios: Looking at student projects as teaching and evaluation devices. *College ESL, 2*(2), 47–51.

Spolsky, B. (1997). The ethics of gatekeeping tests: What have we learned in a hundred years? *Language Testing, 14*(3), 242–247.

Sternberg, R. J. (1990). T & T is an explosive combination: Technology and testing. *Educational Psychologist, 25*, 201–222.

Wardle, E., & Roozen, K. (2012). Addressing the complexity of writing development: Toward an ecological model of assessment. *Assessing Writing, 17*, 106–119.

Ware, P. (2011). Computer generated feedback on student writing. *TESOL Quarterly, 45*(4), 769–774.

Warschauer, M., & Ware, J. (2006). Automated writing evaluation: Defining the classroom research agenda. *Language Teaching Research, 10*(2),1–24.

Weigle, S. C. (2002). *Assessing writing.* Cambridge, U.K.: Cambridge University Press.

Weigle, S. C. (2010). Validation of automated scores of TOEFL iBT tasks against non-test indicators of writing ability. *Language Testing, 27*(3), 335–353.

Weigle, S. C. (2013a). English as a second language writing and automated essay evaluation. In M. D. Shermis & J. Burstein (Eds.), *Handbook of automated essay evaluation: Current applications and new directions* (pp. 36–54). New York: Routledge/Taylor & Francis.

Weigle, S. C. (2013b). English language learners and automated scoring of essays: Critical considerations. *Assessing Writing, 18*(1), 85–99.

White, E. M. (1994). Portfolios as an assessment concept. In L. Black, D. A. Daiker, J. Sommers, & G. Stygall (Eds.), *New directions in portfolio assessment: Reflective practice, critical theory, and large-scale scoring* (pp. 25–39). Portsmouth, NH: Boynton/Cook.

Yancey, K. B. (Ed.) (1992). *Portfolios in the writing classroom: An introduction.* Urbana, IL: National Council of Teachers of English.

Yancey, K. B. (1996). Dialogue, interplay, and discovery: Mapping the role and rhetoric of reflection in portfolio assessment. In R. Calfee & P. Perfumo (Eds.), *Writing portfolios in the classroom: Policy and practice, promise and peril* (pp. 83–102). Mahwah, NJ: Lawrence Erlbaum.

Yancey, K. B., & Weiser, I. (Eds.). (1997). *Situating portfolios: Four perspectives.* Urbana, IL: National Council of Teachers of English.

Zhang, B., Xiao, Y., & Luo, J. (2015). Rater reliability and score discrepancy under holistic and analytic scoring of second language writing. *Language Testing in Asia, 5*, 5.

Chapter 8

Miscellaneous Controversies: Critical Thinking, Individualism, and Voice

"[C]ritical thinking appears to be something more universally relevant than just a social practice. If some cultures differ in their present ability to appropriate the tools of critical thinking, it is probably only a difference in the degree to which critical thinking is tolerated in certain spheres of life." (Davidson, 1998, p. 122)

"[T]here are people with collectivistic tendencies in individualistic cultures and people with individualistic tendencies in collectivistic cultures." (Gudykunst et al., 1996, p. 529)

"...[C]ertain writing features may be more a matter of socialized discourse conventions than directly attributable to differences in collectivist or individualist ideation." (Wu & Rubin, 2000, p. 148)

"...[I]t remains questionable whether L2 students' writing success depends upon an individualized voice." (Helms-Park & Stapleton, 2003, p. 246)

"...[W]riting always has voice in the sense that it conveys a representation of the writer" (Hyland, 2008, p. 5).

LEADING QUESTIONS

- How do you define critical thinking in the context of L2 writing activities? Do you think it is a culturally loaded concept?
- What is your current understanding of the concepts of individualism and collectivism when you think about L2 students from Western and non-Western cultures?
- What is your notion of voice? How important is it to your understanding of successful writing for L1 and L2 students? Does genre or type of writing make a difference?

Introduction to the Issues

A number of unresolved issues with a cultural and ideological aspect face L2 writing teachers as they make decisions about how best to design and carry out instructional activities. I have discussed some of these issues in Chapter 4, ones having to do with whose standards should be taught and emulated in L2 writing. As I discussed in that chapter, these arguments contrast proponents of Western-style standard written English with those who wish to see more fluidity and flexibility in our expectations for L2 writing, more reflective of the great diversity of usages in lingua franca oral language and World Englishes. In this concluding chapter, I review several other controversies that have been around for some time, all of which also have somewhat of a cultural and ideological edge in the sense that they concern what have been described as Western and nonWestern values. The issues discussed in this concluding chapter include the debates on critical thinking, individualism, and voice, and the extent to which these are cultural concepts imposed by Western values that suit, or do not, L2 writing in school settings worldwide.

Critical thinking has been defined in a variety of ways, leading some to say that it is difficult to proceed with productive
discussions when we can't even define our key terms (e.g.,
Atkinson, 1998). But there do seem to be threads of agreement that focus on similar kinds of practices and processes,
such as those that involve analyzing, synthesizing, reflecting
skeptically, identifying flaws in reasoning, drawing conclusions, presenting a point of view, and evaluating (Cottrell,
2011, pp. 2–3; Stapleton, 2001). Students sometimes mistake
the term *critical thinking* for negative commentary, so one of
the writing teacher's first tasks is to clarify that the definition
does not connote negativity, but a questioning, skeptical, and
evaluative attitude.

Two other related concepts that have been labeled Western
are those of individualism and voice as goals for L1 and L2
writing. Both received a great deal of attention during and after
the process-writing era in the United States (begun in the late
1960s and peaking in the mid-1990s; Tobin & Newkirk, 1994),
partly thanks to the so-called expressivist movement and also
to the work of L1 writing educator Peter Elbow, among others.
Educators became more interested in how people wrote than
in what they wrote (hence the process-product debates; see
Chapter 5, this book), and in how they could express themselves individually in their writing. Individualism has been
touted as a quintessential American (if not Western) value,
linked to related values of autonomy, liberty, and privacy.
Voice is also linked to an individual sense of self in the views
of some scholars and should be aimed for in at least some kinds
of writing. Elbow (1994), for instance, distinguished between
the literal meaning of the term *voice* (sound coming from the
vocal cords) and the metaphorical use (the "sound" of a person's voice in a piece of writing, recognizable as that person).
He spent many decades of his career arguing that students
do not always need to adhere to the person-less conventions
of academic discourse, what Geertz (1988) called "author-
evacuated prose." Voice, however, is now thought to be an
inherent part of all academic writing (Hyland, 2008; Tardy &

Matsuda, 2009; Zhao, 2013). These concepts of critical thinking, individualism, and voice continue to play a large role in L1 and L2 writing and composition classes, and educators continue to ask to what extent they are Western-imposed values that many L2 students might have trouble with. I discuss some of these ideas in more detail in the next section.

Discussions in the Literature

An ideological topic in L2 writing that has been debated for some time concerns the role of culturally constructed notions such as critical thinking, individualism, and voice in the kinds of writing activities teachers ask students to do and the ways that teachers expect students to write and talk about their ideas. As I said in the introduction, a common assumption is that these notions are Western, not universal, and that in the world of English language teaching they are imposed on students as the most important way to think and write in academic contexts (Canagarajah, 2013; Fox, 1994). Not only educators from L1 English language backgrounds, but also many L2 writers and educators have bought into this idea, even describing their own culture's thinking as imitative rather than critical, as group-oriented or collectivist rather than individual, and as lacking in appropriate authorial voice for writing in English. I discuss each of these subtopics in turn, despite their interrelatedness.

Critical Thinking

Expressed in the simplest terms, the debate about critical thinking contrasts two sets of beliefs. The first set holds that critical thinking is a culture-specific construct encompassing a questioning, reasoned stance that is taken for granted as a skill that people develop as they are socialized and educated in particular cultures such as Anglophone Western cultures (Atkinson, 1997). People who hold this belief question whether L2 educators should be imposing what they see as a uniquely

Western way of thinking on L2 students. The second set of beliefs constructs critical thinking in broader ways, characterizing it as a basic human survival mechanism used by all societies, even if applied minimally in some educational settings. Those who hold this set of beliefs argue that all students, including those who are minorities or speakers of a nondominant language, need to develop the critical-thinking skills of questioning and analyzing in order to understand and perhaps resist dominance and injustice, as well as to solve problems at home, school, and the workplace (Benesch, 1999, 2001a, 2001b; Delpit, 1988).

Does critical thinking come naturally to students from certain cultures? Certainly in the United States, all undergraduate university students face critical thinking tasks in their first-year composition classes, indicating that even though some of them have been immersed for a lifetime in U.S. culture, they still don't know how to read and write critically. As a simple internet search will reveal, educators in the United States have long addressed the lack of and need for critical-thinking skills in U.S. students. Composition textbooks intended for L1 students (Bean, 2011, and Cottrell, 2011, are just two examples) routinely address critical thinking, indicating that lack of critical-thinking skills is not just a problem facing L2 students. However, in spite of evidence that U.S. L1 students lack critical-thinking skills, the view was put forth in the mid- and late-1990s that L1 students in composition classes were ready for critical thinking and the L2 students were not.

Arguing that critical thinking is a peculiarly Western construct, characteristic of U.S. middle class socialization practices, Atkinson, Ramanathan, and Kaplan (Atkinson, 1997; Atkinson & Ramanathan, 1995; Ramanathan & Atkinson, 1999; Ramanathan & Kaplan, 1996a, 1996b) all urged TESOL educators, and L2 writing teachers in particular, to consider whether the kinds of critical-thinking activities often found in L1 writing classrooms are suitable for L2 populations, particularly those from Asian countries. Perhaps one of the strongest statements in this regard appeared in Ramanathan and Kaplan (1996b, p. 232):

> L2 student-writers, given their respective sociocultural and linguistic socialization practices, are more likely than native English speaking (NES) students to encounter difficulty when being inducted into CT [critical thinking] courses in freshman composition classes. They are not "ready" for CT courses in either L1 or L2 writing classrooms.

The following year Atkinson (1997) published his much discussed critique of critical thinking in TESOL. In this article, he laid out four major points, all of which, he argued, suggest that TESOL educators should refrain from unthinkingly adopting critical-thinking pedagogies in their classrooms. He first noted that critical thinking is a social practice in which "an individual is automatically immersed by virtue of being raised in a particular cultural milieu and which the individual therefore learns 'through the pores'" (p. 73). (I wish this had happened to me, but it did not!) For this reason, critical thinking is especially difficult to define, although educators seem to have a felt sense of what it is. In response to the evidence that U.S. children lack critical-thinking skills, Atkinson noted that "mainstream schools have become progressively more accessible to nonmainstream groups over the past 30 years," thus provoking a sense of crisis (p. 77). In other words, because the nonmainstream students cannot think critically, they are skewing the assessment of critical-thinking skills in the United States. Atkinson suggested here, citing Shirley Brice Heath's 1983 book *Ways with Words* in this and other publications, that, because critical-thinking skills result from early socialization, they are probably impossible to teach.

Second, Atkinson described critical thinking as "exclusive and reductive" (pp. 77–79). When critical-thinking skills are reduced to (in)formal logic and argumentation as they seem to be in some L1 composition textbooks (noted by Ramanathan & Kaplan, 1996b), many groups are left behind, including women, who may not be comfortable with adversarial thinking (Belcher, 1997). Third, he pointed out that thinking styles of L2 writers have been shown to differ from Western ideas about the values of individualism, self-expression, and language as a tool for learning (see Fox, 1994). Finally, he asked whether critical-thinking skills are generalizable and transferable and found little evidence that they are, other than perhaps within very similar domains and tasks. Atkinson then suggested that a possible solution is to teach critical-thinking skills only within specific disciplines, using a cognitive apprenticeship approach in which experts and novices work together to learn what skills are needed in that context (Lave & Wenger, 1991). He referred to such an approach as "pan-cultural" (p. 89).

Such a discipline-specific approach is also promoted by Ramanthan and Kaplan (1996b), who found that the approaches to critical thinking in the 12 (U.S.) first-year composition textbooks they analyzed do not suit L2 writers. In those textbooks, the authors claimed, emphases on informal logic, creating knowledge, taking a stand, and developing awareness of public issues in U.S. contexts will create special problems for L2 writers. These problems are exacerbated by the questionable transferability of critical-thinking skills. Learning thinking skills within academic disciplines, on the other hand, is a not only more "situated" (Brown, Collins, & Duguid, 1989), but it is also a more culturally neutral approach given that disciplines are "freer of cultural constraints" and have relatively language-neutral ways of analyzing problems according to the "paradigms of the discipline" (Ramanathan & Kaplan, 1996b, p. 242–243).

Not surprisingly, these articles sparked vigorous debate among more "critically" oriented L2 specialists. There has been wide agreement that critical thinking should not be a buzzword that refers to a bandwagon fad, but that it deserves thoughtful analysis and application (Davidson, 1998). However, other aspects of the anti-critical thinking argument have garnered much criticism. In the first place, Davidson (1998) pointed out that without the tool of critical thinking, Atkinson (1997) could never have made his own critique of its use with L2 learners.

He also disagreed with Atkinson (1997, 1998) that useful definitions of critical thinking do not exist. Most definitions share a focus on reasoned, reflective, and skeptical thinking (p. 121), a point also made by Stapleton (2001). Davidson also rejected the portrayal of critical thinking as cold, masculinist, and Western, citing his own observations of the "basic rationality of Japanese people" (Davidson, 1998, p. 121). He also pointed out that if indeed students from countries such as Japan have not been trained to question, critique, and analyze to the extent that students from Western countries have, then this is all the more reason for explicitly offering such students the tools for thinking that will allow them to participate in international communications (p. 122).

In another response to Atkinson (1997), Gieve (1998) made an important distinction between two kinds of critical thinking, only one of which he claimed Atkinson referred to. Critical thinking, which is characterized as informal logic, and which is the target of criticisms by Atkinson (1997) and Ramanathan and Kaplan (1996b), is labeled a monological view by Gieve. A second type is labeled dialogical critical thinking and is inherent to the kind of discourse that people engage in when they uncover and examine "the taken-for-granted assumptions and presuppositions that lie behind argumentation" (p. 125). In a later article, Benesch (1999) took up Gieve's (1998) distinction between monological and dialogical critical thinking to argue why and how dialogical critical thinking might be taught in L2 classes. In short, according to Gieve, by restricting his argument to a narrowly (and culturally stereotyped?) perspective of cross-cultural academic writing, Atkinson and others

> . . . deny the enormous power of this [dialogical] use of language and the power that it brings to those capable of using it for their own ends. Analytical precision and critical insight massively enhance the power of dissent, whether the argument is against the location of a nuclear power station in the U.S. by local citizens or against human rights abuses in China or Iraq by aggrieved minorities, and the critical attitude is by no means restricted to the West. (Gieve, 1998, p. 125)

Finally, Gieve claimed to be puzzled by numerous contradictions in Atkinson's (1997) arguments, including his assertion that a cognitive apprentice approach within disciplines is somehow more culturally neutral or universalist. If cultures differ so radically, and if socialization happens from earliest childhood, then it makes little sense, according to Gieve, to argue for a "pan-cultural" approach to critical thinking. (I might add here that disciplinary practices themselves, far from being culturally neutral, evolved out of Western traditions of intellectual and educational practices, and that disciplinary thinking is nothing if not critical.) In the end, Gieve (1998) was unsure what Atkinson was suggesting: Should L2 students, especially in English-dominant contexts, be given different kinds of writing instruction than L1 students? Do we eschew debate and analysis in favor of students' culturally preferred modes of learning and thinking, assuming we know what these are? And, I would add, is anyone asking the students what they want?

In her response to Atkinson (1997), Hawkins (1998) spoke from the U.S. context, and argued that it is precisely because critical-thinking skills are expected to be displayed by participants in U.S. culture that they need to be taught, if only by apprenticeship, to nonmainstream students. Hawkins (1998, p. 131) asserted that "[b]y denying access and exposure to students already marginalized by virtue of not having mainstream language and cultural behaviors, teachers are complicit in ensuring their failure." Like Benesch (1999, 2001a, 2001b), and Delpit (1988) long before, Hawkins (1998) wanted L2 teachers to help "render [...] transparent the workings of status and power through cultural and educational practices, language use, and behaviors" (p. 132). This does not mean either denying L2 students their own cultures or supplanting their cultural practices with ones foreign to them. The critical-thinking game is a both-and endeavor. It can include many different ways of knowing (e.g., Belcher, 1997).

The discussion has continued on what the place of critical thinking should be in L2 writing classes including in EFL and minority or working class contexts. The thinking abilities and predispositions of L2 students in ESL versus EFL settings have still not been fully researched, although the body of literature on EFL students and critical-thinking practices is growing. Some of these EFL educators have noted, following earlier depictions, that their junior high (Liaw, 2007), high school Ghahremani-Ghajar & Mirhosseini, 2005), and university students (Alagozlu, 2007) have not been educated to think critically but instead have learned through memorization and repetition, and that writing instruction therefore needs to focus on critical and reflective thinking. Alagozlu (2007), for example, analyzed 76 essays by Turkish undergraduate students, blaming the education system for the students' apparent inability to think and write critically. Expressing a commonly held view in many parts of the world where students might not be expected to do more than memorize and paraphrase existing ideas, she explained:

> For long, it has been observed that Turkish EFL (English as a Foreign Language) students have great difficulties when writing essays in English as they can not easily integrate their own ideas. The difficulty seems to stem from mere loyalty to texts given as course materials (coursebooks, reference books, hand-outs, reports on the net and so on). (pp. 118–119)

On the other hand, Ghahremani-Ghajar and Mirhosseini (2005) found that the dialogue journal entries of 30 Iranian high school students helped the young writers develop critical reflection and an individual voice, which the authors deemed as valuable skills. Other EFL educators have taken a different stance, and point out that choice of topic for discussion and writing greatly influences students' ability to take a critical stance. Stapleton (2000, 2001, 2002a), for one, provided evidence that his undergraduate students in Japan, when writing about controversial topics familiar to them, were able to express a variety of critical attitudes that they were not able to express on an unfamiliar topic as well as to demonstrate they understood basic concepts of critical thinking.

Several authors who contributed to a book on risk in academic writing (Thesen & Cooper, 2014) also addressed relevant questions about critical thinking. Two of the authors were international African graduate students writing doctoral theses at universities in South Africa (Hunma & Sibohama, 2014). Hunma and Sibohama, from two different African countries, admitted to their difficulties thinking and writing according to the thesis standards imposed by their South African universities, but at the same time, expressed clearly their belief that critical and analytical thinking were essential for them. From a working class northern England background, Cadman (2014), writing from Australia, wrote on her anguish at the constraints imposed on her own dissertation and professional writing by what she called northern hemisphere conventions, and on the thinking and writing of her African students. (For another working class perspective, see Costley's, 2008, struggles with her own academic writing as a graduate student.) Many other ways of knowing were being ignored, Cadman pointed out. Yet her lament is itself deeply critical and scholarly even while not being fully conventional in Western terms: It is both personal and emotional. She readily admitted that as a senior scholar she can take such risks but would not recommend that novice scholars do so. In fact, it is possible that novice scholars such a dissertation writers will not find ways of reconciling their voices and identities until after they are safely through the dissertation defense (Carter-Tod, 2002). In another chapter in this book on risk in academic writing, two non-white scholars from the United States and Canada wrote about constraints on publishing in English (Canagarajah & Lee, 2014). Lee was trying to write and revise an article in the style of a personal narrative for *TESOL Quarterly*, a journal that Canagarajah was editing at the time. However, Lee gave up revising after several rounds of reviews seemed to be asking her to let go of her personal and emotional voice and become more critical and analytical in her treatment of her topic, even though the topic was about herself. Canagarajah concluded that journal gatekeepers continue to demand a kind of conventional critical thinking and objectivity that Lee was trying to counter.

It seems, then, that the open debates from the 1990s on critical thinking have subsided, but the issues remain. Schools, universities, and applied linguistics/TESOL journals in particular continue to expect a kind of thinking and writing that exhibits a questioning, rational, analytical stance and that takes certain conventional forms in writing and not others. This is in spite of strong cases being made for alternate kinds of writing to be accepted in academia (see Schroeder, Fox, & Bizzell, 2002, and Chapter 4, this book, on standards in writing) and for inclusion of alternate modes of knowing in academia (Cadman, 2014). Every writing teacher, therefore, will continue to need to consider how they define critical thinking and what the place of critical thinking is in their pedagogy. Such considerations include querying students as to what their background learning experiences are, what they want and expect in their L2 writing classes particularly when engaging with content in readings and discussions, and what kinds of thinking they can do when writing about issues they are or are not familiar with. In all cases it seems unjustified to claim that students from certain cultures cannot think critically.

Individualism

Individualism has been touted as a fundamental Western value that contrasts with the collectivist values of some other cultures (most often mentioned are those from East Asia, such as China, Korea, and Japan). Researchers in intercultural communication studies have influenced our views greatly on individualism and collectivism in Western and Eastern cultures, introducing these abstract terms and others into common parlance (e.g., high- and low-context cultures according to how much contextual information is required for meaningful communication; Hall, 1976). In this work, which consists mostly of large-scale surveys, whole cultures are labeled according to these concepts, providing us with broad and compelling truisms that are difficult to refute. Here are characterizations of individualism-collectivism by two well-known intercultural communication scholars, based on their own reviews of the literature:

> As members of individualistic cultures are socialized into their culture, [people] learn the major values of their culture (e.g., independence, achievement) and acquire preferred ways for how members of the culture are expected to view themselves (e.g., as unique persons). Members of collectivistic cultures learn different major values (e.g., harmony, solidarity) and acquire different preferred ways to conceive of themselves (e.g., as interconnected with others). (Gudykunst et al., 1996, pp. 512–513)

> Individualism as a characteristic of a culture opposes *Collectivism* (the word is used here in an anthropological, not a political sense). Individualist cultures assume that any person looks primarily after his or her own interest and the interest of his or her immediate family (husband, wife and children). Collectivist cultures assume that any person through birth and possible later events belongs to one or more tight "in-groups," from which he or she cannot detach him- or herself. The "in-group" (whether extended family, clan, or organization) protects the interest of its members, but in turn expects their permanent loyalty. A collectivist society is tightly integrated; an individualist society is loosely integrated. (Hofstede, 1986, p. 307)

Threads of individualistic values understandably run through the previous section on critical thinking and the next section on voice, given that they are all linked to (stereotypical) Western stances like those described that continue to be promoted in educational settings. In fact, taking a critical stance in a piece of writing might require an individualistic perspective due to the very nature of critical thinking. However, much like Kaplan's (1966) oversimplified and misleading commentaries on paragraph organization in different languages and cultures (see Chapter 2 on Contrastive and Intercultural Rhetoric), equally oversimplified views of cultures have been perpetuated in intercultural communication studies such as those reviewed by Gudykunst et al. (1996) and Hofstede (1986) and picked up uncritically by others ever since. We can all recognize ourselves and our students in these descriptions, so powerful have the characterizations become. It has become difficult to see how complex and individually variable we all are when the descriptions of cultures and writing styles are so compelling and full of partial truths.

Such characterizations persist in their uncomplicated forms despite the findings of some large-scale survey research (e.g., Gudykunst, et al., 1996) that patterns of collectivism and individualism across cultures are not clear, and that "individual level factors (i.e., self construals and values) are better predictors of low- and high-context communication styles across cultures than cultural individualism-collectivism" (Gudykunst, et al., 1996, p. 510). The point is that individualist and collectivist tendencies are found within, not just across, cultures, making broad generalizations open to critique.

Debates in the late 1990s between Atkinson (1997) and Spack (1997) and Zamel (1997) among others tried to apply the concepts to L2 writing practices. These arguments contrasted the cultural and individualist perspectives and are still worth reading. Spack (1997) for example claimed that at the level that teachers deal with in their own classrooms, the individual stands out as unique in ways that broad cultural generalizations drawn from survey research might not fit. Atkinson (1997, 1999) argued that it makes no sense to dispose of the notion of culture into which individualist and collectivist perspectives fit, even if at the level of the individuals in our classes we cannot apply these perspectives accurately. Another way to look at this dilemma is to understand that statistical generalizations (e.g., about individualism and collectivism from large-scale surveys), no matter how well a survey has been conducted, say nothing about individuals.

Still, the search continues, and assumptions are put forward that are difficult to refute. In writing studies, for instance, no one can deny that learning to write in a second language involves more than learning grammar, syntax, and spelling—it also "requires assimilation of far more subtle yet pervasive cultural knowledge about ways of arguing, ways of addressing an audience, ways of expressing authority, and much more (Wu & Rubin, 2000, p. 148). As Wu and Rubin pointed out, many studies have highlighted Western-Eastern (Confucian-oriented) cultural differences that seem to point to differences in individual and collective orientations (p. 148). It is worth going back and reading some of these studies that emphasize the influence of culture and the importance of individualism and voice in L2 writing (e.g., Fox, 1994; Matalene, 1985). It is also worth studying some of the survey research carefully for its methods and conclusions, and seeing the extent to which authors comment in broad, and hence inaccurate, terms about large complex and multilingual-multidialectical cultures like China ("Chinese students do/do not do xyz...") and even the English-speaking world without acknowledging the vast variability within these broad groups. Importantly for the L2 writing field, we need to pay attention to whether researchers and educators attribute problems in writing to cultural differences, or to other factors as well such as developmental factors, topic knowledge, task, language proficiency (e.g., Mohan & Lo, 1985; see Chapter 2, this book), in addition to individual idiosyncracies (Spack, 1997; Zamel, 1997).

However, although scholars for many years have warned against essentializing cultures, when it comes to individualism and collectivism, we just can't seem to help ourselves. As Wu and Rubin noted (2000, p. 150), when we notice differences in the writing of Chinese- and English-dominant students, we presume the differences are cultural. To help correct the broad cultural presumptions made by many scholars, Wu and Rubin undertook a study designed to look at a large sample of individual L2 writers within groups broadly characterized as individual and collective: Americans in the United States and

Taiwanese. They framed their study broadly according to the descriptions we are all familiar with: Chinese culture values harmony, interdependence, cooperation, deference, and self-sacrifice; U.S. culture values individualism, independence, privacy, autonomy, and personal liberty (p. 151). As the authors explained based on the review of theoretical literature, "The guiding principle of individualism is the interest of the individual. In contrast, people from collective societies are more concerned with effects of their actions on others, sharing benefits, and loss of face" (p. 152). Ramanathan and Atkinson (1999) had the year before offered a thoroughly referenced review of literature supporting the view that individualism is a cultural value of the West, unfamiliar to and even inappropriate for L2 writers from the East (China and Japan in particular). Wu and Rubin did find differences in the writing features of the Taiwanese (who wrote in both Chinese and English) and U.S. students, but the differences did not always fit the expected patterns. Under greater influence from Western conventions than in the past, half of the Taiwanese students "wrote Chinese essays that were as direct as the prototypical Western model" (Wu & Rubin, 2000, p. 172). The authors attributed most of these differences to socialized discourse conventions rather than to collectivism or individualism. See Kubota (1998) and Kubota and Shi (2005) for similar findings from studies of writing and writing instruction in Japan and China.

These matters do have cultural dimensions, of course, so our challenge is how to retain yet complicate our views of culture (Atkinson, 1999, 2003a) and to determine the extent to which a construct like individualism or collectivism is a broad cultural construct or one also influenced by task, purpose, and personality. The broad generalizations might not help us understand particular groups of L2 writers as we would hope. We should therefore apply the concepts to studies and practices in L2 writing with caution. Linked to these questions is that of voice, another construct that has cultural overtones and that is used by some to generalize about who L2 writers are, what they can do, and what our writing assignments require of them.

Voice

Voice is not just the sound from our vocal cords when we speak, but also a quality of our writing that reveals the presence of an author, whether or not we believe that such a presence reflects an authentic self. To what extent is the concept of voice a cultural one? To what extent does it reflect the presence of an individual in a piece of writing? Is it related to writing quality? Do some kinds of writing exhibit voice and others not?

Conceptualizations of voice in L1 composition and writing in the United States before and during the process-writing movement many years ago gave the impression that voice was a feature of writing that promoted an authentic and individualistic self, and that one goal of writing instruction was to help students learn to express this individual self (e.g., Elbow, 1981; see the discussion of the process-product debate in Chapter 5). Many educators in the West presumed that an authentic and original self existed and could be expressed in free writing and reflective journals. However, postmodernists denied the notion of an essential or core self, favoring a hybrid, changing, and fluid perspective instead. In another view of voice, Bakhtin (1981), too, wrote about the inevitable plurality and heteroglossia of voices in speech and writing, which are made up of the words and thoughts of others. Still, many of us, whether we are L1 or L2 writers, feel that we have a core self of some kind—and a voice in speech and writing that distinguishes us from others. These differing views have not been resolved.

Importantly for L2 writing teachers, often the debate distinguishes between a personal expressive voice and an academic voice. These differences were debated some years ago by Elbow and Bartholomae within the context of (primarily) L1 university composition classes in the United States. For his part, Elbow (e.g., 1973, 1981, 1991) has always tried to help his students lose their fear of writing, discover something about themselves through the act of writing, and find a self in their writing that they can identify as uniquely theirs and that they can express freely. He also hoped to bring into writing some qualities of a more natural spoken voice that was freed from the many constraints of academic conventions (Elbow, 1994, 1995, 1999). Bartholomae (1985), on the other hand, contended that learning to write in a university setting means learning to take on the voice of an academic—to "learn to speak our language" (p. 135). He also believed that any writing we do in a school context is by definition academic (Bartholomae, 1995). He was referring to students in U.S. universities, not necessarily to L2 writers who were studying outside the United States.

If L1 English users as well as L2 writers need to learn this kind of academic voice in their university writing, we need to ask to what extent an academic voice and critical thinking are learned through cultural socialization in English-dominant cultures. As I discussed earlier, Atkinson (1997), for one, argued along with Heath (1983) that mainstream children in the U.S. are imbued from childhood with Western concepts such as the importance of critical thinking and individual voice. If this is so, then it is odd that so much attention is devoted to critical thinking and to voice in U.S. university settings and education literature. As I indicated in the section on critical thinking, perhaps it is not only L2 (ESL and EFL) students who are not prepared to take on these concepts in the U.S. composition class (Ramanathan & Kaplan, 1996a, 1996b), but many L1 students as well.

Some scholars have asked whether the presence or absence of individual voice is related to writing quality. Helms-Park and Stapleton (2003), for instance, tried to measure voice in the writing of mainly Chinese undergraduate L2 students in Canada and relate it to writing quality but found no relation using the measures they did (a "Voice Intensity Rating Scale," itself open to scrutiny). This scale included features of assertiveness, self-identification, reiteration of a central point, and authorial presence and autonomy of thought (Helms-Park & Stapleton p. 245). The authors referred to voice as a personal style of writing and argued that for novice L2 writers it is more important for teachers to help them with their ideas, argumentation, and reasoning skills than to help them develop an individual voice (Stapleton, 2002b). The Voice Intensity Rating Scale was used by others to try to measure voice in academic writing of L2 students (Zhao, 2013) and L1 high school students (Zhao & Llosa, 2014). These two studies found significant correlations between this same voice measure and writing quality on argumentative essays (Zhao, 2013; Zhao & Llosa, 2014), countering the findings of Helms-Park and Stapleton (2003).

The view of voice as a personal style has been refuted by Matsuda and Tardy (2007, 2008; Tardy & Matsuda, 2009), who investigated a very different context to learn whether journal manuscript reviewers could guess anything about an author's identity in anonymous manuscripts from rhetorical constructions of voice (reviewers claimed they could). This study did not, however, make any claims about links between writing quality and voice. Hyland (2008), too, views voice in scholarly academic writing not so much as personal style as an inevitable feature of writing unrelated to quality: We cannot write without it, whether or not it represents an author's individual and authentic self. In short, countering Helms-Park and Stapleton (2003), including their critique of Matsuda and Tardy's (2007) study that appeared in a 2008 article (Stapleton & Helms-Park, 2008), Matsuda and Tardy firmly stated that Stapleton and Helms-Park (2008) had misunderstood their notion of voice, and that "voice is not a trivial element of writing" (Matsuda & Tardy, 2008, p. 101). Novices and aspiring academic writers alike are steeped in it and work to develop it (Matsuda, 2003), as are mature multilingual writers (Hirvela & Belcher, 2001).

Other work in academic English, especially with adult and minority students, has linked discoursal features of writing with "identity"—perhaps another version of (authentic) self that is expressed as voice (Ivanič, 1994, 1995, 1998; Ivanič & Camps, 2001). Analyses of discipline-based published work, too, reveals a variety of author voices both within and across disciplines—voices that are unrelated to conceptualizations of a personal expressive self or even to writing quality (Hyland, 2008, 2010, 2012). Hyland found that in some disciplines an overt self appearing as *I* commonly appeared whereas in other disciplines authors' voices were not expressed as personal pronouns, but embedded in the seemingly objective and neutral style of academic prose. In short, a question persists as to whether writing teachers perceive voice as tied to self-expression, authenticity of identity, and writing quality, or as an inevitable feature of all writing no matter what forms it takes or which of many possible roles we play as authors and how well our writing succeeds.

Still, the views of L2 writing teachers, students, and some scholars persist that individual voice and its companion critical thinking are not taught or expected in many non-Western contexts such as China and Japan. L2 writing teachers will continue to need to study the issues themselves. The point made by scholars on all sides of the debate is that broad cultural sweeps will always miss many things such as contextual and individual variability, educational (i.e., taught) factors as opposed to inherent ways of thinking, and the likelihood that all students can learn to practice the kinds of writing expected in their circumstances. Doing some perspective taking, if I participate in an educational system that requires memorization, rote learning, and exam preparation rather than critical and individual thinking, I will need to follow those practices in order to succeed. If I am expected, on the other hand, to reveal something of myself in my writing (display a personal voice) or to take on the authoritative voice of a disciplinary expert, I will need to learn to take on these voices regardless of my cultural background.

These issues apply beyond the students in our L2 writing classes. We can also ask whether L1 and L2 scholars themselves have an individual voice. The responses differ, often depending on how published writers define voice. Atkinson (2003b), as a sometime skeptic of modernist views, found the whole question of whether he has a personal voice "vexing" given that his self is so intimately tied to theoretical issues. Kubota (2003), on the other hand, found that her "original voice" was often altered as reviewers and editors commented on or changed her writing for publication (see also Hartse & Kubota, 2014). As I discussed earlier, Cadman (2014) agonized about pressures on her as a scholarly writer and on her doctoral students as well to eliminate overt references to an authentic self in their writing. Likewise, Starfield (2015) told a fascinating story of being forced to eliminate first-person references in an article for publication even when the article was about herself. For his part, Hyland (2008) defined voice in academic writing as "the ways writers express their personal views, authoritativeness, and presence" (p. 5). He acknowledged that stereotypical academic and scientific writing often aims to remove any semblance of a personal voice or presence (what Helms-Park and Stapleton, 2003, consider part of style), leading students and their teachers to avoid references to the self and to their agency as writers (hence the ubiquitous passive voice in some writing).

However, as Hyland (2008) pointed out, "writing always has voice in the sense that it conveys a representation of the writer" (p. 5). Writers cannot write voiceless academic prose. In one interesting example, Hyland (2010) analyzed the published writing of two well-established scholars (Deborah Cameron and John Swales) and found distinctive textual characteristics in each, leading him to conclude that writers do have identifiable voices that can be linked to their identities. Hyland's large body of work over many years (e.g., 2008, 2012; Hyland & Tse, 2012) shows how writers use textual resources to convey identities, stances, membership and alliances, positions and counter positions, and so on in different disciplines, all of which are expressed in a kind of voice. Ivanič, too, (e.g., 1994, 1995, 1998) studied links between identity and academic writing but, in her case, focusing on the writing of adult and minority students in the U.K. In her work, we can presume that voice helps establish identity. In other words, all writers, whether published authors or struggling novices, have personal choices in how they represent themselves in the social act of writing, and do this more or less skillfully whether we are L1 or L2 writers. It seems that not everyone believes that academic writing is neutral and objective, and that even this kind of writing displays voice in many ways, not just with personal pronouns.

Current questions about voice now extend to studies of digital and multimedia-multimodal composition in which writers construct, compile, and mix-remix electronic texts from a wide variety of sources, sometimes in very creative ways (Hafner, 2013, 2015; Hafner, Chik, & Jones, 2013). These studies raise questions about voice, authorship, and ownership in writing (see also Chapter 6, this book) in an era when voices, texts, images, and sounds are so readily culled from internet sources and creatively, or not, remixed into works that might be considered original. These more recent sources as well as past misunderstandings and tensions in various views of voice continue to make worthwhile reading (e.g., Atkinson, 2000; Elbow, 1999; Ramanthan & Atkinson, 1999; Yancey, 1994), important if L2 writing teachers have unintentionally adopted facile cultural interpretations of who their L2 writers are. Thus, writing teachers would be wise to think carefully about what they mean by voice, particularly if they cling to notions of authentic and original voice or to the presumed neutrality of academic writing. A question for L2 writers, then, is how they can learn to manage their self-representations effectively, with or without the use of first-person pronouns.

Classroom Perspectives

Of the main culturally influenced topics discussed in this chapter, the one most widely written about from a classroom perspective, is critical thinking. Some of the research that has examined critical thinking in a classroom context has already been cited earlier in this chapter. Techniques for teaching critical thinking in both reading and writing appear in textbooks for university students and teachers (particularly L1 students) (e.g., Bean, 2011; Cottrell, 2011; many other sources can be found through internet searches) and for adolescent English language learners and minority students (e.g., Gibbons, 2009). At least in English-dominant school settings, a common belief is that students need to learn to think critically in order to engage deeply with content and to write argumentative essays and succeed on essay exams. At more advanced levels of schooling, students who are writing master's or doctoral theses in English are also required to write critically, skeptically, and analytically about their topics (see Li's, 2008, experiences learning to "write a thesis with an argumentative edge" in her chapter in the Casanave and Li edited volume on learning the literacy practices of graduate school). Whether or not we find these norms unfairly imposed by the "northern hemisphere West" (Cadman, 2014) and would prefer to expand accepted styles of writing beyond these conventions (see the discussion in this book, Chapter 4 on standards for writing), it seems that both L1 and L2 writing instruction for students from adolescence on still emphasizes critical-thinking and writing skills. Classroom teachers thus need to decide if they will resist teaching conventional norms or follow conventions in the hope of providing students what they might need in high-stakes writing. Time permitting, it makes sense to do both by helping students develop a critical (at least aware) stance toward critical thinking, such as where this mode of thought comes from, what forms it takes in different cultures, why it might be important, and how to resist narrow definitions of it, even in small ways.

In my own history of undergraduate- and graduate-level writing instruction, I have always asked students to explain why they held certain views and, where appropriate, to provide some kind of evidence for them. I have also asked students to look at multiple sides of issues—to do some perspective-taking as they try to learn about a topic. Debate classes typically do this in oral form, although debate classes in my experience tend to be set up in rather simplistic dichotomous ways (one issue, two sides). Even in students' journal writing, which typically I have used as a type of reflective free writing (Casanave, 2011), I have sometimes asked in my comments to students why they hold certain beliefs and whether they have looked at other sides. I can't seem to help myself—this approach seems so deeply embedded in my psyche. However, unlike Atkinson's (1997) claim that middle class Americans like me are socialized into this kind of thinking from childhood, I do not recall being indoctrinated in this way. My parents did not ask me why questions about my beliefs and opinions or even encourage me to develop reasoned opinions. My interest in and skills at critical thinking developed much later, I believe, becoming part of me gradually over many years in my adult life.

In light of pervasive digital technologies and growing attention to multimodal-multimedia writing (see Chapter 3), including ePortfolios, Neal (2011) too found ways to ask his students important "why" questions that inspire a kind of critical thinking. He developed reflective prompts designed to help students develop meaningful self-reflections and self-assessments of their ePortfolios that went beyond the usual "What did you like about this portfolio or this writing?" Instead, his questions asked "why?" Such questions can be asked of students on any of their writing, but seem particularly well suited to multimedia projects that have interrelated parts, whether or not they are part of ePortfolios. Neal's prompts to his students for reflective self-assessments of their ePortfolios include the following:

> Why did you narrow your topic the way you did in light of your other alternatives? Why did you design your navigation the way you did? Why did you include each piece of writing in this portfolio? The *why* questions suggest to students that the choices they make should have a reason that can be articulated within a larger vision for the project, whatever it may be. (p. 87; italics in the original)

Questions about individualism and voice can also be asked in our L2 writing classes. If, for example, we ask students to state and support their individual views, we need to be prepared for some students to claim that they do not have individual views yet because they do not know enough about a topic to have developed an individual opinion or because in their cultures individual opinions don't matter as much as the views of authorities. Beyond any beliefs we might have about individualist and collectivist cultures, this could be the case if we are asking students to write about topics they are just starting to learn about. Students are not the only ones who might hesitate to express an individual view in such a situation. After decades of learning and studying, I still resist taking a strong individual stand about many topics that I am thinking and writing about because I feel I simply have not read enough yet, and so wish to rely on the views of authorities (the perpetual problem as well of doctoral dissertation writers). Not only L2 learners but also accomplished L1 scholars might secretly fear taking an individual stand that could display their incomplete knowledge. Thus, in our L2 writing classes, it makes sense, on the one hand, to help students take an individual stand on topics they are deeply familiar with and, on the other hand, not to force them to take strong positions on topics they are just beginning to learn about. Helping students to express incomplete and uncertain knowledge in appropriate ways in their writing could be a middle ground that L2 writing teachers can take. Likewise, if teachers wish to help students develop an individual and critical stance in a piece of writing, then topic familiarity will be important, as Stapleton (2001) learned with his Japanese students.

As for helping students develop a way of representing themselves in their writing that will be recognized as their voice, writing teachers first need to decide whether they believe that voice is a quality that appears only in personal expressivist writing and that academic writing has no recognizable voice, or if (as Hyland and some others would claim) all writing represents a writer's voice. If L2 writers and their teachers study features of texts of accomplished writers that indicate voice and identity (see Hyland, 2008, 2012, for examples from academia), they will certainly increase their awareness of how voice is a presence of self in all writing conveying certain identities, intentionally or not. For writers who are not yet fully proficient, they still can understand that, unless they are copying directly from another source, all their writing represents choices they have made, resulting in the rudimentary beginnings of a voice.

Ongoing Questions

It is likely that most scholars and educators would agree that both L1 and L2 students in English-dominant schools and universities are expected in at least some kinds of writing and engagement with subject matter to practice critical thinking, take and support an individual stand, and express some kind of voice that can be identified as theirs, even if they use no personal pronouns. However, the origins and definitions of these conventions of thinking and writing probably merit further inquiry as to their cultural, disciplinary, genre, and individual influences. Such inquiry is important especially if we are to dismantle facile stereotypes about cultural groups. Some of this inquiry can be done by scholars doing formal research, but for writing teachers, inquiry with their own students can lead to insights that pertain directly to what happens in their own classes. We need to know how to alert students to the issues, ask pertinent questions that lead to increased awareness, and listen and observe well.

Moreover, many questions remain about writing teachers themselves. Speaking for myself, I know that sometimes I do not reflect enough on where my own habits and beliefs come from. I take for granted that as an educator, critical thinking is an asset for me, but I don't often query why I hold to these beliefs and practices. My beliefs about self-representation and voice in academic writing have evolved over the years in favor of a more signature voice and less so-called neutrality in my writing and scholarly work (e.g., Casanave, 2017). But not everyone agrees with me, especially those who adhere to traditional scientific values of objectivity and neutrality in scholarship and writing (see the experiences that Starfield, 2015, had with editors of some of her writing). Questions therefore remain as to what kinds and degrees of individualism and voice suit an individual writer, a discipline, an institution, a department, a genre, and different tasks, purposes, and venues for writing.

Beliefs and Practices

Beliefs

1. What factors do you believe affect an L2 writer's ability or willingness to think and write critically? Try to think beyond cultural stereotypes.

2. Considering your own experiences with school-based writing and/or those of your students, how important do you believe it is to teach some version of critical thinking to L2 students? Do you believe that your response depends on the country and culture you reside in? On something else?

3. Do you believe in some version of the culturally-based individualism-collectivism argument? How have your beliefs changed, if at all, since studying the issues raised in this chapter? Do you believe that your L2 writing students see themselves in individualist-collectivist terms?

4. What kinds of voices, if any, do you believe are revealed in your own L1 writing? Your L2 writing? What do you believe the characteristics are of your individual voice in different kinds of writing? Can voice be taught in a writing class?

5. Considering critical thinking, individualism, and voice in your own experiences and cultures, what evidence do you have of variability within settings, tasks, and even individuals? How important do you believe within-context variability is?

Practices

1. In your L2 writing classes, present or future, do you, or do you plan to, teach critical thinking skills? How might you do this, and for what kinds of reading and writing? With a classmate, design at least two activities (linked to reading if needed) that are designed to do the following:
   (a) first, to introduce students to the concept of critical thinking, from your perspective, and to learn students' views from their perspectives;
   (b) second, to help students practice some aspect of critical thinking that is needed in your class (or in a class you hope to teach in the future).

2. Design an activity in which you engage students in discussion about their views (including their own possible stereotypes) of individualistic or collectivist aspects of their cultures. Do their views fit the stereotypes? Can they provide counter examples? How do they see themselves as fitting or not fitting within these views? Be sure to consider not only broad generalizations but also individual variability. Try to learn from students if their views influence the choices they make, or risks they might take, in their writing.

3. To what extent have you tried to convince your L2 writing students that they have an original and individual voice, if this is a construct you believe in? How have you done this? If you believe that writers have an original and individual voice, design a handout (electronic or print) that offers students some specific options for representing themselves in their writing, beyond phrases like *In my opinion…* See work by Hyland for ideas on language, and work in multimodality (see this book, Chapter 3, Writing in an Digital Era) for other ideas, including design factors such as font and formatting. As you design this activity, distinguish between academic writing and literary or creative writing.

References

Alagozlu, N. (2007). Critical thinking and voice in EFL writing. *The Asian EFL Journal, 9*(3), 118–136.

Atkinson, D. (1997). A critical approach to critical thinking in TESOL. *TESOL Quarterly, 31*, 77–94.

Atkinson, D. (1998). The author responds. *TESOL Quarterly, 32*, 133–137.

Atkinson, D. (1999). TESOL and culture. *TESOL Quarterly, 33*, 625–654.

Atkinson, D. (2000). On Peter Elbow's response to "Individualism, Academic Writing, and ESL Writers," by Vai Ramanathan and Dwight Atkinson. *Journal of Second Language Writing, 9*, 72–76.

Atkinson, D. (2003a). Writing and culture in the post-process era. *Journal of Second Language Writing, 12*, 49–63.

Atkinson, D. (2003b). Writing for publication/writing for public execution: On the (personally) vexing notion of a (personal) voice. In C. P. Casanave, & S. Vandrick (Eds.), *Writing for scholarly publication: Behind the scenes in language education* (pp. 159–175). Mahwah, NJ: Lawrence Erlbaum.

Atkinson, D., & Ramanathan, V. (1995). Cultures of writing: An ethnographic comparison of L1 and L2 university writing programs. *TESOL Quarterly, 29*, 539–568.

Bakhtin, M. M. (1981). *The dialogic imagination: Four essays.* (C. Emerson & M. Holquist, Trans.; M. Holquist, Ed.). Austin: University of Texas Press.

Bartholomae, D. (1985). Inventing the university. In M. Rose (Ed.), *When a writer can't write* (pp. 134–165). New York: Guilford Press.

Bartholomae, D. (1995). Writing with teachers: A conversation with Peter Elbow. *College Composition and Communication, 46*(1), 62–71.

Bean, J. C. (2011). *Engaging ideas: The professor's guide to integrating writing, critical thinking, and active learning in the classroom* (2nd ed.). San Francisco: Jossey-Bass.

Belcher, D. D. (1997). An argument for nonadversarial argumentation: On the relevance of the feminist critique of academic discourse to L2 writing pedagogy. *Journal of Second Language Writing, 6*(1), 1–21.

Benesch, S. (1999). Thinking critically, thinking dialogically. *TESOL Quarterly, 33*(3), 573–580.

Benesch, S. (2001a). *Critical English for academic purposes: Theory, politics, and practice.* Mahwah, NJ: Lawrence Erlbaum.

Benesch, S. (2001b). Critical pragmatism: A politics of L2 composition. In T. Silva & P. K. Matsuda (Eds.), *On second language writing* (pp. 161–172). Mahwah, NJ: Lawrence Erlbaum.

Brown, J. S., Collins, A., & Duguid, P. (1989). Situated cognition and the culture of learning. *Educational Researcher, 18*(1), 32–42.

Cadman, K. (2014). Of house and home: Reflections on writing and knowing for a 'Southern' postgraduate pedagogy. In L. Thesen & L. Cooper (Eds.), *Risk in academic writing: Postgraduate students, their teachers and the making of knowledge* (pp. 166–200). Bristol, U.K.: Multilingual Matters.

Canagarajah, A. S. (2013). *Translingual practice: Global English and cosmopolitan relations.* New York: Routledge/Taylor & Francis.

Canagarajah, A. S., & Lee, E. (2014). Negotiating alternative discourses in academic writing and publishing: Risks with hybridity. In L. Thesen & L. Cooper (Eds.), *Risk in academic writing: Postgraduate students, their teachers and the making of knowledge* (pp. 59–99). Bristol, U.K.: Multilingual Matters.

Carter-Tod, S. L. (2002). In search of my "jingle": Reconciling voice and identity after the dissertation defense. In N. Welch, C. G. Latterell, C. Moore, & Carter-Tod, S. (Eds.), *The dissertation & the discipline: Reinventing composition studies* (pp. 137–146). Portsmouth, NH: Boynton/Cook.

Casanave, C. P. (2011). *Journal writing in second language education.* Ann Arbor: University of Michigan Press.

Casanave, C. P. (2017). Representing the self honestly in published research. In J. McKinley & H. Rose (Eds.), *Doing research in applied linguistics: Realities, dilemmas and solutions* (pp. 235–243). London: Routledge/Taylor & Francis.

Costley, T. (2008). "You are beginning to sound like an academic": Finding and owning your academic voice. In C. P. Casanave & X. Li (Eds.), *Learning the literacy practices of graduate school: Insiders' reflections on academic enculturation* (pp. 74–87). Ann Arbor: University of Michigan Press.

Cottrell, S. (2011). *Critical thinking skills: Developing effective analysis and argument (2nd ed.).* New York: Palgrave MacMillan.

Davidson, B. W. (1998). Comments on Dwight Atkinson's "A Critical Approach to Critical Thinking in TESOL": A case for critical thinking in the English language classroom. *TESOL Quarterly, 32*(1), 119–123.

Delpit, L. (1988). The silenced dialogue: Power and pedagogy in educating other people's children. *Harvard Educational Review, 58*(3), 280–298.

Elbow, P. (1973). *Writing without teachers.* New York: Oxford University Press.

Elbow, P. (1981). *Writing with power.* New York: Oxford University Press.

Elbow, P. (1991). Reflections on academic discourse. *College English, 53*(2), 135–155.

Elbow, P. (1994). What do we mean when we talk about voice in texts? In K. Yancey (Ed.), *Voices on voice: Perspectives, definitions, inquiry* (pp. 1–35). Urbana, IL: National Council of Teachers of English.

Elbow, P. (1995). Being a writer vs. being an academic: A conflict in goals. *College Composition and Communication, 46*(1), 72–83.

Elbow, P. (1999). In defense of private writing: Consequences for theory and research. *Written Communication, 16*(2), 139–170.

Fox, H. (1994). *Listening to the world: Cultural issues in academic writing.* Urbana, IL: National Council of Teachers of English.

Geertz, C. (1988). *Works and lives: The anthropologist as author.* Palo Alto, CA: Stanford University Press.

Ghahremani-Ghajar, S., & Mirhosseini, S. A. (2005). English class or speaking about everything class: Dialogue journal writing as a critical EFL literacy practice in an Iranian high school. *Language, Culture and Curriculum, 18*(3), 286–299.

Gibbons, P. (2009). *English learners, academic literacy, and thinking: Learning in the challenge zone.* Portsmouth, NH: Heinemann.

Gieve, S. (1998). Comments on Dwight Atkinson's "A Critical Approach to Critical Thinking in TESOL": A reader reacts. *TESOL Quarterly, 32*(1), 123–129.

Gudykunst, W. B., Matsumoto, Y., Ting-Toomey, S., Nishida, T., Kim, K., & Heyman, S. (1996). The influence of cultural individualism-collectivism, self-construals, and individual values on communication styles across cultures. *Human Communication Research, 22*(4), 510–543.

Hafner, C. H. (2013). Digital composition in a second or foreign language. *TESOL Quarterly, 47*(4), 830–834.

Hafner, C. H. (2015). Remix culture and English language teaching: The expression of learner voice in digital multimodal compositions. *TESOL Quarterly, 49*(3), 486–509.

Hafner, C. H., Chik, A., & Jones, R. H. (2013). Engaging with digital literacies in TESOL. *TESOL Quarterly, 47*(4), 812–815.

Hall, E. T. (1976, 1981). *Beyond culture.* New York: Random House. (1989, Anchor Books edition)

Hartse, J. H., & Kubota, R. (2014). Pluralizing English? Variation in high-stakes academic texts and challenges of copyediting. *Journal of Second Language Writing, 24,* 71–82.

Hawkins, M. R. (1998). Comments on Dwight Atkinson's "A Critical Approach to Critical Thinking in TESOL": Apprenticing nonnative speakers to new discourse communities. *TESOL Quarterly, 32*(1), 129–133.

Heath, S. B. (1983). *Ways with words: Language, life, and work in communities and classrooms.* Cambridge, U.K.: Cambridge University Press.

Helms-Park, R., & Stapleton, P. (2003). Questioning the importance of individualized voice in undergraduate L2 argumentative writing: An empirical study with pedagogical implications. *Journal of Second Language Writing, 12*(3), 245–265.

Hirvela, A., & Belcher, D. (2001). Coming back to voice: The multiple voices and identities of mature multilingual writers. *Journal of Second Language Writing, 10*(1–2), 83–106.

Hofstede, G. (1986). Cultural differences in teaching and learning. *International Journal of Intercultural Relations, 10,* 301–320.

Hunma, A., & Sibohama, E. (2014). Academic writing and research at an Afropolitan university: An international student perspective. In L. Thesen & L. Cooper (Eds.), *Risk in academic writing: Postgraduate students, their teachers and the making of knowledge* (pp. 100–128). Bristol, U.K.: Multilingual Matters.

Hyland, K. (2008). Disciplinary voices: Interactions in research writing. *English Text Construction, 1*(1), 5–22.

Hyland, K. (2010). Community and individuality: Performing identity in applied linguistics. *Written Communication, 27*(2), 159–188.

Hyland, K. (2012). *Disciplinary identities: Individuality and community in academic discourse.* Cambridge, U.K.: Cambridge University Press.

Hyland, K., & Tse, P. (2012). 'She has received many honours': Identity construction in article bio statements. *Journal of English for Academic Purposes, 11*(2), 155–165.

Ivanič, R. (1994). I is for interpersonal: Discoursal construction of writer identities and the teaching of writing. *Linguistics and Education, 6,* 3–15.

Ivanič, R. (1995). Writer identity. *Prospect, 10,* 1–31.

Ivanič, R. (1998). *Writing and identity: The discoursal construction of identity in academic writing.* Philadelphia: John Benjamins.

Ivanič, R., & Camps, D. (2001). I am how I sound: Voice as self-representation in L2 writing. *Journal of Second Language Writing, 10*(1–2), 3–33.

Kaplan, R. B. (1966). Cultural thought patterns in intercultural communication. *Language Learning, 16*, 1–20.

Kubota, R. (1998). An investigation of L1-L2 transfer in writing among Japanese university students: Implications for contrastive rhetoric. *Journal of Second Language Writing, 7*(1), 69–100.

Kubota, R. (2003). Striving for original voice in publication?: A critical reflection. In C. P. Casanave & S. Vandrick, S. (Eds.). *Writing for scholarly publication: Behind the scenes in language education* (pp. 61–69). Mahwah, NJ: Lawrence Erlbaum.

Kubota, R., & Shi, L. (2005). Instruction and reading samples for opinion writing in L1 junior high school textbooks in China and Japan. *Journal of Asian Pacific Communication, 15*(1), 97–127.

Lave, J., & Wenger, E. (1991). *Situated learning: Legitimate peripheral participation.* Cambridge, U.K.: Cambridge University Press.

Li, X. (2008). Learning to write a thesis with an argumentative edge. In C. P. Casanave & X. Li (Eds.), *Learning the literacy practices of graduate school: Insiders' reflections on academic enculturation* (pp. 46–57). Ann Arbor: University of Michigan Press.

Liaw, M.-L. (2007). Content-based reading and writing for critical thinking skills in an EFL context. *English Teaching & Learning, 31*(2), 45–87.

Matalene, C. (1985). Contrastive rhetoric: An American teacher writing in China. *College English, 47*, 789–806.

Matsuda, P. K. (2003). Coming to voice: Publishing as a graduate student. In C. P. Casanave & S. Vandrick (Eds.), *Writing for scholarly publication: Behind the scenes in language education* (pp. 39–51). Mahwah, NJ: Lawrence Erlbaum.

Matsuda, P. K., & Tardy, C. M. (2007). Voice in academic writing: The rhetorical construction of author identity in blind manuscript review. *English for Specific Purposes, 26*(2), 235–249.

Matsuda, P. K., & Tardy, C. M. (2008). Continuing the conversation on voice in academic writing. *English for Specific Purposes, 27*, 100–105.

Mohan, B., & Lo, W. A.-Y. (1985). Academic writing and Chinese students: Transfer and developmental factors. *TESOL Quarterly, 19*(3), 515–534.

Neal, M. R. (2011). *Writing assessment and the revolution in digital texts and technologies*. New York: Teachers College Press.

Ramanathan, V., & Atkinson, D. (1999). Individualism, academic writing, and ESL writers. *Journal of Second Language Writing, 8*, 45–75.

Ramanathan, V., & Kaplan, R. (1996a). Audience and voice in current L1 composition texts: Some implications for ESL student writers. *Journal of Second Language Writing, 5*, 21–34.

Ramanathan, V., & Kaplan, R. (1996b). Some problematic "channels" in the teaching of critical thinking in current L1 composition textbooks: Implications for L2 student-writers. *Issues in Applied Linguistics, 7*, 225–249.

Schroeder, C., Fox, H., & Bizzell, P. (Eds.). (2002). *ALT DIS: Alternative discourses and the academy*. Portsmouth, NH: Boynton/Cook Heinemann.

Spack, R. (1997). The rhetorical construction of multilingual students. *TESOL Quarterly, 31*, 765–774.

Stapleton, P. (2000). Culture's role in TEFL: An attitude survey in Japan. *Language Culture and Curriculum, 13*(3), 291–305.

Stapleton, P. (2001). Assessing critical thinking in the writing of Japanese university students: Insights about assumptions and content familiarity. *Written Communication, 18*(4), 506–548.

Stapleton, P. (2002a). Critical thinking in Japanese L2 writing: Re-thinking tired constructs. *ELT Journal, 56*(3), 250–257.

Stapleton, P. (2002b). Critiquing voice as a viable pedagogical tool in L2 writing: Returning the spotlight to ideas. *Journal of Second Language Writing, 11*(3), 177–190.

Stapleton, P., & Helms-Park, R. (2008). A response to Matsuda and Tardy's "Voice in academic writing: The rhetorical construction of author identity in blind manuscript review." *English for Specific Purposes, 27*(1), 94–99.

Starfield, S. (2015). First person singular: Negotiating identity in academic writing in English. In D. N. Djenar, A. Maboob, & K. Cruickshank (Eds.), *Language and identity across modes of communication* (pp. 249–262). Berlin: De Gruyter Mouton.

Tardy, C. M., & Matsuda, P. K. (2009). The construction of author voice by editorial board members. *Written Communication, 26*(1), 32–52.

Thesen, L., & Cooper, L. (Eds.). (2014). *Risk in academic writing: Postgraduate students, their teachers and the making of knowledge*. Bristol, U.K.: Multilingual Matters.

Tobin, L., & Newkirk, T. (Eds.). (1994). *Taking stock: The writing process movement in the 90s*. Portsmouth, NH: Boynton/Cook Heinemann.

Wu, S.-Y., & Rubin, D. L. (2000). Evaluating the impact of collectivism and individualism on argumentative writing by Chinese and North American college students. *Research in the Teaching of English, 35*(2), 148–178.

Yancey, K. B. (1994). Introduction: Definition, intersection, and difference— Mapping the landscape of voice. In K. B. Yancey (Ed.), *Voices on voice: Perspectives, definitions, inquiry* (pp. vii–xxiv). Urbana, IL: National Council of Teachers of English.

Zamel, V. (1997). Toward a model of transculturation. *TESOL Quarterly, 31*, 341–352.

Zhao, C. G. (2013). Measuring authorial voice strength in L2 argumentative writing: The development and validation of an analytic rubric. *Language Testing, 30*(2), 201–230.

Zhao, C. G., & Llosa, L. (2008). Voice in high-stakes L1 academic writing assessment: Implications for L2 writing instruction. *Assessing Writing, 13*(3), 153–170.

Index